Fundació Joan Miró

Fundació Joan Miró Barcelona

Fundació Joan Miró
Guidebook

Edited by Rosa Maria Malet

SKIRA
CARROGGIO

Cover illustration
Joan Miró: *Flame in space and naked woman*, 1932

Coordination
Victòria Izquierdo Brichs

Documentation
Carme Escudero

English translation
Joanna Martinez

Design
Marcello Francone

Maquette
Monica Temporiti

Photographs of Miró's works
Jaume Blassi
Gallery K. AG

Parc de Montjuïc
08038 Barcelona
Tel. 34 934 439 470
Fax 34 933 298 609
www.bcn.fjmiro.es
fjmiro@bcn.fjmiro.es

I.S.B.N.: 84-7254-788-4
D.L.: B-14.217-2002
Printed in Spain

Contents

Joan Miró at the entrance to
the Foundation

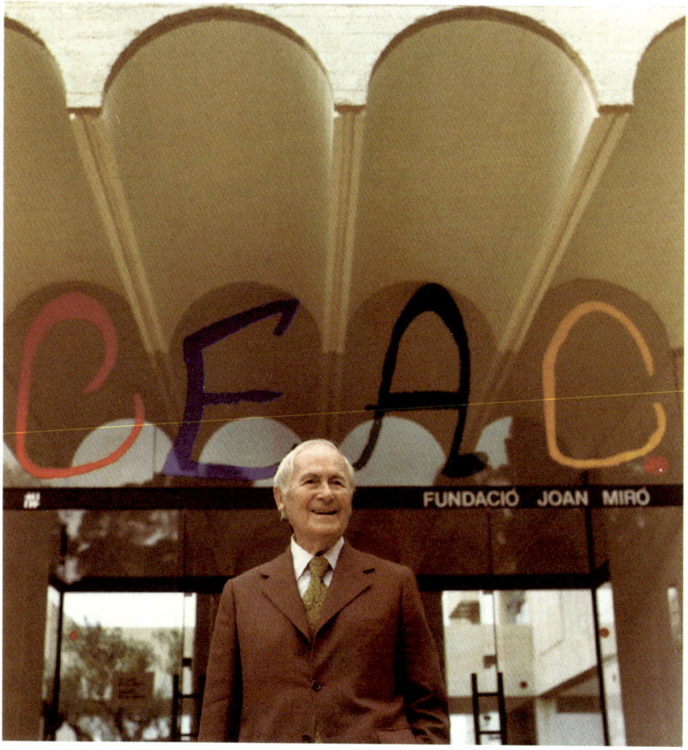

What is the Joan Miró Foundation?

Origins

The Joan Miró Foundation was the first public institution set up in Barcelona to focus entirely on contemporary art.

In 1968, the year of Joan Miró's seventy-fifth birthday, the City Council organised a large retrospective exhibition of his work at the Antic Hospital de la Santa Creu. The remarkable selection of works on show – some from museums and private collections and others from the artist's studio in Majorca – was proof of the interest in his oeuvre and of the importance of his contribution to the art of the twentieth century.

Realising that it would be relatively easy to make his work accessible to the public on a permanent basis, Miró, with the encouragement of his friend Joan Prats, decided to set up the Foundation. His intention was to create a dynamic centre where art experts and the public in general would come in contact not only with his own work but also with the main currents in twentieth-century art, and where support would also be provided for the creative talents of young artists.

The idea of a foundation, a form of institution with a long tradition in Catalonia, seemed to be the most suitable way of ensuring complete independence.

Josep Lluís Sert, a founder member of GATCPAC (Grup d'Arquitectes i Tècnics Catalans per al Progrés de l'Arquitectura Contemporània) and a friend of Joan Miró, drew up the plans for the building and supervised its construction. The City Council provided the land and paid for part of the construction costs.

The Building

Joan Miró and Josep Lluís Sert had first met in 1932, and became close friends in 1937 when they both worked on the Spanish Republican Government's pavilion at the Paris World Fair.

The pavilion, designed by Josep Lluís Sert and Luis Lacasa, contained among other pieces Picasso's *Guernica, Montserrat* by Julio González, the *Mercury fountain* by Alexander Calder and *The reaper* by Joan Miró. It was the first building by Sert designed specifically to house works of art, and was followed some years later by Miró's own studio in Majorca (1956), the Fondation Maeght at Saint-Paul-de-Vence (1964) and finally the Joan Miró Foundation in Barcelona (1975). In the Joan Miró Foundation, Sert created an open-plan structure where the interior space communicated with the exterior, producing a perfect balance between architecture and landscape.

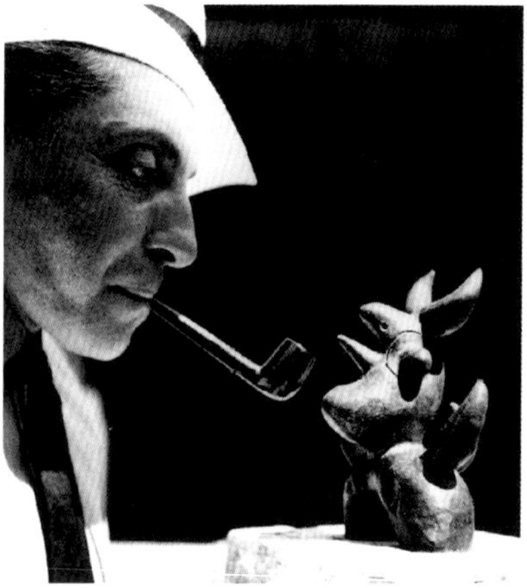

Joan Prats contemplating the *Moon bird*

From the outset, he gave considerable thought to resolving the two main difficulties affecting places in which works of art are exhibited: lighting and the way visitors circulate.

In order to make the maximum use of daylight, he decided to construct skylights in the form of quadrants through which reflected sunlight penetrates the building from above in such a way that no shadows are produced and no rays of light shine directly on to the works of art or into the eyes of visitors, whatever the height of the sun above the horizon according to the time of day or season of the year.

The circulation of visitors was organised around the central patio – the origin of which can be found in the impluvium of a Roman house and in medieval cloisters – so that the same point need not be passed more than once.

The basic material is reinforced concrete painted white. On the outside, the marks left by the shuttering are combined with prefabricated panels of a granular texture, while the white interior walls create a restful atmosphere that is conducive

The Joan Miró Foundation

The central patio and roof terrace

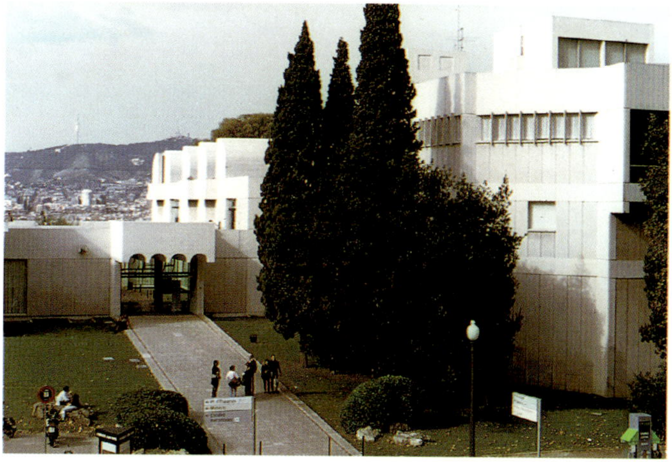

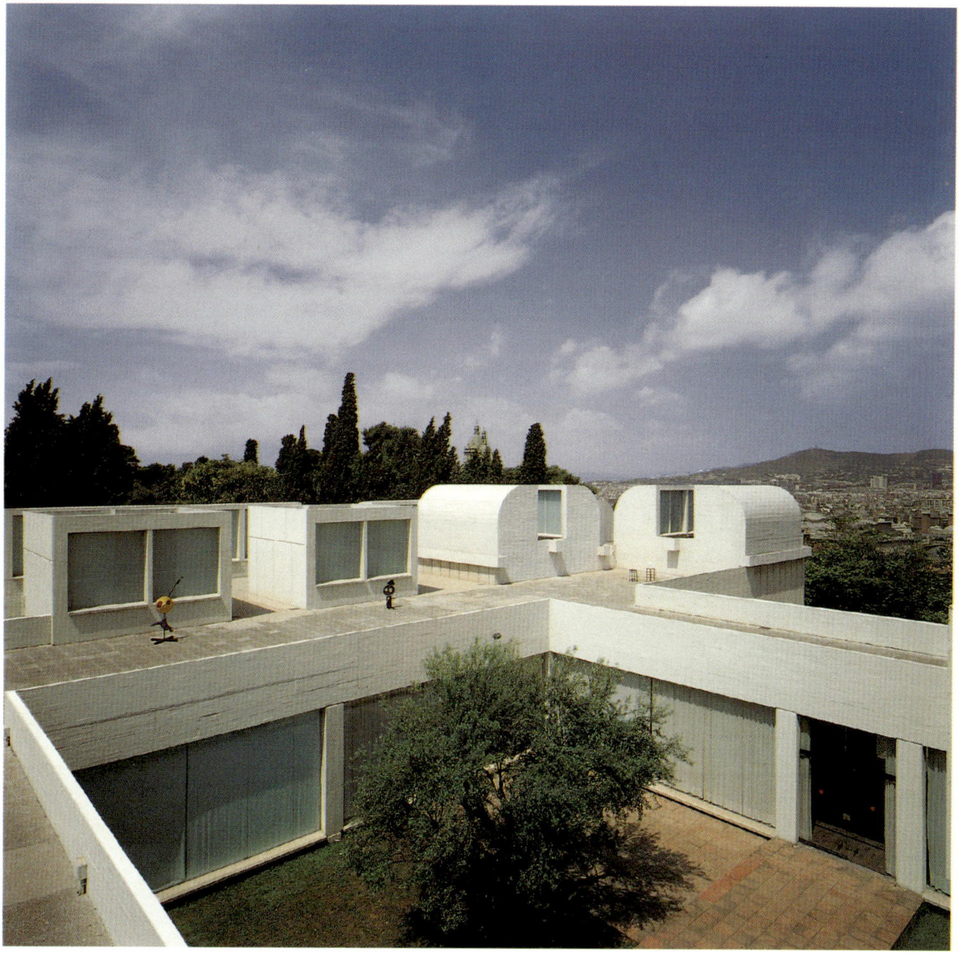

to contemplation. Other features – such as the terracotta tiles, the wooden edgings to the steps, etc. – are, like the colour of the building itself, typical of vernacular architecture in the Mediterranean. The austere yet pleasing forms of Sert's designs are of similar origin: the central patio, the apertures linking the interior and the exterior, and the shallow vaulted ceilings. One of the distinctive features of the building is the octagonal tower housing the Auditorium, the Library and an exhibition room.

Ten years after the opening of the Foundation, and as a result of the increasing number of activities and the need for a permanent exhibition area, the Board of Trustees decided to enlarge the building. The architect commissioned to carry out this task was Jaume Freixa, a pupil of Sert's who had worked with him for eleven years at Harvard and had played an active part in the creation of the Foundation.

The original design, of Rationalist inspiration, was modelled on Mediterranean domestic buildings, where the houses blend into the landscape and are adapted to the needs of those living in them. In line with Sert's idea that one of the essential characteristics of these buildings is the possibility of adding extensions to meet specific needs as they arise, Freixa's design clearly respected the overall uniformity of the building.

Since then, the Foundation has consolidated its status on an international level and the number of visitors has increased considerably. In addition, there was the need for more exhibition space in order to display the 23 works by Miró from the Gallery K. AG as well as two more paintings on permanent loan from the Miró family, which have added greatly to the quality of the permanent collection. This resulted in a second extension to the building in 2000-2001, also designed by Jaume Freixa.

The Collections

The most important aspect of the Foundation's collections is without doubt its valuable stock of works by Joan Miró, consisting of over 11,000 items: 217 paintings, 178 sculptures, 9 textiles, 4 ceramics, the almost complete graphic works, and a collection of around 8,000 drawings, sketches and notes. Practically all these pieces were donated by Miró himself.

Alexander Calder: *Mercury fountain*, 1937

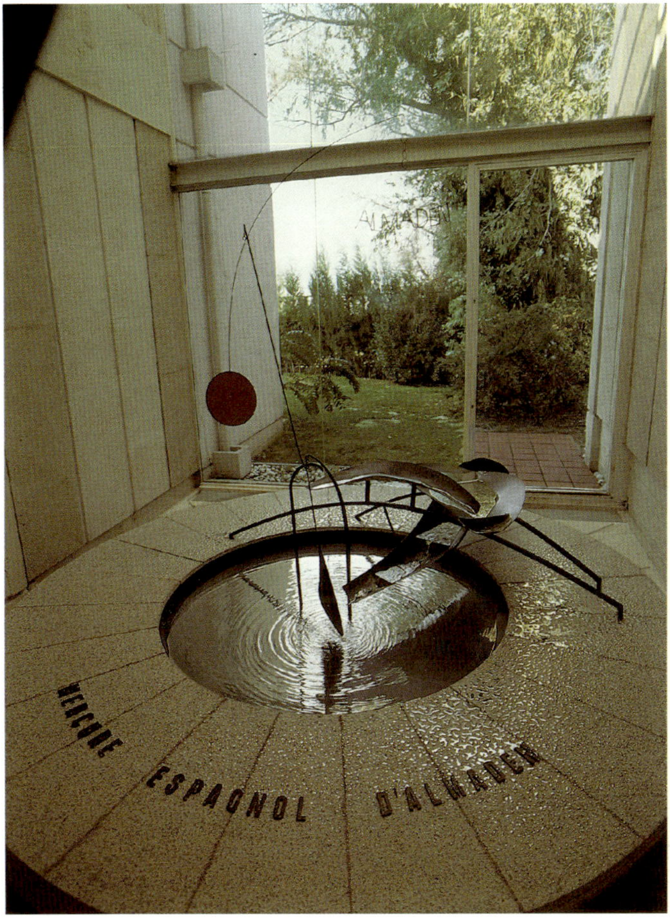

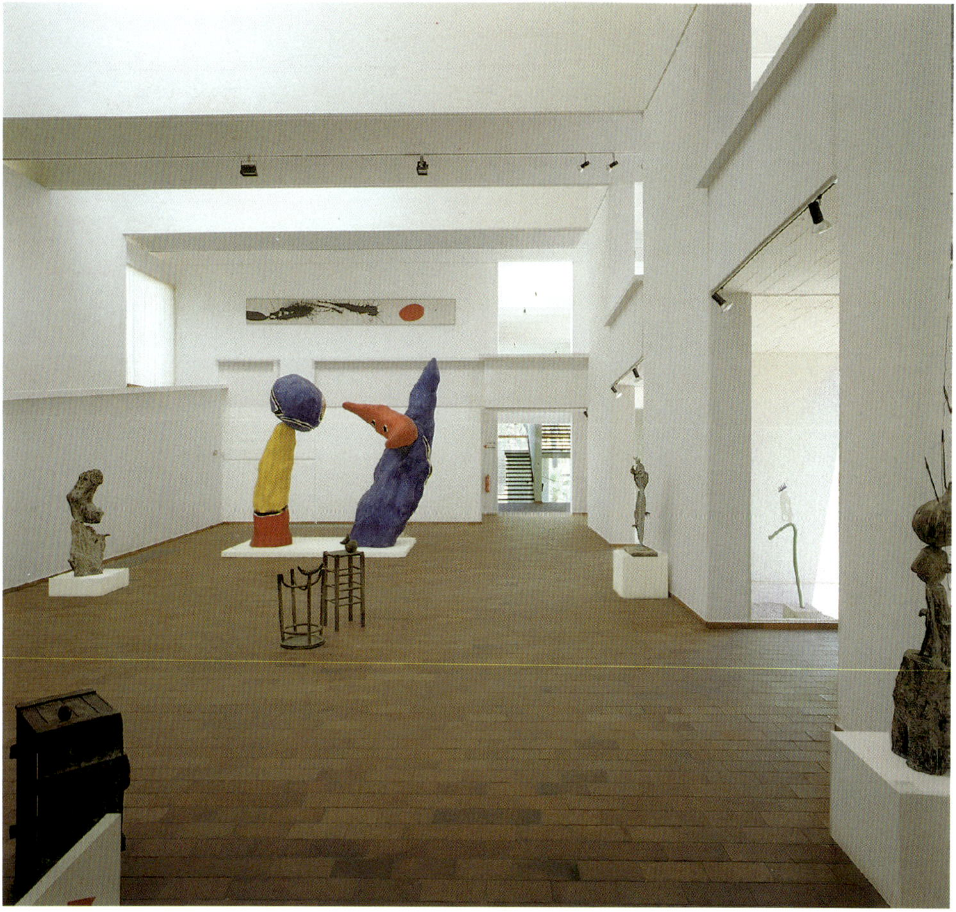

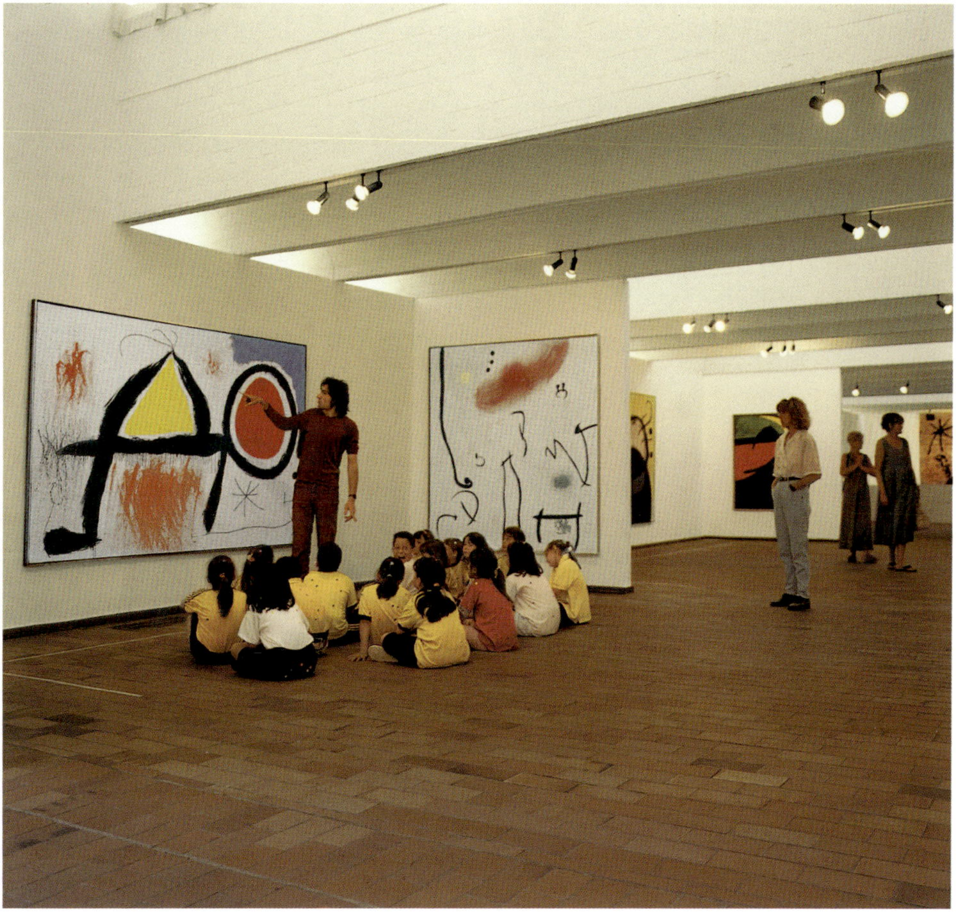

In addition, there are the works from her personal collection on permanent loan from Miró's wife, Pilar Juncosa de Miró. After her death, these passed to her heirs, but have continued on permanent loan to the Foundation in order to respect the founder's initial intentions. Consisting of a number of paintings from different periods, this collection gives a good overall view of the development of the artist's work.

The private collection of Miró's works assembled by Joan Prats, his close friend and the driving force behind the idea of setting up the Foundation, was donated at the outset and also shows the process of consolidation of the artist's pictorial language.

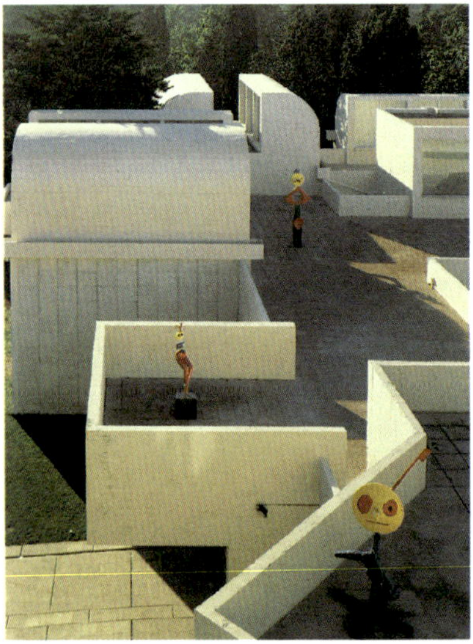

The roof terraces

The Foundation also holds works that Miró donated to Barcelona City Council with the stipulation that they should be kept at the Foundation after the closure of the 1968 exhibition at the Antic Hospital de la Santa Creu.

Further works by Miró have been donated to the Foundation by Marguerite and Aimé Maeght, Pierre Matisse, Manuel de Muga, David Fernández Miró, Josep Lluís Sert, Francesc Farreras, Josep Royo and Gérald Cramer.

The Foundation has a representative selection of the bronze sculptures produced by Miró between the mid-1940s and the late 1970s. It also has one object-sculpture dated 1946 and four from the 1950s, in addition to the maquettes of two of his later large-format sculptures: the monumental group for the district of La Défense in Paris (1975) and *Woman and bird* (1981-82) in the Parc de Joan Miró in Barcelona.

It was not until 1972 that Miró began to work with textiles. In the innovative spirit that characterises his entire oeuvre, and with the technical assistance of Josep Royo, he produced a number of pieces – *sobreteixims* and sacks – that although similar to tapestry cannot strictly speaking be classed as such. The Foundation has four examples of each type. The large *Tapestry of the Foundation*, dated 1979, clearly shows the artist's desire to transport colours and textures from a painted surface to one formed of warp and weft.

Although Miró's contacts with the theatre were sporadic, the very varied material in the Foundation connected with this facet of his work is eloquent proof of its importance.

Firstly, there is the entire collection of drawings, sketches and maquettes related to the world of ballet. From this we can see how closely Miró's work was linked to the movements of the dancers on stage when he designed the sets and costumes for *Jeux d'enfants,* performed by the Ballets Russes de Montecarlo in 1932.

Secondly, there are the figures used in the performance of *Mori el Merma,* which were created by the Teatre de la Claca group on the basis of the typical forms found in Miró's drawings and were painted by the artist himself. These show the effects of his work in conquering not only the third dimension but movement too.

Of Miró's extensive output of graphic works, the Foundation holds at least two copies of practically every one of the original prints, books and posters he produced. In some cases, in addition to the two copies – one in the archives and the other for display – the Foundation has all the proofs and maquettes where these have survived.

The graphic works held by the Foundation include one item that is unique in the world: the complete *Barcelona series.* Consisting of fifty lithographs in black and white, of which only five prints were pulled of each one, it was published as a result of the enthusiastic help of Joan Prats.

Nevertheless, the single factor that sets the Foundation apart from other museums containing a representative selection of the artist's work is unquestionably the total of almost 7,000 items that Alexandre Cirici named the "Miró papers" – the drawings, sketches and notes of various kinds made by Miró during the course of his life. It is thanks to this material that we can today follow the development of the artist's forms of expression, the concerns that led him always to explore new paths, his reflections on his own work, and so forth.

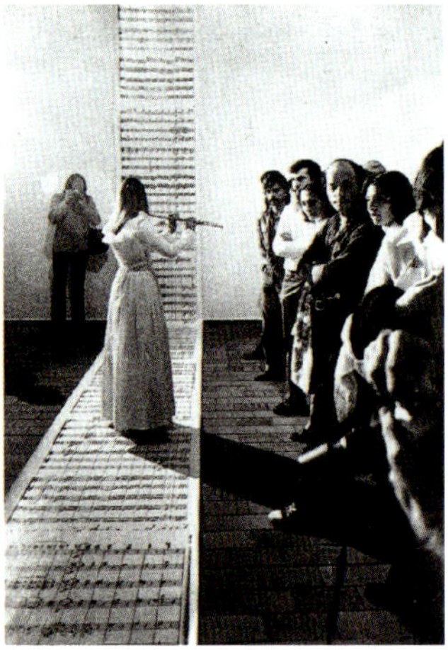

Recital by the Grup Instrumental Català, 1977

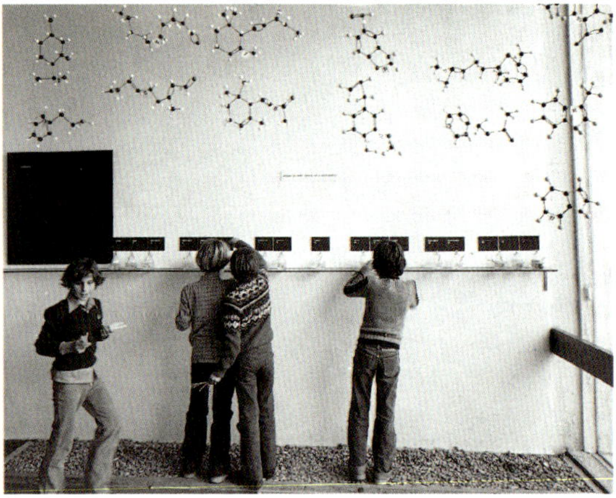

"Olfactory suggestions" exhibition, 1978

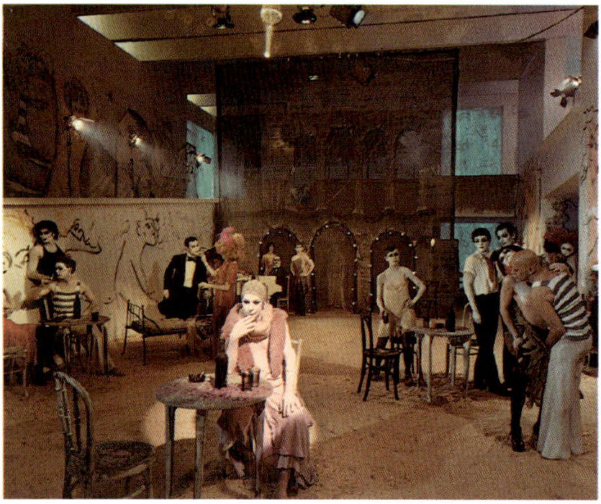

"Lindsay Kemp" exhibition, 1980

The main room in the west block is known as the forge, and it may have served this purpose at some time. Originally it would have been a formal apartment wherein Sir William and his guests might gather to discuss and appraise the horses to be exercised in the adjoining Riding School.

The two buildings were similar, five bays long with two windows on either side of the entrance on the north wall and, here, four similar windows in the south wall. The roof trusses have the same structural form as those of the Riding School. Only those in the eastern half are original, the remainder are modern. The present ceiling and the fragments of a plaster entablature, interrupted by the window openings, belong to the 1635–40 alterations.

Two fireplaces, back to back in the centre of the south wall, were inserted with a light cross wall whose scar can still be seen. Each one formed a small corner hearth. To the south of the doorway in the east wall is a further wide fireplace. It has a segmental arch springing from jambs with IMPOST and plinth moulds.

Beyond the forge, to the west, is the ruined stair to the private apartments, to be described later.

Terrace Range: interior

Access to the interior of the Terrace Range will be restricted for reasons of safety until consolidation work has been completed.

State rooms

Sir William's new rooms of 1635–40 are entered through the columned and rusticated door facing the Great Court. Roofless and bare, they now present a bleak appearance but sufficient remains to recall their former state.

First is an entrance hall, an early appearance for such an apartment, entirely symmetrical with, opposite the entrance, a great rusticated stone doorcase of 1617–20 reset in the altered east wall of the gallery, and flanked by two fireplaces once of blue and white marble slab, severely classical in form and not unlike those in the gallery at Hardwick Hall. On the north–south axis, but not centrally placed in the end walls, are large stone doorcases with frieze and cornice hoods, the cornice only being broken forward over baroque consoles.

The windows, of which there are four in the east wall, have ashlar internal SPLAYS finished with a bold STAFF BEAD. The walls appear to have been fully panelled in wood up to the height of the windows, above which ran a deep plaster entablature with pulvinated frieze. Immediately over the cornice were four smaller upper windows.

To the north rises the gable of the great hall of 1617–20 which, until the state rooms were built, was external. On it are the remains of an iron sundial. A blocked door of the earlier period may be seen to the west of the inserted doorway. In 1710 this room was called the dining room and contained a large equestrian portrait of William, Duke of Newcastle.

En suite with the entrance hall is the withdrawing room to the south, once similarly decorated. Its two windows looking eastwards on to the Great Court, the fireplace and door surrounds repeat the detail of the entrance hall. South again lies the State Bedchamber, the third of the state rooms added in 1635–40. The general scheme of panelled rooms and plaster cornice continued into this room, with similar windows set in the south wall overlooking the Outer Court and a further fireplace opening, shorn of its marble surround, in the west wall. In the north wall are indications of the unfinished work of 1617–20.

Among the pictures known to have decorated these rooms were two of Charles II, one of him as a young man, perhaps painted when Newcastle was his governor.

There were also portraits of the duke, his father and his son. The inclusion of Frances, Duchess of Newcastle, wife to the second duke, suggests that it was he who arranged the pictures.

In the northeast corner of the bedchamber a small doorway with classic architrave forms the entrance to a suite of rooms which lie to the east and which are partly accommodated in the Riding School Range. The provision of these private rooms off the formal state bedchamber may be compared with the similar layout at Hampton Court and points to the regal state for which Bolsover was planned.

The partition walls between the rooms have fallen but enough remains to show that they were provided with plaster cornices over wood panelling and had fireplaces with simple classic surrounds. They were on two floors connected by a staircase to the east. The bedroom was doubtless the larger of the two first-floor rooms; that below has a private entry from the court. These rooms mark the junction of the work of Huntingdon Smithson with that of his successor in 1634–35, when work was started on the state rooms.

The gallery

Returning to the bedchamber, a plain opening in the southwest angle leads into the great gallery, substantially John Smithson's work of 1617–20 and a part of the unfinished scheme for which his plan survives. In its final state, however, the interior was much altered.

With the completion of the state rooms along its east side in 1635–40 the gallery was lengthened by two bays to include the two ante-rooms originally planned at its north and south ends; the door from the bedchamber was moved slightly to the south and the partition walls across the gallery removed, leaving the scars that are still visible. At the same time the door in the centre of the north wall was blocked and the south wall rebuilt to include a large opening reaching to the ground, semi-circular outside and square within. The two fireplaces were also altered; the northern had a new smaller fireplace inserted within the old opening and the southern was blocked and a new opening formed further south.

In its revised state the decoration of the gallery would have been similar to that of the state rooms – panelled walls with marble fireplace surrounds and a flat ceiling over a deep plaster cornice of which a number of fragments survive. The remodelling left the gallery some 220 by 23ft (67 by 7m) with a range of ten large windows overlooking the valley, each divided into four lights by a cross mullion and transom of which the lower lights opened and had internal shutters.

On the axis of the entrance hall was the great doorway to the Terrace, formerly hung with double doors. Yet another large equestrian portrait of William, Duke of Newcastle, was hung in the gallery. The picture, now in the possession of the Duke of Portland, shows Newcastle in armour with a truncheon in his hand and below 'men and horses in several postures as of an army defeated.' Beneath it was the title *La Bataille Gaignée*.

The northern end of the gallery is now divided off by a low wall, beyond which the floor over the rooms below is missing. The wall is modern and marks the limit of a two-storey conversion of this end of the gallery some time after the rest of the building was abandoned. In the east and west walls are the joist holes of the floor inserted during these alterations, at which time the northern of the gallery fireplaces was blocked. From this point can be seen the elaborate chimney stacks contemporary with the state rooms. They are two-stage compositions with angle pilasters and console cornice.

New dining room

Returning through the entrance hall into the Great Court, the door beneath the first gable to the north gives on to a formerly enclosed landing at the head of a stair leading to the basement. In 1635–40 this door and the small window to the south were transposed so that the stair might be redesigned to clear the door to the entrance hall to the south. The SPRINGING of the BARREL VAULT to its upper landing can be seen on the west wall.

At ground level to the north, now lacking its floor, is the new dining room, remodelled as such in 1635–40 out of Smithson's earlier great hall. John Smithson's hall had an open timber hammer-beam roof which was removed, the slots on the east and west walls for its wall posts filled, a new flat ceiling inserted and the serving hatch in the north wall blocked. The four two-light hall windows, each divided by two transoms, remain unaltered.

In the west wall, beyond the former great stair, is first a large sideboard recess; next comes the fireplace of 1617–20 with heavy diamond rustications to jambs and VOUSSOIRS of a straight-arched opening, surmounted by architrave and pulvinated cornice; then in the northwest angle are twin openings to the entry and service passage. On John Smithson's plan for the hall these openings and the service hatch are shown as being hidden behind a screen with two openings.

Kitchens

Descending, the staircase turns through a right-angle at the bottom to enter the two kitchens which lie beneath the north end of the gallery and which, in common with the remainder of the rooms at this level, are part of Sir Charles Cavendish's unfinished work of 1608–17 (see page 18).

The first of these kitchens has its main fireplace on the east wall, a plain chamfered segmental-headed opening. There are the remains of a small hot plate in the northwest angle and, partly covering this, a later brick oven. The two windows to the west, once divided by mullion and transom, have deeply splayed sills. Flanking the fireplace are two doors to wine or beer cellars of which the southern is the shorter to accommodate the foundations of the great stair above and has a small fireplace in the northwestern angle. There is a hatchway between them and a STILLAGE for casks across the east end of the northern cellar.

The great kitchen lies beyond the first and is double the size, being divided by a central column identical in detail to that in the Little Castle. From this spring two arches with projecting block voussoirs. The west arch springs from a corbel carried on the hood of a fireplace, similar to that in the south kitchen, with plain recesses on either side set beneath two three-light windows. Within the fireplace may be seen the remains of the iron supports for two pot cranes. A further fireplace, now ruined and partly blocked, is to the south.

In the north wall are the door and blocked hatch to the servery. In the east wall are two small recesses, the bakery hatch and a door. The bakery, lit by two high windows in its east wall, is similar to, though more spacious than, its comtemporary in the Little Castle where the triple oven, here partly ruined, is complete. Service was through a hatch to the north of the ovens which was fitted with a top-hung inner shutter. To the north of the great kitchen is the servery, a door in the west wall of which, now blocked, opened into the space beneath the former north staircase.

East of the servery is the north kitchen, lit by two windows looking on to the Great Court. A segmental arch with plain chamfers spans the main fireplace, into which a later oven and hot plate have been

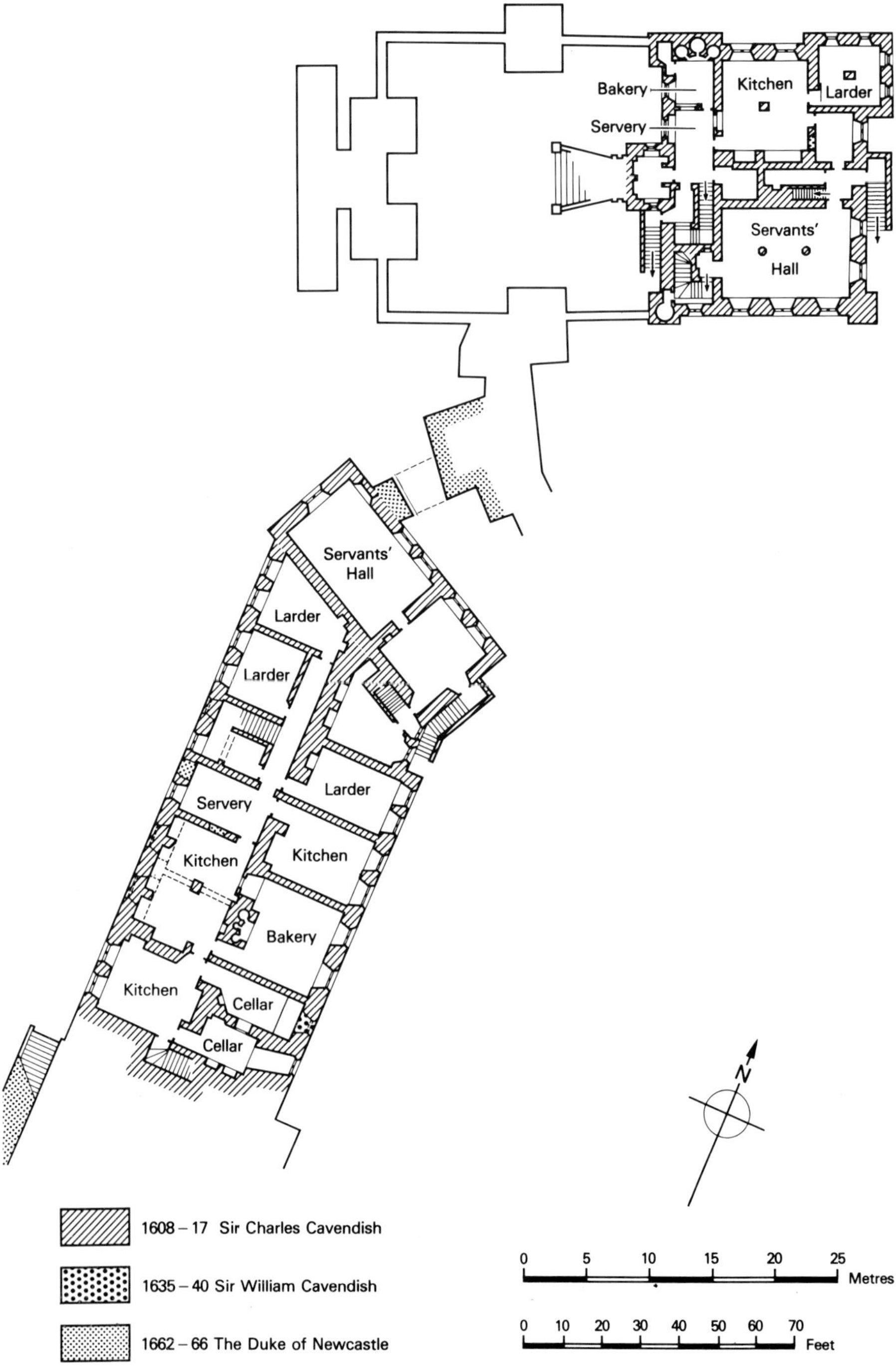
Bakery
Servery
Kitchen
Larder
Servants' Hall
Servants' Hall
Larder
Larder
Larder
Servery
Kitchen
Kitchen
Bakery
Kitchen
Cellar
Cellar
N
1608 – 17 Sir Charles Cavendish
1635 – 40 Sir William Cavendish
1662 – 66 The Duke of Newcastle
0 5 10 15 20 25 Metres
0 10 20 30 40 50 60 70 Feet

fitted. The servery passage runs northwards from the servery. Three larders or store rooms open off the servery passage, one to the east and two to the west, the northern of which has a curiously small fireplace in its northeast corner. They retain portions of their stone paving and floor drainage channels.

Immediately to the north of the servery are the remains of the main staircase which also formed the service stair from the kitchens to the hall and the apartments on the upper floors. Like the northwest stair in the Little Castle, it was a stone stair rising round a central rectangle block, the upper flights being carried on transverse arches over the lower. A store with a barrel vault is contrived beneath the lowest stage.

Upper floors

The first- and second-floor rooms to which this stair led have lost their floors and can be viewed only from basement level. Above the servery, on the first floor, was the entry leading to the SCREENS PASSAGE of Sir William's Great Hall of 1617–20 and formerly approached through its west door by a double flight of stairs from the Terrace. A door in the south wall, blocked in the 1635–40 alterations, led to the north ante-room and another, square-headed with ovolo- and ogee-moulded jambs and head, formed the principal entrance to the Great Hall.

The remaining rooms, to the north and east of the staircase, were completed before Sir Charles's death in 1617. A central passage once divided the range, with a secondary passage, now ruined, along its east side which connected with the servants' rooms in the basement of the north block by means of a staircase surviving only in its lower stages.

To the east of this secondary passage was a servery next to the hall, its hatch now blocked, and a pantry or store room. Both were lit by windows on to the court and were without fireplaces. On the west side of the passage, overlooking the Terrace, are two rooms, probably for pages or household officials, as the northern had a small internal window commanding the door at the end of the central passage which led to Sir Charles's private suite on the first floor of the north block.

The uppermost, or second, floor follows the lines of that below, with a central passage from which the staircase and four guest rooms open, and a further guest room over the entry. These have angle fireplaces with plain square-headed surrounds and each has a two-light window divided by a transom. Once again, a door at the end of the passage leads to a suite in the north block.

Above the west windows may be seen the remains of the gables obliterated by John Smithson when he remodelled the Terrace façade. On the courtyard side a range of attics, probably servants' rooms, was contrived in the roof space and later extended over the great hall when this was converted into a dining room in the 1635–40 alteration.

North block

Returning through the Great Court, the north block of the Terrace Range is entered by a stair which leads down from courtyard level to an area door in the east wall. On each floor this block, also completed by Sir Charles before 1617, is divided into two rooms. On the lowest level the western of these probably formed the servants' hall. It has high windows in its north and west walls, one in the north wall being blocked by the bridge to the wall walk. Beneath the window in the west wall is a blocked door which led out on to the Terrace.

The outer or eastern room was, perhaps, the office of the official in charge of the household. From a lobby in the southeast corner rose the stair by which servants would have reached the hall, servery and guest rooms and, to the south of the lobby, is a store room or wine cellar with deep recesses beneath the stair in its west and north walls.

On the upper floors are pairs of rooms, with a principal room by which the suites were entered to the west and an inner room to the east. On the first floor the smaller room has a fireplace, square-headed, with ogee- and ovolo-moulded surround and the larger a similar fireplace but with four-centred head, both set in the dividing wall between the rooms. There are recesses for wall cupboards, three in the smaller rooms and one in the larger.

Four windows light the principal room, of which one in the north wall is half blocked by the bridge to the wall walk. The inner room has three windows. The arrangement is repeated above but with plainer fireplaces set in the angles between the outer wall and the cross wall.

In 1633, on the completion of the Fountain Garden wall walk, this was connected by a bridge with the principal room of the upper suite and a door inserted in the place of the western window of the north wall. The exterior of this doorway, which has a four-centred arch with a keystone, is flanked by rusticated pilasters; these supported an entablature, now missing, on the frieze of which is inscribed 'CAVENDO TUTUS' and between these words the date, Ao DMI 1633.

Terrace

From the northeast of the Great Court a narrow way leads to the Terrace. On the left is the northern end of the Terrace Range containing the Cavendish apartments on its upper floors and the servants' hall below, on the right the wall of the Fountain Garden. The stone bridge with a plain two-centred arch which spans between the two was rebuilt and the block from which its northeast end springs altered when the castle was repaired in 1666 following the damage done during the Civil War. The alterations have obscured the original purpose of this block which now contains a small room to which there is no access.

Some projecting stones in the masonry of the Terrace Range at this point are inscribed with letters and dates: HS 1629, GD 1629, MC 1629, MW 1630, and EL 1630. These probably commemorate the completion of the work to the Terrace Range and record the initials of the masons engaged. If the initials HS do, indeed, refer to Huntingdon Smithson they suggest that he was then working as a mason under his father. The stonework in which they are cut is earlier.

Beyond the arch is the Terrace crowning the steep western slope of the promontory. Over 400 by 50ft (122 by 15m), it gives a commanding impression of space successfully relating the castle to the scale of the landscape in which it is set. To the south, rising out of the same ridge, can be seen the towers of Hardwick Hall, yet another Cavendish mansion built by Sir Charles's mother, 'Bess of Hardwick' and, westwards, the long empty façade of Sutton Scarsdale faces across the valley.

The outer wall rises some 3ft (1m) above terrace level and continues downwards to form a retaining wall for the made ground on which the Terrace is built. It is probable that the wall of the medieval outer bailey here ran on the line of the west wall of the buildings, which is founded on the bed rock, rather than that of the Terrace, curving in at the north end to meet the wall of the inner bailey and thus dictating the curious angle assumed by the northern end of the Terrace Range.

At the southern end of the Terrace is the southwest gateway, part of the 1630–35 build. The gate piers, the western of which has fallen, had square inner piers with short wing walls, against which are set attached CORINTHIAN columns surmounted by half a broken segmental pediment on each side, all heavily rusticated.

Overlooking the Terrace is the long western façade of the Terrace Range. In its final form this is substantially the compromise reached by John Smithson in 1618–20 when he extended the work started by his father for Sir Charles Cavendish. Nearly three-quarters of the length is taken up by the ten large windows of the great gallery. Their treatment is highly characteristic, employing interrupted triangular and segmental pediments with a heavy crown moulding that marks John Smithson's work at Bolsover.

Equally individual is the treatment of the central doorcase to the gallery, where flanking rusticated pilasters support a curious mixed segmental and triangular pediment enclosing an arched opening with block rustications. So too is the balconied feature above, which can never have served any purpose other than to form an architectural accent breaking the long straight line of parapet above the principal entrance. Designs for both the doorcase and the balcony above are among John Smithson's surviving drawings.

The most striking feature of this elevation must surely be the series of unusual cannon-like pilasters that are placed between the windows. Their purpose may best be appreciated by standing at the southern end of the terrace and looking northwards, from which viewpoint the entire façade appears as one coherent design, the powerful punctuation provided by the pilasters concealing the variations in fenestration at the northern end.

Smithson utilised the parapet to the gallery to the same purpose. By removing the gables of his father's uncompleted work at the north end and, in their place, continuing his crenellated gallery parapet, he added to the unifying effect achieved by the pilasters. He was to use the same parapet detail for the balustrade to the Fountain Garden wall walk in 1633.

The landing before the great doorway to the Gallery is reached from the Terrace by opposing flights of stone steps with an arched recess below the steps flanked by niches. These stairs, which originally had balustrades on both sides, were part of the Duke of Newcastle's repairs of 1666 and replaced a detached staircase of Smithson's, similar in overall size but with return lower flights.

Three bays to the north of the entrance the building becomes two-storeyed; the lower windows, which light the kitchens, have a hood mould which continues between them to form a string course. They are part of Sir Charles Cavendish's work of 1617 which stopped at the point at which the string course ends when only the basement was completed. Beyond the last gallery window is a further doorcase at first-floor level. Semicircular headed and set within a rectangular frame, it is yet another characteristic design of John Smithson. This door and the window and niche above it mark the point at which he recommenced building after 1618 for Sir William.

To the north the building is in the main the work of his father Robert, for Sir Charles. There is now no means of reaching the door which formed the entrance to the great hall of 1618–20 as the staircase, similar to that first provided for the gallery entrance, was later removed. The original stair had an iron balustrade (the stumps of which may still be seen on either side of the door) and beneath it an area from which a door, now blocked, led into the servery.

Northward again, the building continues for three bays, the lower windows lighting the kitchens and larders, and the upper windows first the staircase and next the apartments. Between these windows John Smithson inserted two pilasters similar to those between the gallery windows. Just above the heads of the upper windows are the water spouts left in position to drain the gutters of the pitched roofs retained behind the new parapet that replaced the gables originally designed by Robert Smithson whose northernmost canted bay remains unaltered, its elevation similar to that on the Great Court.

Little Castle

On the highest part of the site, a dramatic culmination to the whole group of buildings, standing the Little Castle. It is approached from the northern end of the Terrace, which here widens to form a platform overlooking the valley.

To the right (northeast), the keep-like building rises above the battlemented walls of its forecourt. It is the view that best captures the theatrical spirit in which the building is conceived, a scenic set for a masque with mock CROSS-LOOPS in walls that flank an impractical gatehouse.

A double stair, now without its balusters, leads to a gate with piers surmounted by scrolls and reclining figures set between square pavilions. The rectangular forecourt beyond has similar pavilions in the centre of each of its north and south sides. Entered by square-headed doors with windows to the court, these have battlemented parapets and small angle turrets with ogee dome heads. Within each is a single room with a corner fireplace in the style of those in the Little Castle itself (see the plan). The Forecourt and pavilions, though part of the original plan, were completed after 1620 to a slightly revised design.

Exterior

The general form of the exterior of the Little Castle and, indeed, the element of sustained romanticism which pervades the whole building, is due to Sir Charles Cavendish and his architect, Robert Smithson. It was begun to his designs some time between 1608 and 1613 and work was well under way when supervision passed into the hands of John Smithson at his father's death in 1614.

The building is almost square, some 95ft (29m) high with turrets surmounted by pyramidal caps at three corners rising above the battlemented parapets. The northeast angle is occupied by the stair tower, projecting boldly to the east, which continues for a further storey topped by a small octagonal cupola with a lead dome. The west front breaks forward over the porch.

A domed octagonal stone lantern with TRACERIED windows in each face crowns the centre of the building. The walling is of fine ashlar with moulded plinth and string courses dividing it into basement and three storeys. Windows are square-headed with two lights; those on the ground and first floor have two transoms and those on the second floor, one. The ground-floor windows have ovolo and fillet mouldings, the remainder plain chamfers.

A straight but tapered stone stair with fretted balustrade leads to the porch. Above the entrance arch the first-floor window is made to appear as a doorway flanked by rusticated columns supporting a pediment containing a circular opening surrounded by strapwork ornament. This composition, which forms the subject of one of John Smithson's surviving drawings, was added when Sir William Cavendish completed his father's work.

Before the window is a balcony, with a contemporary iron railing supported on three carved corbels, partly recessed in niches, representing Hercules in the centre with the arms of Ogle flanked by lions. A somewhat similar balcony, again with a false doorway above, is placed in the centre of the south wall.

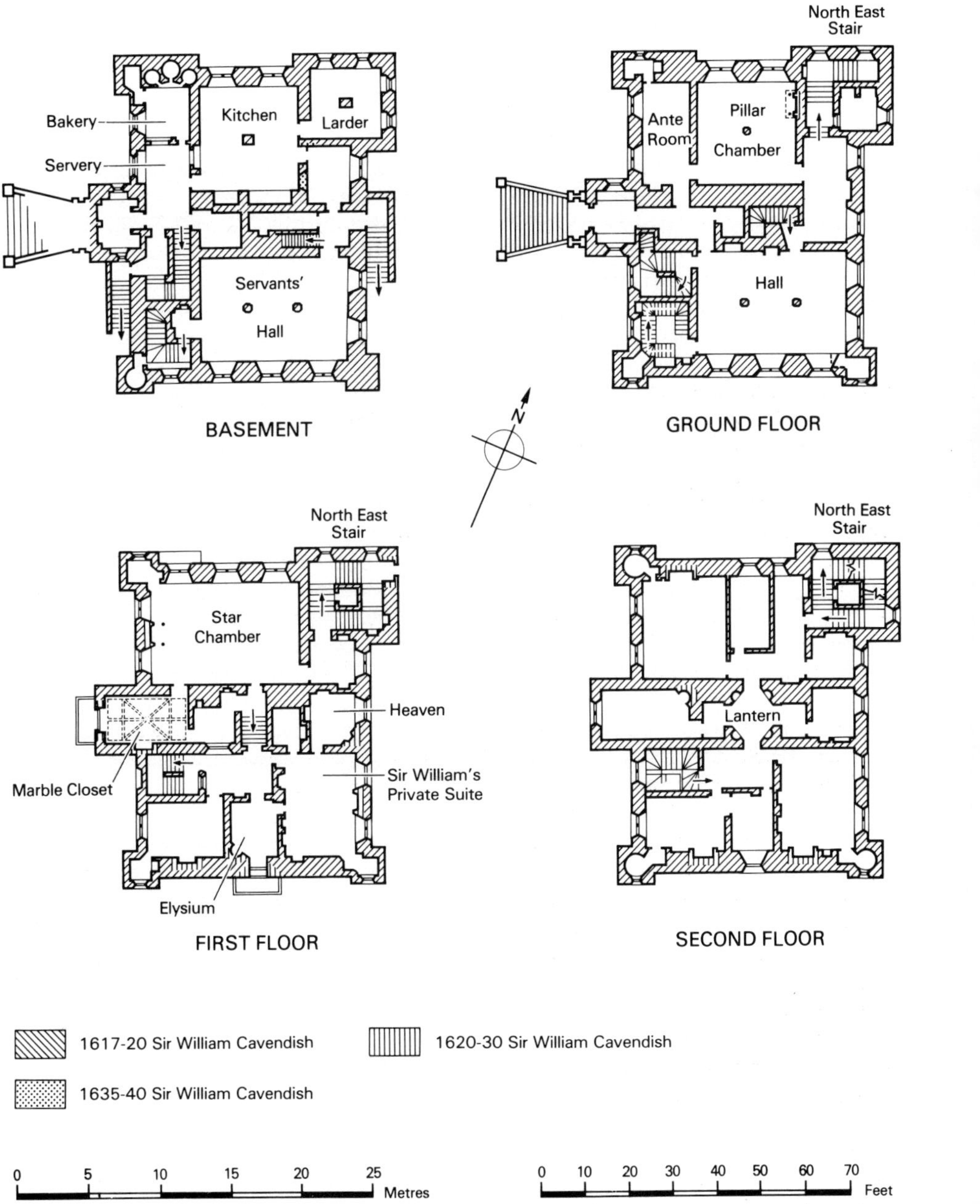
Bakery
Servery
Kitchen
Larder
Servants' Hall
BASEMENT
North East Stair
Ante Room
Pillar Chamber
Hall
GROUND FLOOR
N
North East Stair
Star Chamber
Heaven
Marble Closet
Sir William's Private Suite
Elysium
FIRST FLOOR
North East Stair
Lantern
SECOND FLOOR
1617-20 Sir William Cavendish
1620-30 Sir William Cavendish
1635-40 Sir William Cavendish
0 5 10 15 20 25 Metres
0 10 20 30 40 50 60 70 Feet

Porch

The vault of the porch immediately strikes the romantic theme of the interior, the stellar arrangement of its ribs being 'gothic' in flavour though the corbels from which they spring and the central foliage BOSS are typically Jacobean in detail. The stone benches beneath the flanking windows have console supports that are repeated in the Fountain Garden wall recess. The door hung within the porch is of Sir Charles's time with planted mouldings to simulate panels and has much of its original ironwork. Above, a small window lights the inner lobby.

The vaulted lobby, like much of this floor, is plastered and lined out to resemble stone jointing above panelling which is slightly later in date. Two small stores occupy the wall opposite the entrance, one above the other. On the left is the door leading to the ante-room.

State Rooms

Ante-room

The paintings in the Little Castle formed part of the completion of the building during Sir William Cavendish's time. In no case is the artist known. There are four paintings in the ante-room, depicting an old man attempting to seduce a somnolent young woman, a soldier and his girl, a fisherman and fishwife, and an architectural composition. They are copied from a set of prints of 'The Four Temperaments', by Pieter Jode, after Martin de Vos (1531–1603). Thus the three figurative paintings illustrate the melancholic, the choleric, and the phlegmatic temperaments. The fourth painting, were it present would be of a couple listening to a musician, to represent the sanguine.

The oak panels have coloured mouldings and stencilled ARABESQUES beneath over-painting.

There is a small stool closet in the northwest angle.

Hall

The hall, the largest single apartment in the Little Castle, was designed to be used as though it were the great hall of a self-contained house, which, indeed, describes the Little Castle. It is the only room completed by Sir Charles though, even here, the panelling and wall decorations were added by his son. On the wall to the right of the entrance is first, an opening to the service stairs, and secondly, a stable door serving the wine cellars. In the southeast angle is a small closet contained in the turret.

There is a square-headed two-light window with single transom in each bay of the east and south walls. Like the porch the hall has quasi-medieval quadripartite ribbed vaulting in three double bays springing from wall corbels and two bastard Doric columns whose cap-moulds are intersected by consoles.

The diagonal ribs are simple, the pointed transverse ribs are double with sunk moulded panels or coffers between them. In the centre of the north wall is the first of a series of remarkable fireplaces designed in a style peculiar to Bolsover. Its projecting hood is corbelled out to a semi-octagon forming a panelled steeple reaching almost to the apex of the vault and inscribed ANO 1616 on its top member. There is a contemporary iron gate.

The wall panelling was added by Sir William Cavendish after 1620. It is now over-painted, but traces of its original blue-grey ground may be seen. On the west and north walls, above the panelling, are paintings depicting the labours of Hercules against a background which contains the vault in perspective. Hercules, a figure from Greek mythology, was set twelve tasks to perform in penance for killing his wife and children. The paintings depict beasts he was forced to subdue: the Nemean Lion, Diomedes' Mares, the Cretan Bull and the Wild Boar of Erymanthus. The scenes are probably intended to symbolise Man overcoming his animal passions. Flanking the fireplace are depictions of Hercules and Vulcan, god of fire.

Beyond the door in the north wall of the hall is a small lobby into which rises the back stair from the servants' hall, so arranged that the personal servants could give direct service to the high table at this end of the hall or, through the east lobby, to the Pillar Chamber.

Pillar Chamber

The Pillar Chamber, which was the parlour or withdrawing room from the hall, owes its appearance, apart from the 'gothic' windows inserted in the north wall by the Reverend Hamilton Grey in 1834, to Sir William Cavendish and his designer, John Smithson.

An unusually complete example of high quality Jacobean decoration, the room is square in plan with a central column supporting four quadripartite vaults of similar rib section to that employed in the hall. The column cap and the half-caps which form the wall corbels have strapwork consoles and enriched ABACI whilst the ruling passion of Sir William, by this time Viscount Mansfield, is honoured in the horse's-head decoration of the vault bosses. Rich panelling rises to the full height of the room and retains its original colouring, much darkened, with gold fillets to the strapwork and painted scenes in the LUNETTES.

The pictures represent the five senses: sight, hearing, touch, taste, and smell. The symbolism is similar in each case. For example, sight is represented by a young woman with a mirror with a sharp-eyed eagle. The paintings closely follow engravings by Cornelius Cort after Franz Floris (1561). In his masque for the visit of Charles I in 1633, Ben Jonson included the lines:

> When were the senses in such order plac'd?
> The Sight, The Hearing, Smelling, Touching, Taste,
> All at one banquet. . . .

He may well have been referring to the decorative scheme in this room.

The design of this panelling was clearly inspired by that in Sir Robert Cecil's house at Theobalds, built some 40 years before and visited and drawn by Smithson in 1618.

The fireplace in the east wall has a projecting rectangular hood with a full entablature which breaks forward over two free-standing columns. Partly of alabaster, it is delicately carved, the frieze and side brackets inset and 'JEWELLED' in marble and TOUCH. Above the cornice the panelled sides slope back to terminate in a strapwork CRESTING rising to the apex of the vault. An achievement of the arms of Cavendish, for Sir William, impaling Basset, for Elizabeth Basset, his first wife, with cherub supporters stands on the face of the hood. On the north side is incised the crest of Sir William as Viscount Mansfield, the Cavendish snake under a coronet; on the south is the Basset crest, a boar.

Northeast stair

From the east lobby the northeast stair rises in short straight runs with quarter landings around a central square, transverse arches supporting the flights above. Among the surviving Smithson drawings is one for the recesses which occur at intervals on the landings, another is of the door which leads out on to the Fountain Garden wall walk from this staircase.

The door surround has a semicircular head with VERMICULATED quoins and voussoirs surmounted by a broken pediment. The door is contemporary and has raised vermiculated panels to simulate

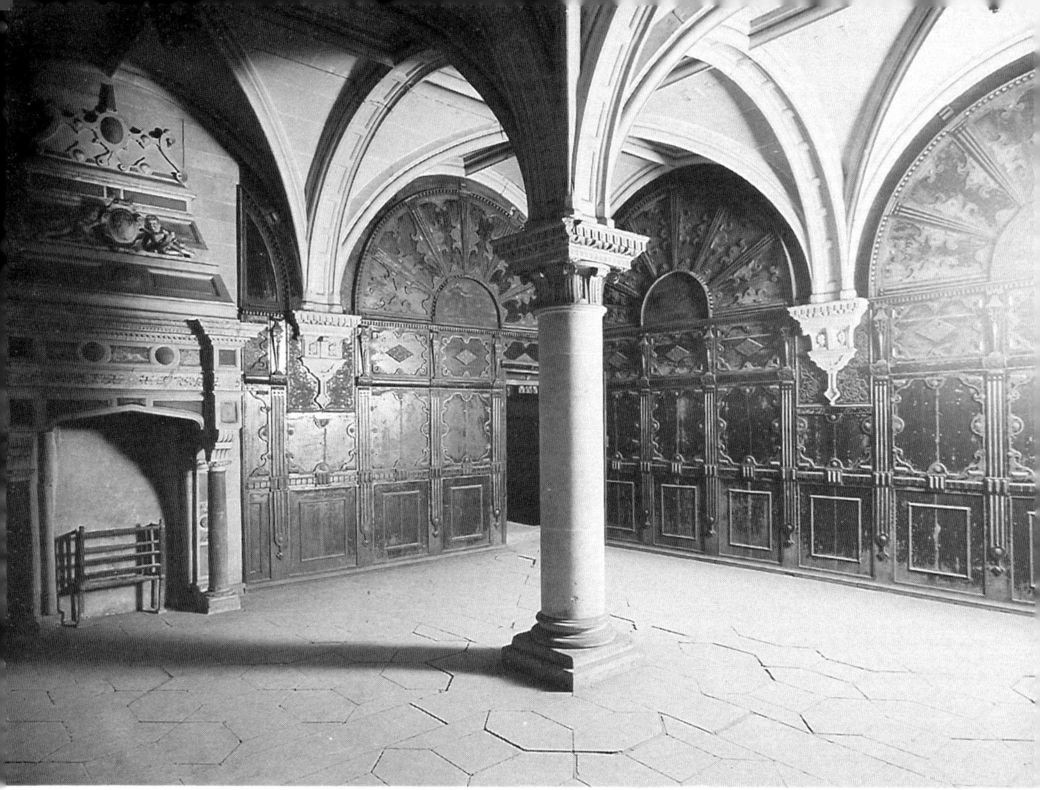

Pillar Chamber

masonry. At this point the wall walk broadens into a landing carried on heavy corbelling and on both sides are short lengths of the battlemented parapet that formerly enclosed the wide wall-top promenade that connected the Terrace Range with the Little Castle.

Returning to the northeast stair, this gives on to a square lobby at first-floor level, panelled to half height and with a full classic cornice in plaster. In the southwest angle is the door to the Star Chamber.

Star Chamber

The Star Chamber is the equivalent of the 'great chamber' of a normal house of the period, being, after the hall, the principal reception room wherein Sir William would have met and entertained his guests. Like the Pillar Chamber below, its rich and colourful decoration is part of the revision of his father's uncompleted work and dates from 1620–30. It has an enriched ceiling, an elaborate fireplace, and on the north and west walls painted panelling.

The east and south walls, now covered with later panelling and rescued window shutters, were designed to be covered with tapestry or other hangings, thus concealing the plain backs of the doors in these walls. The ceiling is divided, within a border, into alternating circular and rectangular panels by flat double ribs looped between each. Their centres are decorated with low-relief arabesques and the background, originally blue, is set with gilded lead stars. In the course of recent repairs one of these stars was found to have been painted on the back of an early playing card.

The panelling on the north and west walls is an important example of Jacobean decorative work. Arcaded panels, their heads, SPANDRILS and surrounds heavily carved, are set above a geometrically panelled DADO. In the window reveals the arcade is in two stages. Over the arcade is a deep frieze of strapwork arabesques and CARYATID figures, the whole richly decorated with green, black, and gold as the predominant colours. The panels contain figure subjects painted direct on to the wood in oil in tones of brown and white by the same hand as the lunettes in the ante-room on the floor below.

The paintings are largely of Old and New Testament figures; David, Solomon and Moses, with apostles in the reveals of the north-wall windows, and female saints each side of the fireplace. The paintings of St Thomas and of St James the Greater have been incorrectly titled as St Josephas and St Bonaventure.

These two are known to have been copied from engravings after Marcantonio Raimondi (*c*1440–1530). The presence of prophets and saints may be intended to demonstrate Man's road to Redemption. Three other paintings, St Ursula and St Katherine, and one of a boy with a cat, were stolen in the 1970s and have not been recovered.

The fireplace between the two windows on the west wall is the most elaborate in the Bolsover series. Built up in freestone, alabaster and varied English marbles, it is in three stages. The lower is open for the fire with free-standing Ionic columns (the intermediate supports are modern), the middle stage has Corinthian pilasters with panels between them displaying to the front the arms of Talbot within a Garter, Cavendish and Talbot on the north flank and Cavendish on the south. The upper stage is a bejewelled strapwork composition.

Marble Closet

To the southwest of the Star Chamber, over the porch, lies the Marble Closet, an inner retiring room to be used in conjunction with the larger room. The decoration of this room also is the work of Sir William, though a surviving drawing by Robert Smithson shows that it is based on a scheme originally intended by Sir Charles to be used in the Elysium Room.

That there was a change of intention after Sir Charles's death is evident from the remains of a plaster cornice which, though not now visible, exists above the vault. The black and white marble floor is original but the walls, now covered with softwood panels, were designed to be hung with tapestry to the level of the vault. Above this, filling the lunettes, are paintings in oil on canvas of the Virtues by an unidentified artist whose hand does not appear elsewhere at Bolsover.

The figures may be identified by the symbols associated with them: Justice and Prudence (sword and scales and twisting serpents), Fortitude and Patience (column and press containing a heart), Faith and Hope (anvil with hammer and anchor). The fourth pair, Concord and Peace, would have been expected over the window. Instead there are the heads of cherubs.

The room takes its name from its marble vault, sexpartite in the middle bay, extended by two barrel half-bays, in contrasting black marble, which springs from white marble corbel caps, three on each wall, with a heavy white foliage pendant boss at the centre. The fireplace is in the south wall, almost flush with the wall, the marble hood supported on flanking pilasters and consoles in black touch and white marble.

Private suite

A door in the east wall of the Marble Closet leads through a small half-panelled room to the short stair that connects the Star

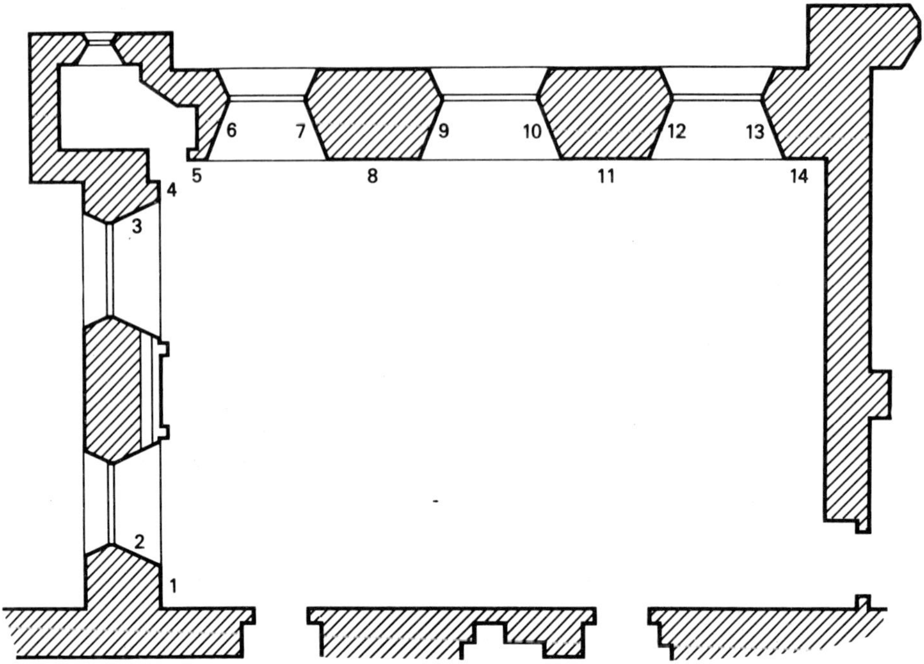

Star Chamber: subjects painted on wall panelling

1 Aaron

2 St Mary Magdalene
St Cecilia

3 St Ursula
St Katherine

4 Old man in armour

5 Young man with a cat

6 St Matthias
St James the Greater

7 St Bartholomew
St Mathew

8 King David

9 St Andrew
St Thomas

10 St Simon
St Jude

11 King Solomon

12 St Peter
St Paul

13 St Philip
St John

14 Moses

Chamber with Sir William's private suite of rooms arranged round an internal lobby. To the west is the back stair communicating direct with the hall and kitchens below. The lobby has a plain ceiling with a classic cornice above three-quarter-height panelling; in its north and west walls are internal windows, the one giving light to the small room next to the Marble Closet, the other borrowing light from the back stairs.

The room to the southwest was designed perhaps for Lady Cavendish or as a withdrawing room. It has panelling and cornice similar to those in the lobby, the former once carried across the windows to disguise the manner in which they are continued below floor level to maintain external symmetry. In the southwest corner is a stool closet, and in the south wall a bolection moulded fireplace similar in detail to that in the ground-floor ante-room.

A stone doorway in the northeast corner of the lobby leads to the principal room of the suite. It is lined throughout in oak wainscot in small square panels decorated with stencil pattern into which are let four cupboards. A plaster frieze and cornice run above the panelling. The fireplace is between the two windows on the east wall, notable for their good iron casement fasteners. This has a semi-octagonal corbelled hood supported on BALUSTER pilasters with alabaster capitals.

Above, the entablature is in alabaster decorated with lion-head masks; the hood in freestone has panelled FACETS set with marble and touch jewels all surmounted by a strapwork cresting. The room retains its original lime-ash floor laid on reed lathing and the marks of the fixings for the matting which once covered it may be seen round the edges.

Leading out of Sir William's Chamber are two richly decorated inner rooms, the Elysium Room to the west and the Heaven Room to the north, their names deriving from the subjects of the paintings on their ceilings. The Elysium Room has wainscot panels painted a dark green, the mouldings ebony with gold fillets. In the north wall a door, contrived in the nineteenth century by the Reverend Hamilton Grey, gives access to the central lobby.

The south wall is occupied by a window, elongated to simulate a door, on to the central balcony of the south façade. West of the window is a corner fireplace, its ogee LINTEL supporting a conical hood inset with marble over an alabaster cornice. Above the panelling the upper parts of the walls and ceilings are painted in oil on plaster.

Pagan deities range round the walls; the window arch contains a figure of Neptune with a scroll inscribed 'All is vanite' and on its SOFFIT the laughing Democritus and weeping Heraclitus. The assembly of gods is continued on the ceiling which owes its composition to an engraving by Cornelius Cort of a ceiling by Primaticcio in the Galerie d'Ulysse at Fontainebleau.

The ceiling of the Heaven Room, to the north of Sir William's Chamber, is by the same anonymous artist who was responsible for the paintings in the hall. It depicts the ascending Christ surrounded by a heavenly choir of cherubs and angels. In the corners cherubs carry music books with parts of *Three country dances in one* written by Thomas Ravenscroft in 1609. In the frieze are angels carrying emblems of the Passion.

Below the paintings the wall panelling is similar to that in the Elysium Room with the unusual variation of romantic vignettes within arabesques on each panel. There are cupboards let into the panelling with good contemporary hinges once gilded. The corner fireplace to the right of the window had a conical hood decorated in touch and alabaster.

Upper floor

Returning through the Star Chamber to the northeast stair, this continues up to the second floor. Apart from the structural walls and the central octagonal space under the lantern, Sir Charles Cavendish must have left this floor incomplete, perhaps even unroofed, to be finished by his successor some time after 1620.

The rooms on this floor, for the use of guests or members of the family, are grouped round an octagonal stone lobby which rises above the roof. The sides of this octagon have alternate openings and arched niches. Over these is a moulded string course, then a blank stage below the eight traceried windows. Finally there is a cornice, from which springs an octagonal dome with a carved foliage boss at its centre. The golden colour of the stone gives a surprising effect of perpetual sunlight.

The largest rooms are those which lie in the northwest and southeast angles. Both were formerly panelled, their bare walls now showing the timber partitions inserted by Sir William into the unfinished structure. Both contain corner closets and in the southeast room there are some original window shutters.

Again the fireplaces are the principal features of these rooms. That in the northwest room displays the arms of Carnaby, for Sir William's maternal grandmother, and Cavendish on the left (west) and Cavendish and Ogle, for his mother, Catherine Ogle, on the right. On the face is Cavendish IMPALING Ogle. The fireplace in the southeast room has a semi-octagonal hood supported on ogee brackets whose spandrils are carved with musical instruments, perhaps a reference to Sir William's reputed skill in that art. The hood is decorated in alabaster and touch and the central knob incised with the Cavendish crest, a snake.

In the centre room on the west façade and in the southwest angle are two more hooded fireplaces, the former a quadrant hood displaying warlike trophies and the latter a rectangular hood with flowers and fruit carved on its frieze. To the south of the octagon is a lobby with the door to the service stairs in its southwest corner. The head of the stairwell is protected by a contemporary balustrade of delicate turned oak balusters and moulded handrail.

Kitchens

The service stair, unlike the main northwest stair, runs the full height of the building, giving access to the guest rooms, to Sir William's private suite and the hall direct from the kitchens in the basement, and from the lowest half landing, to a small wine cellar beneath the porch. The whole of the basement floor had been finished before the pause in the work following Sir Charles's death, and thus dates before 1617.

At the foot of the stair is the servery, a groin-vaulted chamber with a high window to the west. To the east is the kitchen and to the north the bakery, both with serving hatches next to their doors. On the west is a game larder contrived beneath the porch and, opposite this, a barrel-vaulted store. Beside the stair is a passage that leads to a door into the Forecourt.

The bakery has a groined vault, plastered like the walls and lined out in masonry joints. The window is set high in the west wall within a lunette; below is a deep recess and next to this a small store set in the northwest angle turret. A plain chamfered recess, spanned by a straight masonry arch encloses the bread ovens which occupy the whole of the north wall. Within the main arch is a three-sided recess with a stone shelf at half-height on which are the segmental-headed openings to the ovens. At ground level was the low fire, probably of charcoal, which would heat the whole mass of stonework. Vents for this rise through the shelf to discharge in front of the ovens into the main flue.

To the east of the servery is the main kitchen with a groined vault springing from a central octagonal pier and from four wall corbels formed as half caps. The floor is of stone slabs channelled for drainage. On the north wall are two windows with deep recesses under. On the west runs a heavy bench (covered with modern board) in front of a hatchway to the servery in which the shutter still hangs. In the northeast angle is a door to the larder and another in the east wall which has at some time been moved away from the fireplace and reversed to open inwards.

The two large fireplace openings fill the south wall. The eastern has a plain chamfer to its jambs and shallow arch. Within may be seen the remains of an iron bracket to support the pivot of a large pot crane on the west side. The aperture above formerly housed a smoke jack, a form of windmill which made use of the rising flue gases to drive the mechanism which turned the spits before the fire. The western fireplace, rather smaller, has been further reduced by the later insertion of a brick arch below the original stonework. A model is displayed showing a reconstruction based on a surviving drawing in the Smithson Collection of the east fireplace. Some of the minor fittings included in the model are of eighteenth-century types.

In the northeast angle of the building is the larder or preparation room. Like the kitchen this is vaulted with a central pier, this time in the form of an elongated octagon. Four windows light the room, two on the north and two on the east. Many of the original fittings survive, such as the end of the lead pipe that carried the water supply from the well in the Fountain Garden and the stone sinks, salting stone and brine tank as well as an oak preparation table. All the sinks have outlets, once fitted with plugs, which discharge into the open floor channels. It requires little imagination to picture the state of the floor when the kitchens were in use.

South of the larder a small barrel-vaulted chamber leads to the east lobby, from which a flight of steps rises to the Fountain Garden. Opposite is a small store which has beside it a stair giving direct communication between the high table in the hall and, through the south door, the great cellar. Like the hall above, this has a plastered groined vault but without ribs, supported on two octagonal piers with ogee caps breaking forward on four sides to take a square abacus. Some of the five windows retain their wooden shutters, two to the east and three to the south.

Originally there was no fireplace (one was inserted later in the north wall when the room may have become a servants' hall, and in turn blocked up). The floor is crossed by the open drain channel from the kitchen and in the northeast angle was a pump or water conduit. In the west wall is an opening to the stair communicating with the hall above, its upper landing forming a buttery, formerly with stable doors for service into the hall.

Fountain Garden

Leaving the Little Castle, the visitor passes through a door in the south wall of the Forecourt to enter the Fountain Garden. Essentially the Little Castle and Garden represent the keep and inner bailey of the medieval castle, although the Little Castle stands rather to the east of the site of the medieval keep which probably occupied the eastern half of the forecourt, overlapping the present building. There are now no visible remains of this keep, nor indeed is there anything visible of the medieval curtain which was entirely recased in new stonework.

This refacing was started by Robert Smithson for Sir Charles Cavendish before 1617, by which time the east side was probably finished, including the east and south garden rooms. Thereafter the work, as on the Little Castle itself, remained in abeyance while the construction of the Terrace Range was pushed forward, to be resumed sometime in the late 1620s and finally completed in 1633, when the connecting bridge between the wall walk and the Terrace Range was built.

A door, already described, from the northeast stair of the Little Castle leads out on to the wall walk, broadened out into a landing at this point on heavy corbelling which may be seen from below. A short length also survives of the crenellated parapet that was continued on both sides to contain a broad and pleasant promenade at wall-top level around the garden and which in detail reproduced the parapet that John Smithson added to the Terrace Range buildings.

Whether the wall was refaced because of its ruinous condition, to conceal the shorn-off remains of the medieval buildings that formerly stood against it or simply to provide a more agreeable background to the garden it is not now possible to say, but the opportunity was taken to include, within its thickness, alcoves and garden rooms doubtless originally related to the PARTERRES of the garden layout. On the east side there are, from north to south, first two simple segmental-headed alcoves set slightly forward from the wall face and containing stone benches on console supports that repeat the detail in the porch of the Little Castle.

Next is the east garden room, entered through a door with a two-light window over. It is vaulted and takes up the full depth of the curtain wall with a fireplace, rectangular with a plain chamfer, a recess to the north and an inserted door in the east wall, later blocked, that led to steps down to the bank below. The position of this room, at a point at which the curtain changes direction, and the gap in the medieval wall which its existence implies both suggest that this would be the site of one of the mural towers built in 1223 and 1228.

South again is a further alcove and, beyond that, the south garden room. This is similar to the eastern room but with the window over the door later blocked and may be, perhaps, the site of the second medieval mural tower. Westward from here is the inner face of Huntingdon Smithson's inserted archway (originally without gates) of similar design to that facing the Great Court. Between the south alcove and the archway may be seen the change of masonry which indicates the point at which John Smithson took up the work left unfinished by his father in 1617.

Westward of the archway is the west garden room which may be attributed to John Smithson between 1620 and 1630. It is, in fact, three rooms, the central one with a groined vault and pendant boss which has a fireplace on its south wall with a vermiculated hood surmounted by strapwork cresting and, through doors in the side walls, two flanking rooms. Both have segmental barrel vaults and the eastern room wall recesses and a small quadrant hooded fireplace in the south-east angle. The west room is featureless; its north and south walls have been forced through to form an opening and later again blocked.

On the garden face the central room is entered through a rusticated arch with a lion mask on its keystone set in a square frame with pierced spandrils. On either side are rusticated piers with sunk panels with a further panel over the arch. The balustrade, which would have had dies over the piers, is missing. Like the east and south rooms, the west room fills a gap in the medieval wall, in this case considerably wider. It was, moreover, built after the adjoining curtain wall was refaced. This suggests that it stands on the site of the medieval gatehouse which was retained till the last moment as a way through the wall for the materials used in building the Little Castle. North of the garden room is the door leading to the stair to the wall walk.

In the centre of the garden stands the Venus Fountain. Among the drawings left by John Smithson is one for a garden fountain that is clearly a preliminary design for that at Bolsover. It shows a square cistern with niches in the sides and four internal angles, and a central square pier with round 'turrets' projecting from the corners with mock crossloops in the manner of his design for the wall to the Forecourt of the Little Castle. Female demi-figures are shown in the niches and PUTTI on the turrets.

The design was altered in execution and the sunk basin made octagonal with a crenellated parapet. There is a niche within a rusticated AEDICULE on each facet and quadrant corbels in each angle with indications that the niches received figures with water jets. The square central pier retains its 'turrets' though without the cross-loops. In each case the upper stone of the turret is missing with the animal (stated in 1785 to be a griffin or satyr) through which the water jet passed. Above this is a basin with a decorated rim displaying the Cavendish crest under an earl's coronet on the north and the Basset crest, also under a coronet, on the south. Above the basin is a square pedestal with lions' masks containing further jets which supports the marble figure of a bucolic Venus ascending from her bath.

Conduit houses

To the south of the castle, along the edge of the hillside, are four small stone conduit houses. They are all similar, about 10ft (3m) square, gabled with a solid stone vault and originally finished with a stone slab roof. The gable ends had projecting KNEELERS. Each has a door facing up the hillside with a small opening above and a similar opening in the opposite gable. They are built on the line of the castle water supply from a spring on Spittle Green to the southeast. Sir William Cavendish secured a right of way to enable him to lay the pipe connecting the conduits in July 1622, so the buildings would date from that time or shortly after.

A slightly earlier and larger conduit house is situated on the hill to the northeast of the castle. This was probably erected by Sir Charles Cavendish some time before 1617 and is still connected by a lead pipe to the well house of the castle.

HISTORY

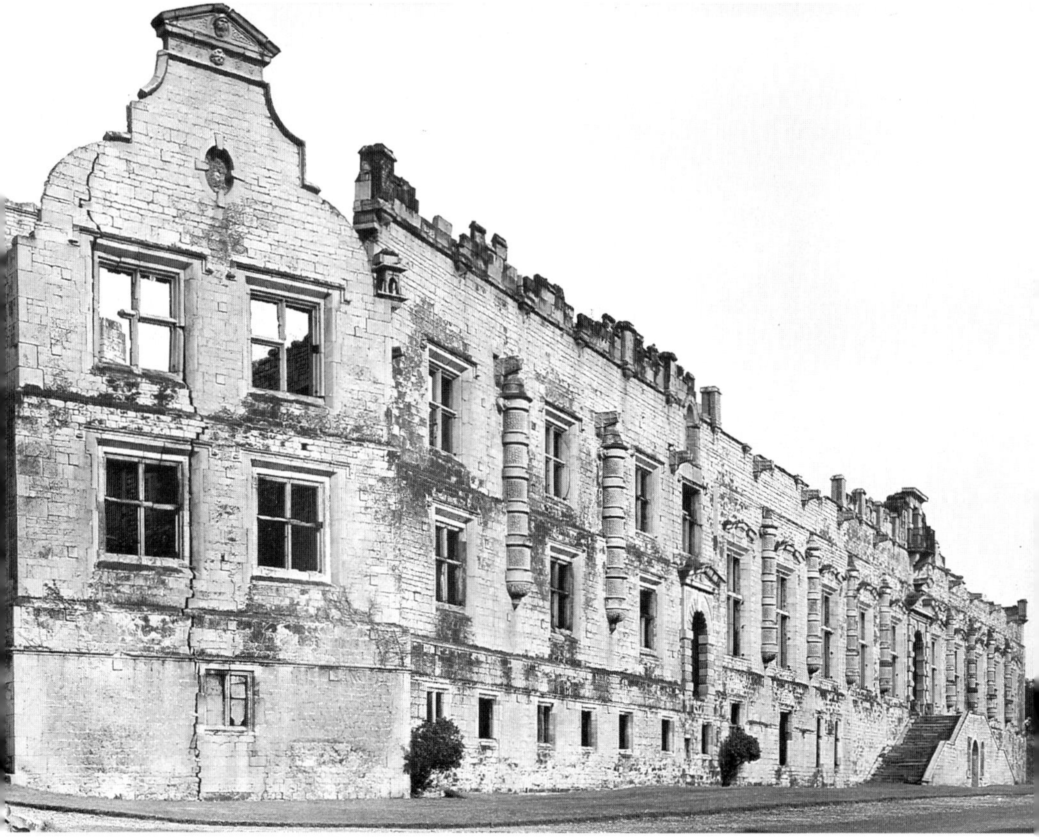

Terrace Range from the Terrace

The present Bolsover Castle is a castle in name only. The surviving buildings are the remains of the mansion erected by the Cavendish family in the seventeenth century on the site of an earlier castle. Nothing is now visible of that castle which had its origins in the late eleventh or twelfth century.

The manor of Bolsover, in common with other lordships in Derbyshire included in the HONOUR (see Glossary) of Peverel, was conferred by the Conqueror on William Peverel the first, bailiff of the royal manors in northwest Derbyshire. At the time of the Domesday survey it was in the tenure of one Robert, under William Peverel. No castle is mentioned as being on the site, although Peverel had been permitted to construct a castle for himself, not far away, in the Peak Forest (Peveril Castle, Castleton).

The property passed first to his son, William the second, the founder of Lenton Priory near Nottingham, and then in 1113 to his grandson William the third. The first stone fortification of the site was probably made by William Peverel the second at the same time as he carried out similar work at the Peak where his simple stone curtain wall without towers survives. The sites of the two castles, both placed at the end of an impregnable bluff, are markedly similar.

In the confused fighting at the end of Stephen's reign Peverel sided with the King and was taken prisoner at Lincoln in 1141; in 1152 his property was granted by Henry of Anjou to Ranulph, Earl of Chester, unless he were to be acquitted of the charge of treason. The following year the earl died and William Peverel was accused of poisoning him. Rather than face the charge Peverel sought refuge by entering the priory of Lenton as a monk. Eventually, on Henry's accession to the throne, he fled the country, and his estates, including the castles of Bolsover and Peak, were confiscated to the Crown by whom they were leased to tenants.

In 1173–74, during or immediately after the Barons' Rebellion, the sum of £116 is recorded as having been spent on the two castles. Two years later a further sum of £135 is specifically stated to have been spent on the construction of the keep at Peveril. It is probable that the earlier sum represents the building of a small keep at Bolsover, similar to that still standing at the Peak. The situation of the two keeps is similar and the ease with which that at Bolsover was demolished in the seventeenth century argues that it was small. Both castles were garrisoned during the rebellion, twenty knights and sixty servants receiving payment at Nottingham, Bolsover and Peak castles in 1174.

Richard I granted Bolsover to his brother John on his marriage in 1189. It was for only five years, until John's rebellion, when the castle reverted again to the Crown for whom it was thereafter held by a long series of governors or constables. John, after he succeeded, visited in 1200 and 1201, dating charters from Bolsover in those years. Minor expenditure continued on repairs during this period in addition to the considerable sum of £134 spent on Bolsover and Horston castles in 1208–09, perhaps marking the construction of the first permanent domestic buildings on the site at Bolsover and thus providing a further parallel with the development of Peak Castle.

At the opening of the thirteenth century the defences of the castle consisted of a curtain wall on the line of the present Fountain Garden wall, towerless, except for a gatehouse on the southwest and a keep or tower to the north with, perhaps, a further ditch to the south to protect this most vulnerable approach. The next fifty years seem to have been the most active in the castle's military history, during which time the defences were further strengthened by the addition of two mural towers on the sites of the south and east garden rooms to cover the south approach. Without them the castle was clearly not considered to be overstrong for, in 1215, instructions were sent to the constable to hold it against the King's enemies or, if that were impossible, to render it untenable by demolition.

In 1216 the King was persuaded to transfer the custody of the castle to William de Ferrars, Earl of Derby, but, before the earl could obtain possession from the existing constable, Gerard de Furnival, he was obliged to besiege the castle and take it by force. Not till seven years later in 1223 was the damage done during this siege repaired and the first of the new towers built to fill the breach made 'when the Earl Ferrars besieged the castle.' Five years later the second tower was built in the place of a section of the curtain which had collapsed. The domestic buildings too were kept in repair.

In 1225–28 a new kitchen and barn were built and a hint that the castle was equipped with the usual hall and royal apartments is given by the expenditure in 1249–53 of

£148-7-4d on repairs to the upper storeys of the great tower and the roof of the queen's chamber. The same sum also covered repairs to the foundation of the wall round the great bailey, where a part had already collapsed in 1228 and which has always tended to be insecure. There is no suggestion at any later date that the outer bailey ever received a stone curtain.

Through the years 1253–57 an annual claim of £5 was made for repairs, but after the close of Henry III's reign no serious attempt appears to have been made to maintain Bolsover as a royal castle. From 1290 the castle and manor were again leased. Its active life was over, and by the end of the fourteenth century the buildings were said to have been allowed to suffer 'waste and strip' by the successive lessees and could have had little value either as a residence or as a military strongpoint.

Later the castle and manor were granted by Henry VI to Edmund Tudor, Earl of Richmond, from whom they passed first to Jasper Tudor, his younger brother, and then in 1495 to the latter's nephew, Henry VII. In 1514 Henry VIII granted them to Thomas Howard, second Duke of Norfolk, Earl Marshal and victor of Flodden, who died in 1524. It is unlikely that Norfolk had any interest in Bolsover, other than in the manorial rents, or that he ever used the castle. It passed with his other estates to the third duke in whose possession it remained until the conviction of his son, the Earl of Surrey, for treason in 1547. With the resultant forfeiture of the Howard estates Bolsover passed into Crown hands for the last time until 1553 when, after 400 years of royal or near-royal ownership, it was granted to Sir George Talbot.

In 1560 Sir George succeeded his father as sixth Earl of Shrewsbury, becoming one of the richest men in England, with vast estates and no fewer than seven great houses in the north Midlands—Sheffield Castle, Sheffield Manor, Rufford Abbey, Wingfield Manor, Worksop Manor, Buxton Hall and Tutbury Lodge—and, in addition, lessee from the Crown of Tutbury Castle. His first wife, Gertrude, daughter of the Earl of Rutland, died in 1566 having borne him seven children.

Two years later Sir George took as his second wife Elizabeth, Lady St Loe, the celebrated 'Bess of Hardwick,' this being her fourth and least satisfactory marriage. Elizabeth of Shrewsbury, as she now was, had two ruling passions: her buildings and the children of her second and only fruitful and really happy marriage, that to William Cavendish. Her building activities were henceforward concentrated on the reconstruction of her father's old house at Hardwick; the rebuilding of Chatsworth had been finished only a short while before.

The marriage contract between Lady St Loe and the earl was designed to secure the future of her children and stipulated that, before her own wedding took place, her eldest son, Henry Cavendish, should marry Grace Talbot, and her daughter Mary, Gilbert Talbot. The double wedding took place on 9 February 1568 at Sheffield and that between Lady St Loe and the earl followed soon afterwards.

Less than a year after his marriage to Elizabeth of Hardwick, Shrewsbury undertook, somewhat unwillingly, the custody of the captive Mary, Queen of Scots. For the next fifteen years till 6 September 1584 Mary remained in the charge of the earl and countess, moving from one Shrewsbury home to another. The cost and inconvenience to the earl were enormous. The former left him so poor that, after his death, his executors were unable to carry out the provisions of his will; the latter culminated in the scandal of his suspected liaison with Mary. The two together resulted in a rift so wide between the countess and himself that the earl spent his last years with his former

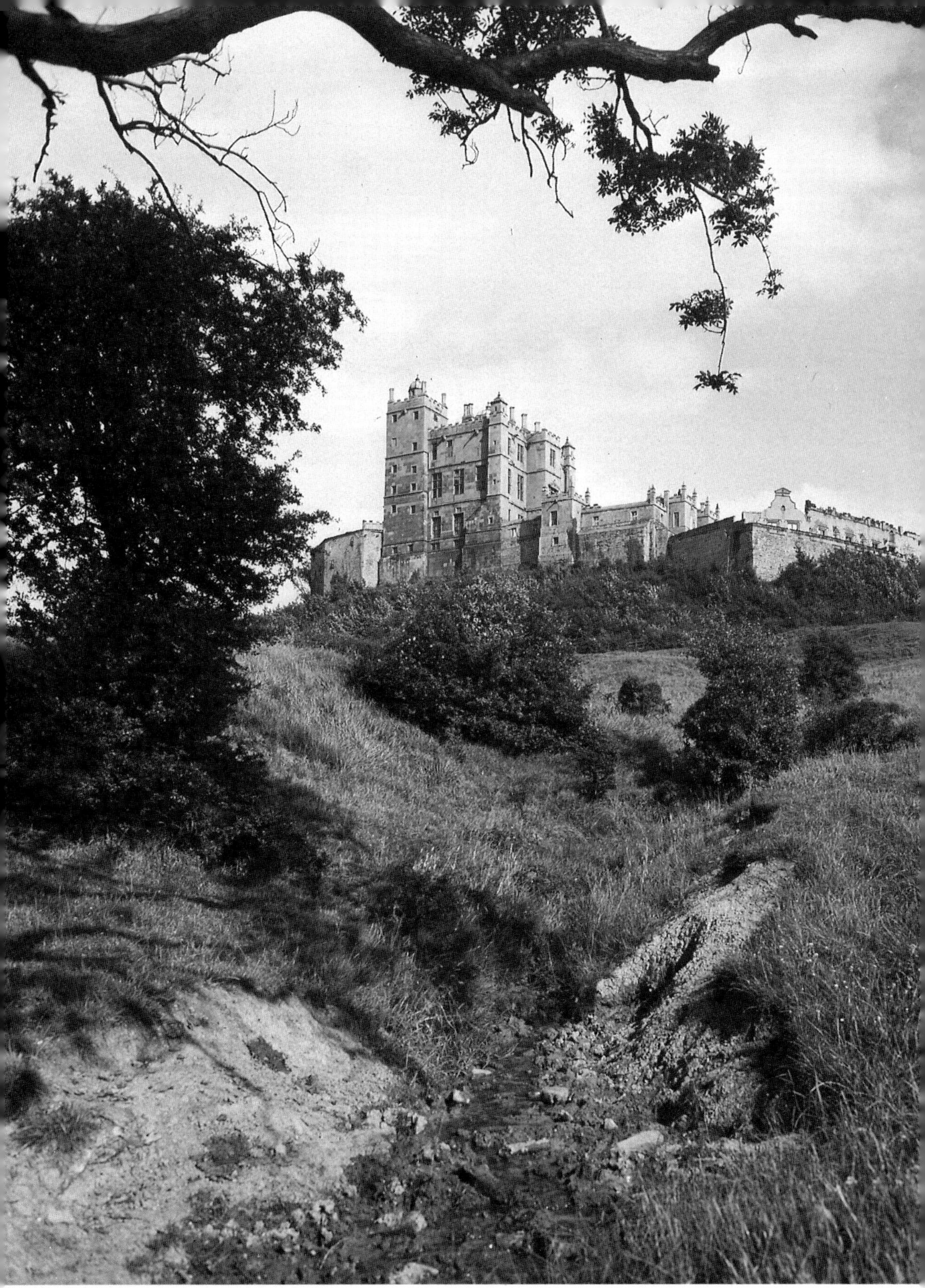

General view from the west, looking up the hill

servant and rapacious mistress, Eleanor Britton, at Handsworth, in Sheffield Park, where he died in November 1590. Thereafter the dowager countess retired to Hardwick where, abandoning work on her father's old house, she started afresh to build the greatest of her houses, Hardwick Hall, in which she died in 1608. She was buried in what is now Derby Cathedral in a tomb erected seven years before to a design by Robert Smithson.

When Gilbert Talbot succeeded as seventh Earl of Shrewsbury to an impoverished earldom, the manor and castle of Bolsover came into his possession. He and Charles Cavendish, the most dashing of Bess of Hardwick's sons, had been close friends in childhood and remained so in later years for Gilbert, like the other Talbot children, had always looked more to his stepmother for sympathy than to the old earl. Some years after their marriage, when the earl was already becoming estranged from his family, Gilbert Talbot and his wife set up house in London and he wrote complaining to the countess that, while his father allowed him only the use of the old furniture from the disused Talbot castle of Goodrich, 'that which your ladyship hath given is worth more than all ... my Lord's bestowing.' In 1608, the year of the countess's death, Gilbert leased Bolsover to his friend and brother-in-law Charles Cavendish for a thousand years at a rent of £10.

As a young man Charles Cavendish had seen service in the Low Countries, where he commanded a regiment and had been knighted. Later he served with Sir Philip Sidney and was present at the battle of Zutphen. He married first Margaret Kitson, by whom he had no issue, and second Catherine Ogle. She was daughter of Cuthbert, Baron Ogle, with whom he was living at Welbeck Abbey at the time he acquired Bolsover, probably with the intention of converting what was then a ruinous castle into a house.

Sir Charles, like his mother before him, was an enthusiastic builder and planned to transform both Welbeck and Bolsover. He employed Robert Smithson as his designer. There is no record of when work was actually started at Bolsover but the plans must have been complete and preliminary demolition work well under way by 1613. On 19 August of that year Sir Charles purchased the manor and castle of Bolsover outright with some six other surrounding manors formerly the property of the Earl and Countess of Shrewsbury.

Although Sir Charles Cavendish and Robert Smithson both died before work on the new Bolsover had proceeded very far, they must be given credit for the conception and the spirit of the buildings that were continued by their successors. There are, in fact, two houses at Bolsover which reflect the duality of the age in which they were built. The Little Castle is a poetic dream castle in which every opportunity is taken to exploit its romantic situation. Even now, viewed from the valley below, its dream-like quality survives, a quality that its creator must have realised could never have been achieved by a mere conversion of the prosaic, if genuine, castle that it replaced. By contrast, the Terrace Range represents the materialism of its time, a great house wherein a magnate might live and entertain in the state and luxury appropriate to his station.

For fifteen months from December 1612 the building accounts survive for Sir Charles's work. By then much of the demolition had been completed and the new buildings had begun to take shape. Most of the work recorded is preparatory. Quarries were opened up at Shuttlewood, Bolsover and Bolsover Moor and masons' lodges were erected there in which stone was worked and finished ready for transport to the site. At the same time

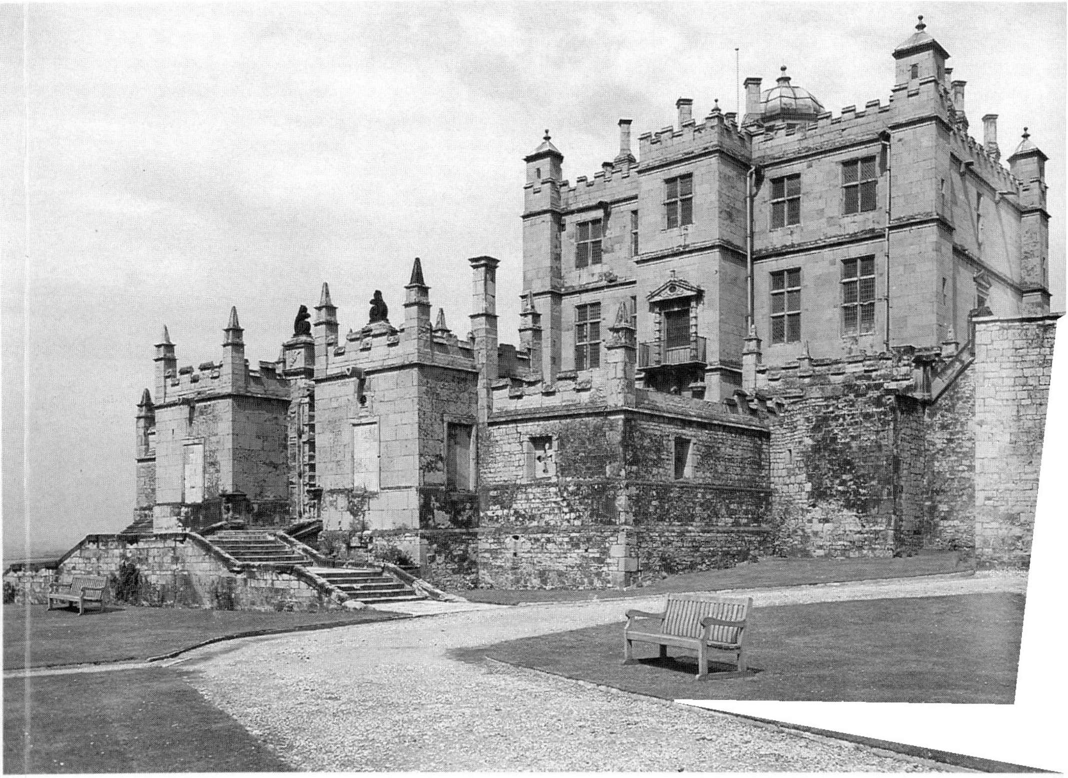

Little Castle

limestone was extracted, kilns built and the carpenters and smiths set to work producing the necessary plant; barrows, hods, shovels and hurdles for scaffolding are all mentioned.

A way was made into the castle, the well was built and provided with windlass, ropes and buckets, and work started on digging out the foundation trenches. Probably it was the Little Castle that was started first though this is not specified in the accounts. In April 1613 scaffolding was erected and the laying of stone commenced. Six months later foundation work started afresh, presumably on the Terrace Range, and thereafter work on the two buildings proceeded concurrently, unfinished work being protected from the winter frosts by a covering of thatch. By the end of the year work was sufficiently advanced for the vaults of the basements to be turned; work on the larder vault is mentioned in the following February. In March 1614 the accounts end.

Throughout the fifteen months covered there are sundry entries relating to further demolition work in taking down old walls. From items which show work being done on 'the old house,' the repair of chimneys and of glazing, it seems that some of the old buildings had been retained as temporary accommodation. It is the last that is heard of the medieval castle.

Studied in detail, the Bolsover accounts give much useful information on contemporary building practice. They were made up each fortnight and show that Smithson personally supervised the works, making frequent visits in each period. His salary would have appeared in the household accounts; here only his expenses are recorded, for which he was allowed 4d a meal for himself and about a shilling (5p) a day for his horse. Most of the work was done by men paid directly from the building account at a daily wage, the number employed rising to about 20 in January 1613 and to over 50 by February 1614. The actual numbers would have been higher as some of the work was sub-contracted to the masons in charge of the lodges at the quarries. Masons, carpenters and other skilled trades received from 10d to 12d a day while the labourers averaged 6d. In addition, boys, women and girls were employed in labouring and carrying at rates between 2d and 4d, mostly in the summer months when about ten women and girls were working.

Materials for the works all came from local sources: stone from Shuttlewood, Bolsover Moor and Bolsover Town quarries, all within 3 miles (4.8km) of the castle, was supplemented by second-hand stone from the demolition of a building in Kirkby-in-Ashfield. There is no mention of re-using ASHLAR from the medieval castle, which suggests that this was mostly constructed in rubble walling that was unsuitable for re-use. Lime was burnt in kilns near the site and sand was obtained from the old buildings. Timber was from Scarcliffe Park, a few miles to the east.

In 1614 Robert Smithson died and for the next three years John Smithson took over the direction of the works for Sir Charles until the latter's death in 1617. During these three years the shell of the Little Castle was completed and considerable progress made on the Terrace Range where the northern end, containing the kitchens below and apartments above, was up to gable height. At this point there was, naturally, a pause before Sir William Cavendish was in a position to continue either at Bolsover or Welbeck.

Meanwhile, John Smithson travelled south for Sir William to see what was new to be learnt in London. Here, through 1618, he visited houses and palaces recently built, made drawings and surveys of those that interested him and returned to his client full of enthusiasm for what he had seen. At Bolsover work was restarted on the Terrace Range for which John Smithson provided a new plan. The great hall, later converted to a dining room, and long gallery were completed to this plan but of the intended range of state rooms and apartments on two floors facing the Great Court, only the foundations were laid. Alterations to the terrace façade of Sir Charles's unfinished building brought this into line with John Smithson's new ideas, which found expression in the design of the central doorcase to the gallery.

Though the refacing of the medieval curtain wall was also proceeding it is probable that, at this stage, there was still some demolition work to be done on the site of the old keep and it was this that held up work on the Little Castle and its forecourt to which Sir William turned his attention in 1620 before the Terrace Range scheme was wholly complete. The effects of Smithson's London visit appear more clearly here. Sir Charles had completed the exterior but, even so, the west and south balcony features were redesigned to suit the new mode. So too, the interior where the fireplaces, the panelling in the Pillar Chamber and Star Chamber, and the mural and ceiling paintings were all completed between 1620 and 1630.

At last the house was capable of being occupied. The water supply was supplemented by a fresh pipe line and

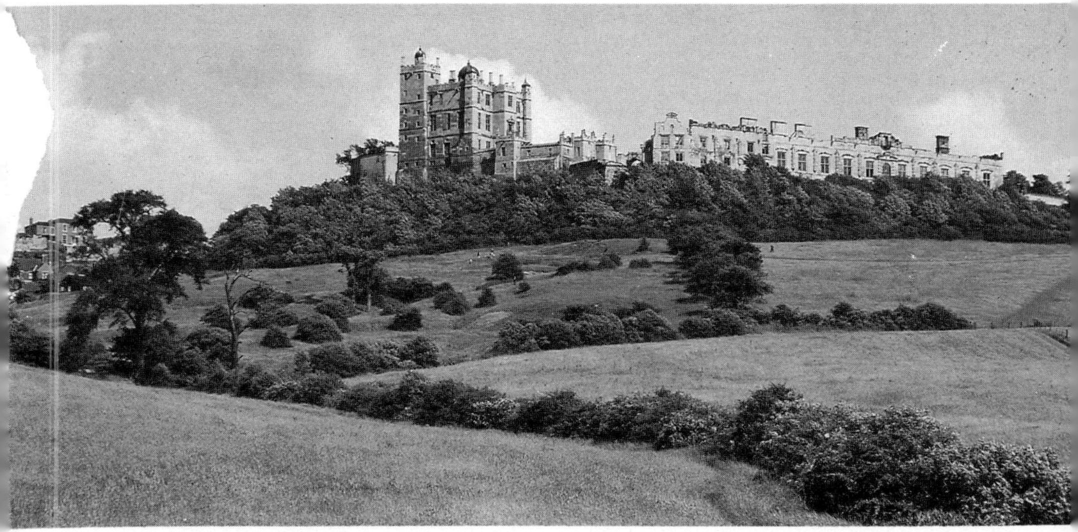

View from the southwest

conduit houses from Spittle Green to the southeast and, by 1633, the Fountain Garden was finished and the Little Castle connected to the private apartments in the Terrace Range by the wall walk. The transformation of the medieval castle was complete.

While these works were going on at Bolsover, Sir William, now Viscount Mansfield, was also carrying out major building works at Welbeck where the great riding school had been completed in 1623 to John Smithson's designs. To a man of his tastes Bolsover must have seemed incomplete without a similar riding school and this, indeed, formed the next project on which work was started about 1630. The hand of a fresh and more sophisticated designer is apparent in the new work and it must have been at this point that Huntingdon Smithson took over from his father, completing the Riding School Range and the boundary wall enclosing the great court, with the southeast and southwest gates.

In 1633 Sir William, created Earl of Newcastle in 1628, was host to King Charles and his Queen, then on progress to the north, at a great entertainment held at Welbeck at which a masque by Ben Jonson was performed. This was to be followed, a year later, by another equally lavish entertainment at Bolsover. Doubtless the completion of the Great Court was hastened in readiness for this event which was held on 30 July 1634. Again there was a banquet and a masque by Jonson, this time entitled *Love's Welcome to Bolsover*.

The banquet would have been held in the long gallery, then the only room large enough; the state rooms were yet to be built. Jonson, it seems, took advantage of the unfinished state of the building to introduce such appropriate characters as Chesil the carver, Maul the freemason, Quarrel the glazier, Fret the plasterer, and so on. The banquet was in two parts, separated by the dancing which may have taken place in the court. In the second part the King and Queen were served by the conventional two loves, Eros and Anteros, equipped with 'bows and quivers, cassocks, breeches, buskins, gloves and perukes.' For lack of accommodation the King and Queen did not stay the night at Bolsover but continued on to Welbeck.

Though another entertainment, proposed for the following year at Bolsover, did not take place, it may have been this proposal that prompted Newcastle to start work on a new suite of state rooms suitable for royal guests. Between 1635 and 1640 the Terrace Range was again transformed. John Smithson's design for rooms facing the Great Court was abandoned and a new, unknown designer was employed to erect the new rooms, refurnish the gallery and alter the old great hall into a dining room.

A further pressing need for the provision of new state rooms may have been Newcastle's appointment in 1638 as governor to Charles, Prince of Wales, the future Charles II. This honour, which the earl had himself sought two years before, he relinquished after three years in 1641 having, it was said, incurred £40 000 in debts as a result.

With the Civil War Newcastle placed his services and resources at the disposal of the King, who appointed him first Governor of Newcastle upon Tyne and then Commander-in-Chief of all forces raised north of the Trent, including his own regiment. The earl immediately set about consolidating Yorkshire and the north for the Royalists. The campaign was successful. He occupied York in November 1642. Such was the Royalist optimism that by the following February it was considered safe for the Queen to return from Holland. Newcastle met her at Bridlington on 22 February and arranged an escort of three to four thousand sorely needed troops for her journey south to meet the King. In the midst of these arrangements he had the news of the death of his wife at Welbeck, to which he returned in April for her funeral.

That summer Newcastle added to the list of his successes the securing of Yorkshire and Lincolnshire for the King, but, towards the end of the year, the tide had begun to turn with the advance of the Scots from the north and of Fairfax from the south. In December he was in Derbyshire and made a short visit to Bolsover to establish a garrison for the castle under Colonel Muschamp. The continued threat from the Scots drew him north again for the campaign that culminated in the long siege of York from April to June 1644.

After the relief of York by Prince Rupert there followed the engagement, fatal to Royalist hopes, of Marston Moor. Newcastle, with the prince present, held no command at the battle but led a troop of his own Whitecoats, so known for their coats of white woollen cloth. Even their famed heroism failed to save the day, which ended with the Royalist commanders, Newcastle among them, taking refuge in York. Here the leaders broke up and Newcastle rode the next day to Scarborough and thence crossed to Hamburg to commence his long exile.

On 12 August 1644 the garrison at Bolsover surrendered and Colonel Muschamp and his troops were allowed to march out with drums and colours, horses, swords and pistols, leaving behind them 'six pieces of ordnance and three hundred firearms,' the castle and manor being sequestrated. The castle was garrisoned by the Parliamentary forces and remained so until 1649 when the Trustees of Delinquents' Estates ordered the Committee of Derbyshire to demolish the outworks and garden walls with the turrets and walls of the frontier-court that were of strength, and ordered that all the doors should be removed and slight ones set in their place.

"Joan Miró: the twenties.
Mutation of reality", 1983

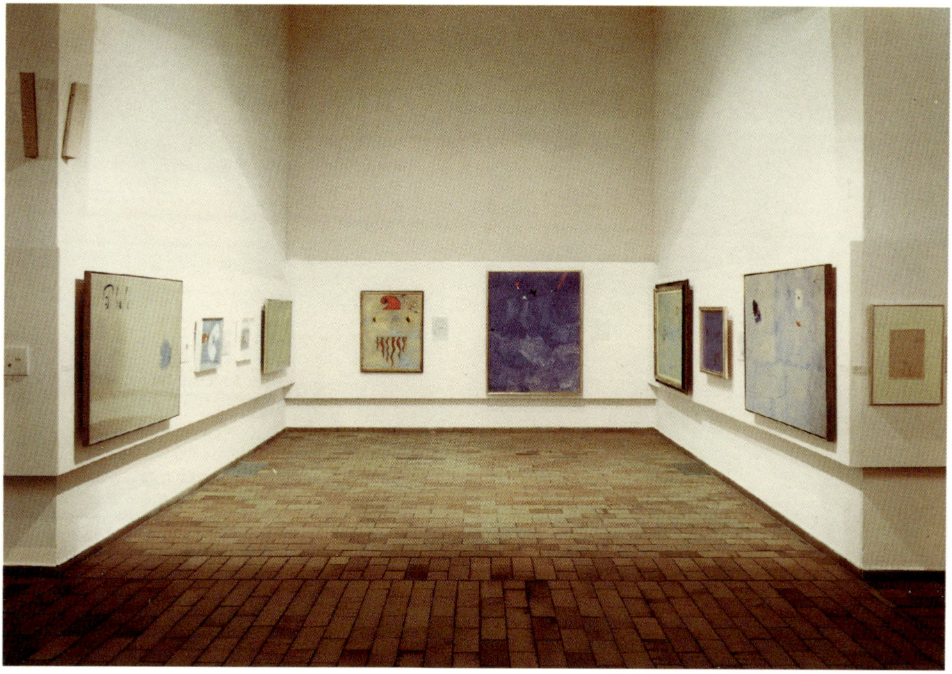

The Foundation, however, does not hold works of art only by Miró. It also has a small collection of contemporary pieces that was formed a year after his death through the generosity of artists, collectors and friends who wished to pay tribute to him.

This collection, consisting of donations and permanent loans, includes paintings, sculptures, photographs and objects by leading contemporaries of Miró such as Balthus, Bissier, Duchamp, Ernst, González, Lam, Llorens Artigas, Manolo, Man Ray, Masson, Matisse, Moore, Penn, Penrose, Tanguy and Torres-García, as well as works by later artists such as Adami, Alechinsky, Brossa, Català-Roca, Chillida, Guston, Motherwell, Newman, Rauschenberg, Saura and Tàpies.

Finally, the Foundation also holds a large collection of original prints by contemporary artists donated by Aimé Maeght in 1976, as well as other pieces contributed by Alfaro, Chillida and Villèlia, among others. An especially relevant place in this section is occupied by two works by Alexander Calder: *Corcovado,* donated by Josep Lluís Sert, and the *Mercury fountain,* originally designed for the Spanish Republican Government's pavilion at the 1937 Paris World Fair and donated to the Foundation by its creator as a token of his friendship with Miró.

Activities

The activities organised by the Foundation have generally been of two kinds, related to its two principal objects: the work of Joan Miró, and contemporary art in all its various manifestations.

Although Miró repeatedly expressed his wish that the Foundation should be a centre of living art and not merely a memorial to his own work, it is an undeniable fact that it possessed from the outset a highly exceptional asset in the shape of the works donated by the artist himself, which constitute the Foundation's permanent collection.

The Foundation has made this important collection accessible to the public through a constantly rotating selection of items on show, through loans to other institutions, and by organising exhibitions on different aspects of the founder's work, namely:

"Wolfgang Laib" exhibition, 1989

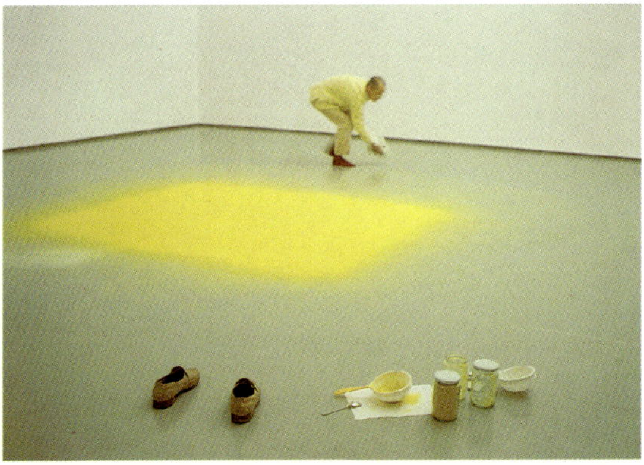

"Joan Miró 1893-1993" centenary exhibition

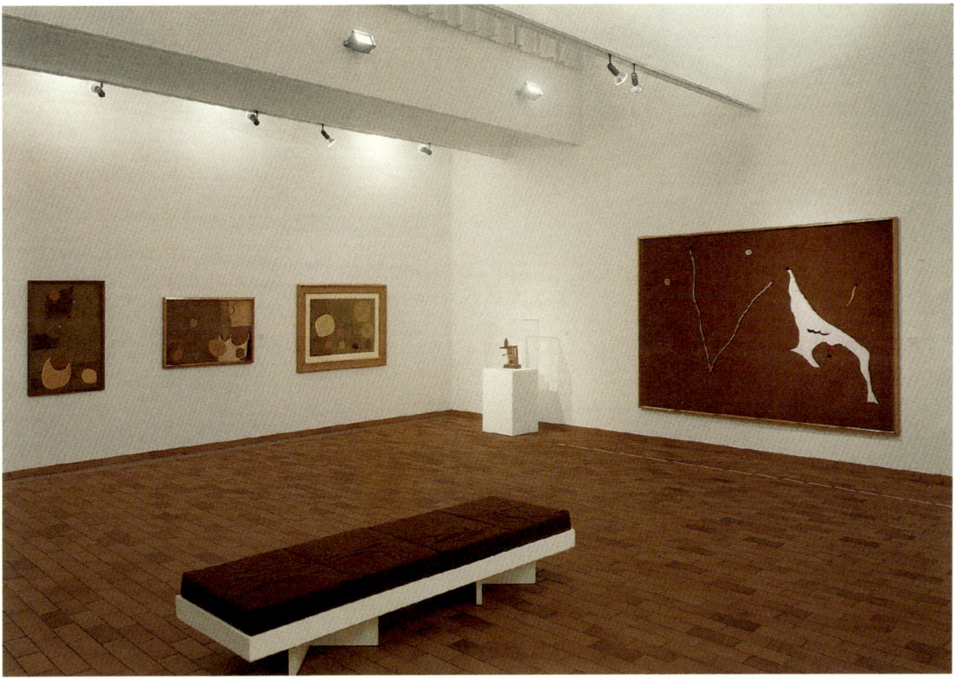

"Miró on stage", 1995

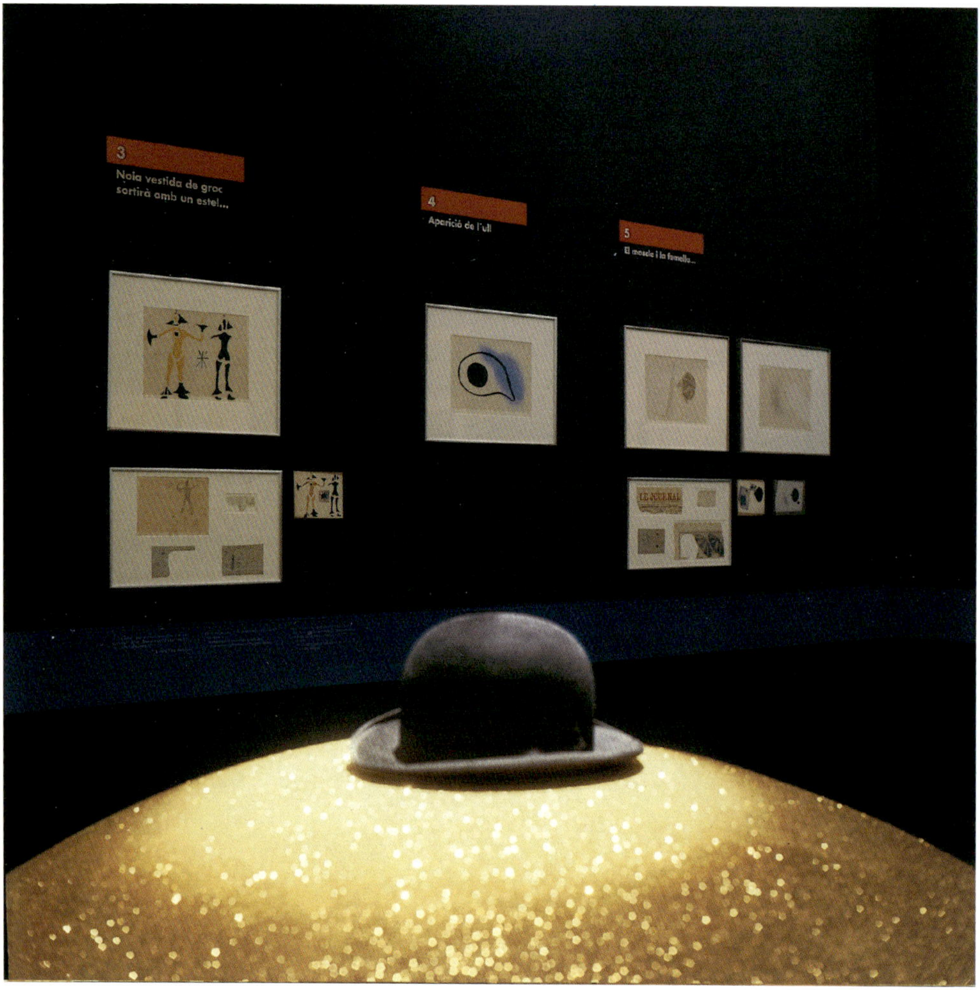

1976: 500 drawings by Joan Miró from the Foundation's collections
1980: Joan Miró: complete graphic works
1982: Joan Miró: painting, sculpture, ceramics, tapestry, theatre
1983: Joan Miró: the twenties. Mutation of reality
1985: Miró in close-up
1988: Impacts. Joan Miró: 1929-1941
1989: 109 books with Joan Miró
1993: Joan Miró: 1893-1993
1995: Miró on stage
1997: Joan Miró: equilibrium in space

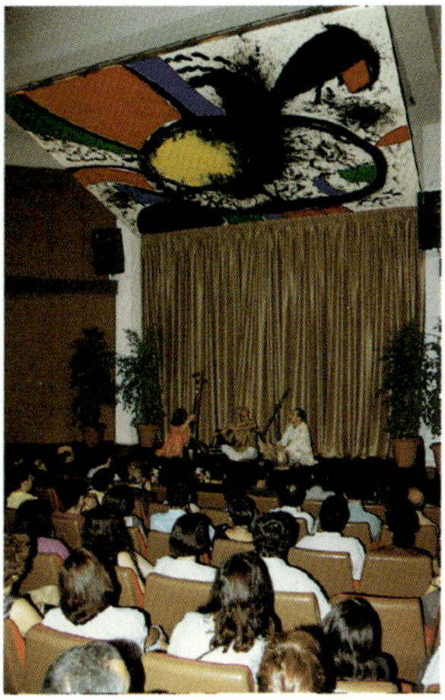
Recital in the Auditorium

When the idea of setting up the Joan Miró Foundation began to take shape in the early seventies, and even when it was finally opened to the public in 1975, the attention paid to contemporary art by official institutions was minimal.

To fill this gap, the Foundation began arranging a programme of temporary exhibitions parallel to its other activities. This programme was planned for the twofold purpose of making known to the public the leading names and movements in twentieth-century art and of publicising the work of younger artists.

The main temporary exhibitions have included:

1975: Tantric art
1976: Antoni Tàpies: works 1955-1976
1977: America, America (US painting 1945-1975)
1978: Olfactory suggestions
1979: The architecture of Josep Lluís Sert
1980: Antonio Saura: retrospective
1981: Henry Moore: sculptures, drawings and prints
1982: The principle of collage
1983: Kurt Schwitters
1984: Marcel Duchamp
1985: Russian avant-garde, 1910-1930
1986: Chillida: sculptures

"Andy Warhol" exhibition, 1996

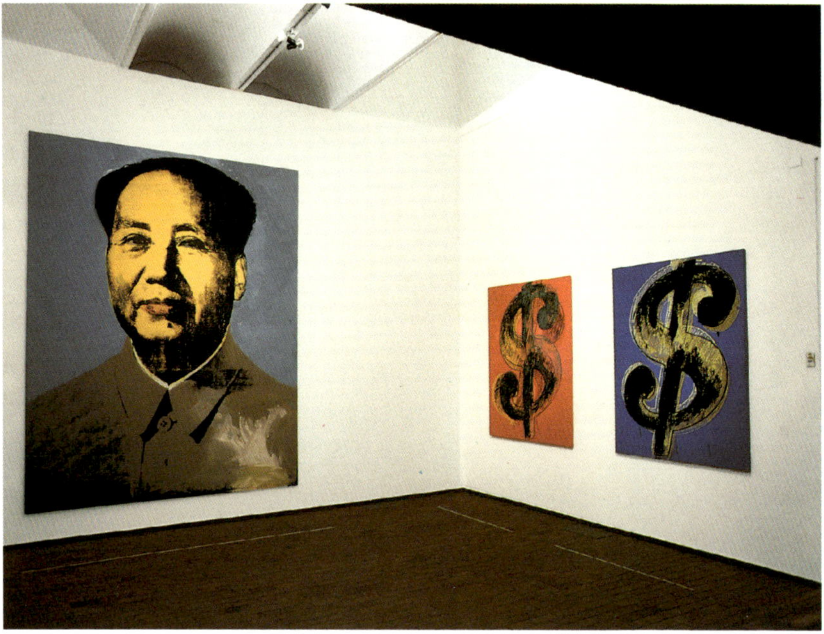

1987: The Giacomettis
1988: Donald Judd: sculpture 1965-1987
1989: 1st Joan Miró Drawing Triennial
1990: Joseph Beuys
1991: Antiquity/Modernity in twentieth-century art
1992: Moving image: Electronic art
1993: Wifredo Lam
1994: Mapplethorpe
1995: China: art of living, art of surviving
1996: Andy Warhol
1997: Alexander Calder
1998: René Magritte
1999: Reality and desire
2000: Mark Rothko

During the first dozen years of the Foundation's existence, the experimental work of younger artists had its own particular venue in the "Espai 10" and later, after the extension was added, in the "Espai 13".

The Foundation's activities, however, extend beyond exhibitions and embrace very diverse sectors of the present cultural scene. Lectures, seminars and panel discussions are regularly held in conjunction with exhibitions. Other events include recitals of contemporary music, film shows, theatrical performances and, occasionally, performances by contemporary dance groups.

The Foundation also organises regular activities for children. It makes a special point of arranging guided tours of the permanent and temporary exhibitions, so that learning about art is treated as a complementary part of the academic programme. Younger visitors can also enjoy the theatrical performances for children held every weekend during term-time.

The Foundation's aim is to make visits by the public as pleasant as possible, not only through the interesting content of its programmes but also through the quality of the facilities available. Visitors are therefore allowed access to the Library specialising in contemporary art, which was initially based on the books donated by Miró but has continued to grow ever since.

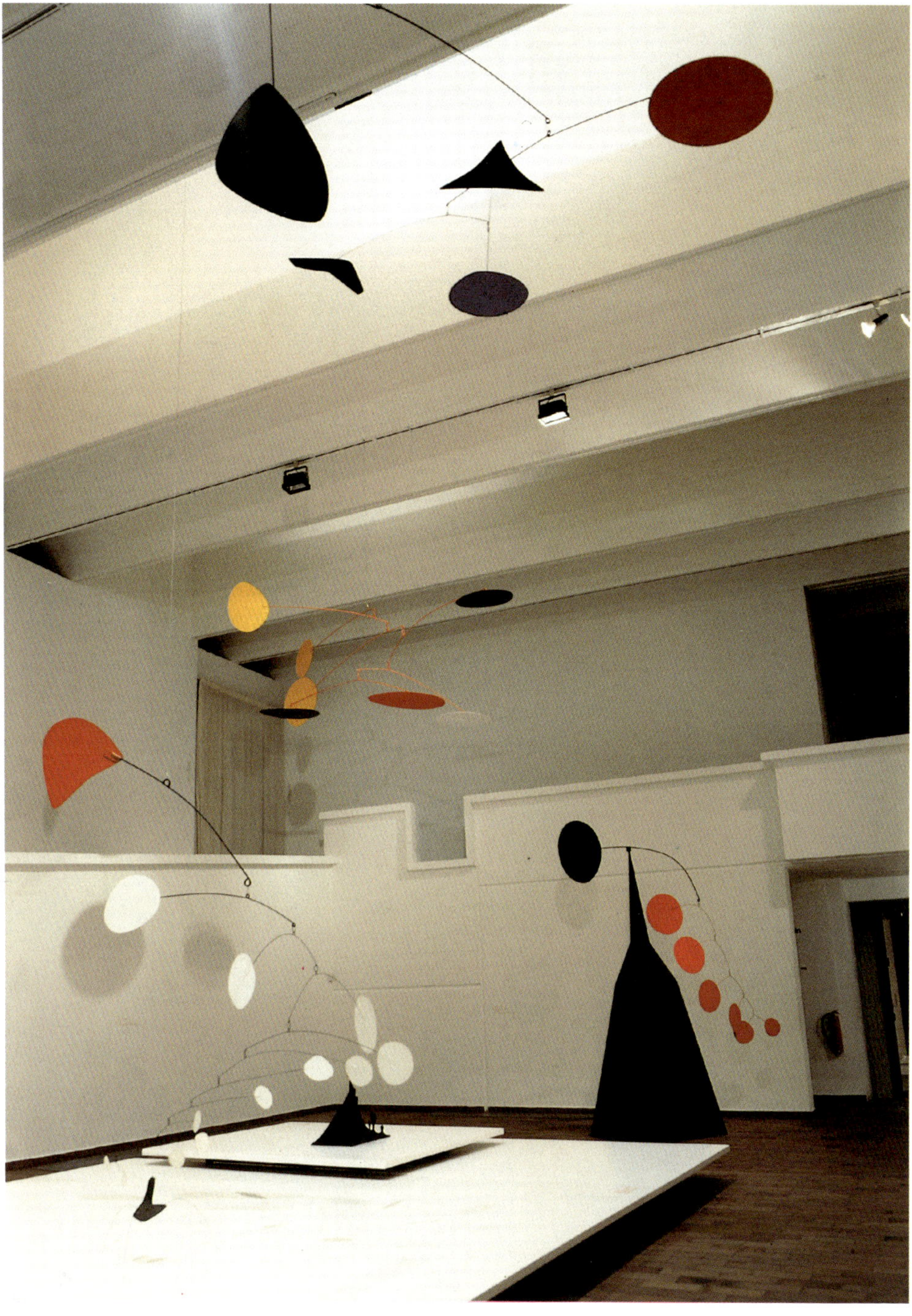

"Calder" exhibition, 1997

The Book Shop and Gift Shop offer a wide selection of the latest books on contemporary art as well as reproductions, designer articles, and other goods.

The Bar-Restaurant is just one more of the services provided by the Foundation for its visitors, where they can relax indoors or outdoors.

The Association of Friends of the Joan Miró Foundation offers a number of advantages, special concessions and activities to those who wish to support the institution set up by Miró.

Miró's works held by the Foundation

The chiropodist, 1901

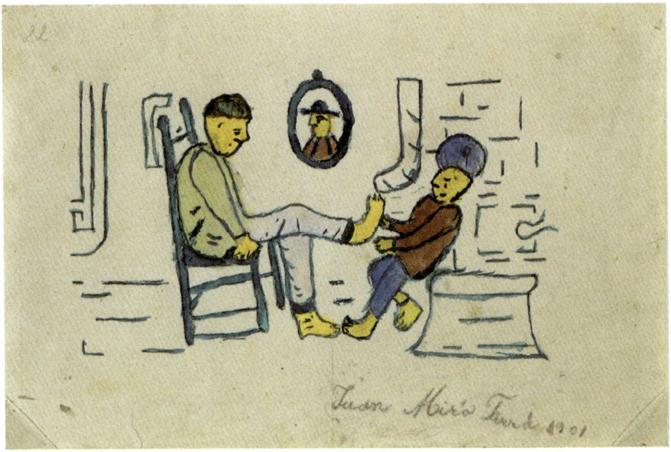

Early Drawings

The earliest reference to Miró's artistic activity comes from the collection of drawings held by the Foundation. This material is a valuable testimony that graphically describes the development of Miró's art, but it also allows us to follow the events and activities connected with his work.

The oldest of these drawings date back to 1901, when Miró was eight years old. They are very simple compositions, always in colour and generally portraying a single object – an umbrella, a flower pot, a tortoise. Among them, one piece stands out on account of its bright tones and the somewhat curious scene depicted: *The chiropodist.* This drawing is almost a prediction of the importance that Miró was subsequently to attach to the foot. According to him, this part of the human body keeps us in contact with the creative force emanating from the earth, and in his pictures it was later to be magnified by distorting its proportions, insinuated by means of an imprint, or sublimated by altering its meaning.

It was probably at school, in 1905, that Miró produced a series of drawings of a markedly romantic nature, a style inherited from the previous century that was very popular in conventional circles. The dominant themes of these pieces are rural landscapes or imaginary medieval scenes.

Contrasting with these drawings, probably done as copying exercises at school, is a sketchbook from the summer of the following year. During the long summer holidays, Miró used to

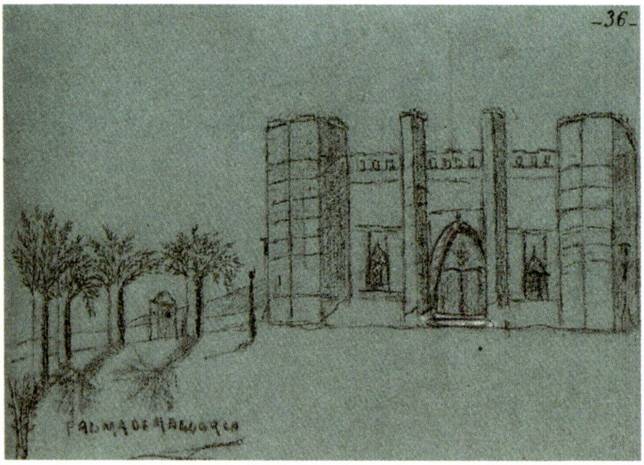

Palma de Mallorca. The Llotja, c. 1906

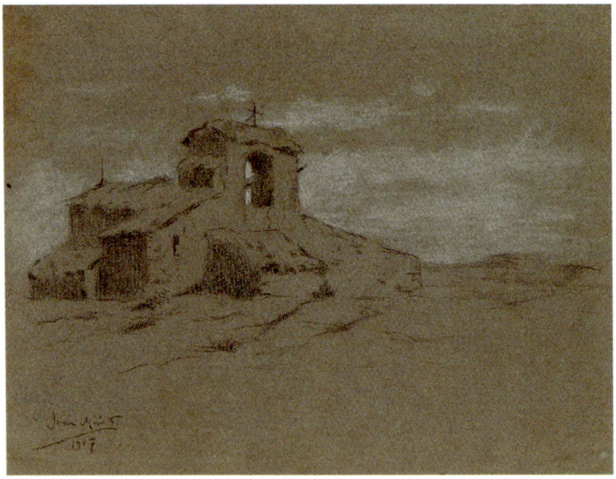

Chapel, 1907

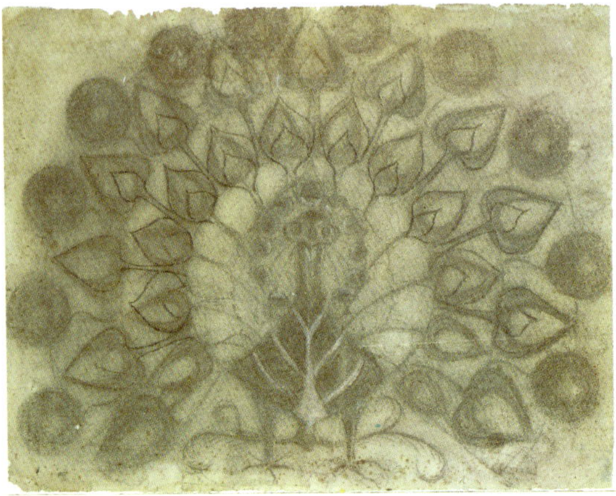

Peacock, c. 1908

Snake, c. 1908

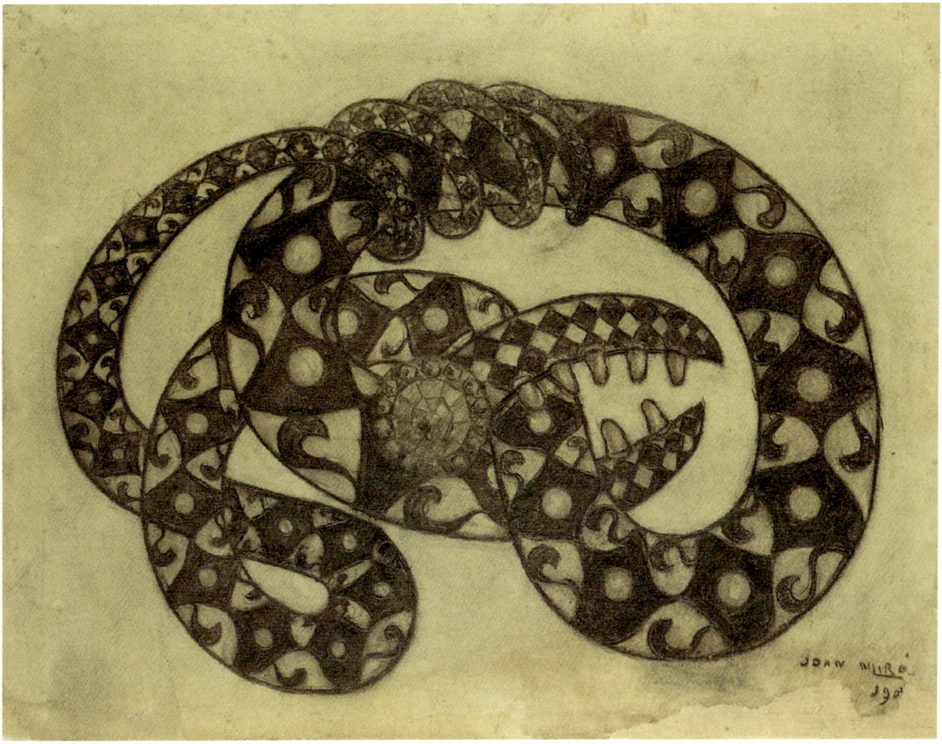

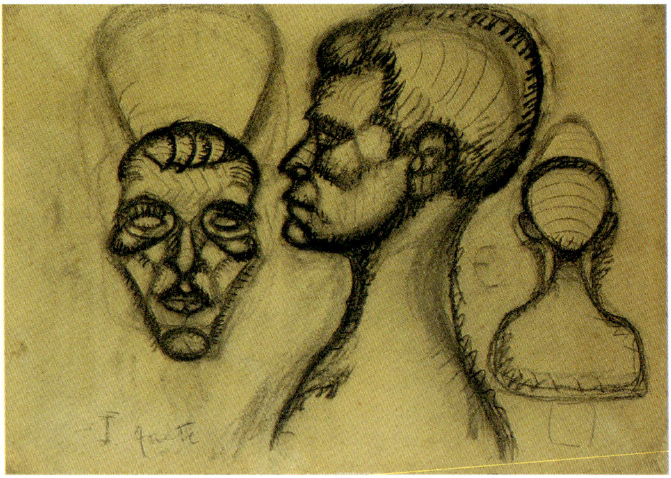

Exercise in touch. Three heads, c. 1912

spend time both at his paternal grandparents' house in Cornudella, and in Majorca where his maternal grandparents lived. The drawings of Prades, Siurana, Porrera and Cornudella bear witness to his holidays in the province of Tarragona, while in Majorca he drew the typical windmills, Bellver Castle, and the port and Llotja (exchange) in Palma.

After finishing primary school in 1907, Miró enrolled in the Escola de Comerç in Barcelona and also in the Llotja school of art. There he combined his commercial studies, undertaken on his father's orders, with his incipient artistic vocation. Although he always rejected anything that did not involve live creation and hated academicism and convention, he always had fond memories of his time at the Llotja, especially his relationship with two teachers, Modest Urgell (1839-1919) and Josep Pascó (1855-1910).

The Foundation holds a good number of drawings done by Miró in Modest Urgell's classes. The subjects represented – landscapes with cemeteries, crumbling walls, cypress trees, etc. – show clearly the influence of the master that was to be evident throughout his work. From Modest Urgell he acquired a taste for empty spaces, for the line of the horizon defining the earth and sky, and for the constant presence of heavenly bodies. References to Urgell became almost an obsession in the final months of Miró's life and confirm the high regard in which he held him as a teacher.

The only records of Josep Pascó's classes are two exceptional drawings, one of a peacock and the other of a snake. In the ornamental style and curvaceous lines of both pieces, which were possibly to be used as designs for jewellery, the influence of the Art Nouveau of the time can be clearly felt.

The panorama of Miró's formative years is completed by the drawings from the period when he attended classes at the art school run by Francesc Galí (1880-1965), a private academy that was more open-minded than the Llotja. The teaching there was not limited to traditional classes on the school premises, but often included sessions spent sketching in the open air, music recitals, poetry readings and debates.

To this period can be dated several curious drawings produced not by viewing the subject but by perceiving it through touch. For the first time, a human figure appears – or part of one, in this case, for the drawings are different studies of heads.

Francesc Galí imposed this particular exercise on his pupil after noting his extraordinary gifts as a colourist but his difficulty in reproducing form. By letting the sense of touch take over, Galí unwittingly provided Miró with a new perspective that he was not to explore in depth until later: the possibility of working in three dimensions.

Mas d'en Poca, 1914

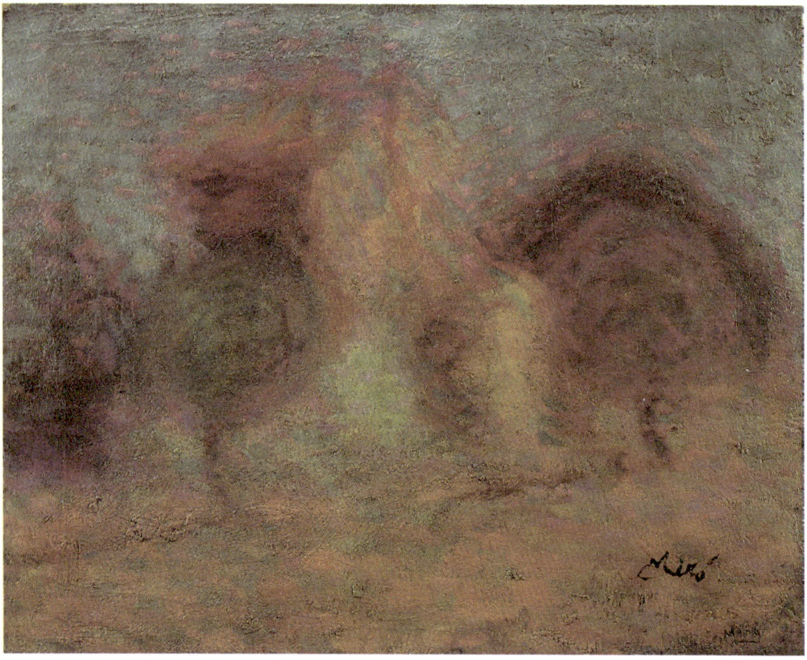

Barcelona / Mont-roig

The first catalogued paintings by Joan Miró date from 1914. In them we again find the subjects that appeared so often in his drawings, especially landscape. One notable work from this period is *Mas d'en Poca,* a representational painting in exuberant colours.

In order to perfect his drawing techniques, Miró left Galí's school in 1915 and joined the Cercle Artístic de Sant Lluc, where he attended lessons in life-drawing until he left for Paris.

Preserved from his days at the Cercle Artístic are three loose drawings and three sketchbooks containing mainly male and female nudes. Produced with very limited materials – paper and graphite pencil or ink – they allow us to follow the artist's progress, concerned at times with capturing a gesture and at others with depicting the precise features of a face or transmitting movement in a rapid stroke.

Aside from their documentary value, these sketchbooks reveal some of Miró's interests at the time, since in addition to the models we find the dancers, clowns and music-hall figures that enlivened Barcelona's night-life and that Miró discovered in the company of Sebastià Gasch. Of particular note among the drawings from this period held at the Foundation is *Female nude,* from the Prats collection.

Once again we find a landscape – a subject that Miró never abandoned – though this time with a certain post-Impressionist influence, in *Beach at Mont-roig,* 1916.

Female nude, 1915

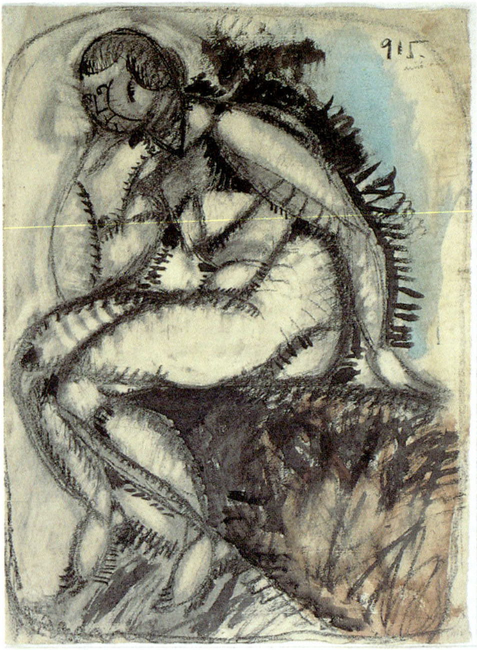

Female nude, 1917. Gift of Joan Prats

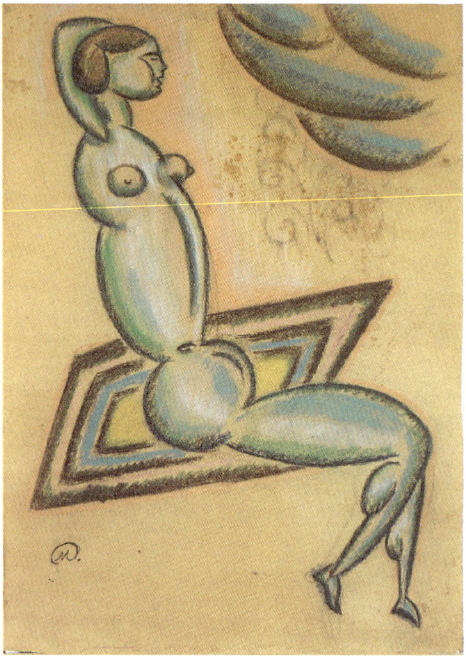

Beach at Mont-roig, 1916

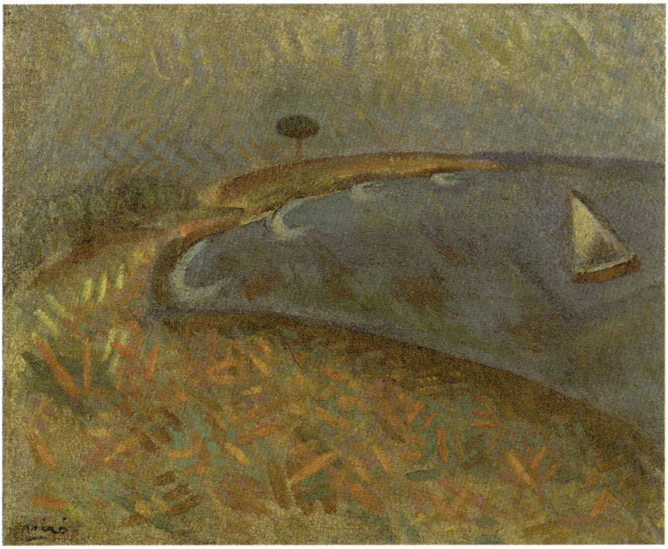

Chapel of Sant Joan d'Horta,
1917. Gift of Joan Prats

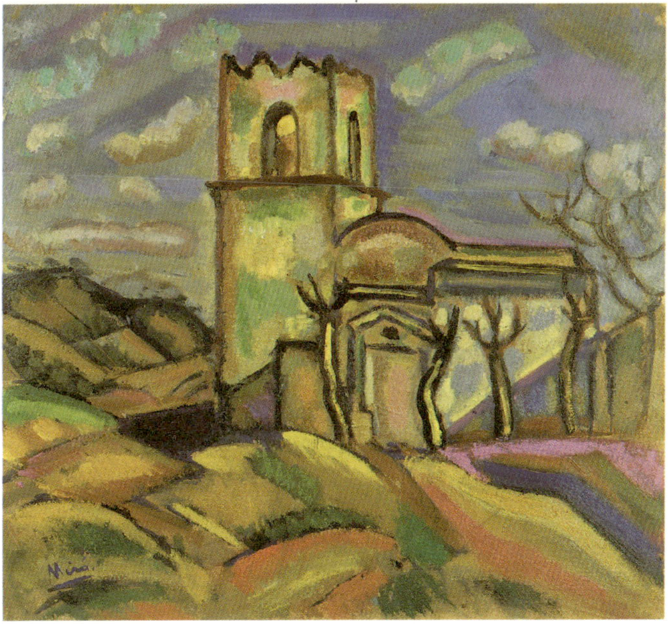

Street in Pedralbes, 1917. Gift of
Joan Prats

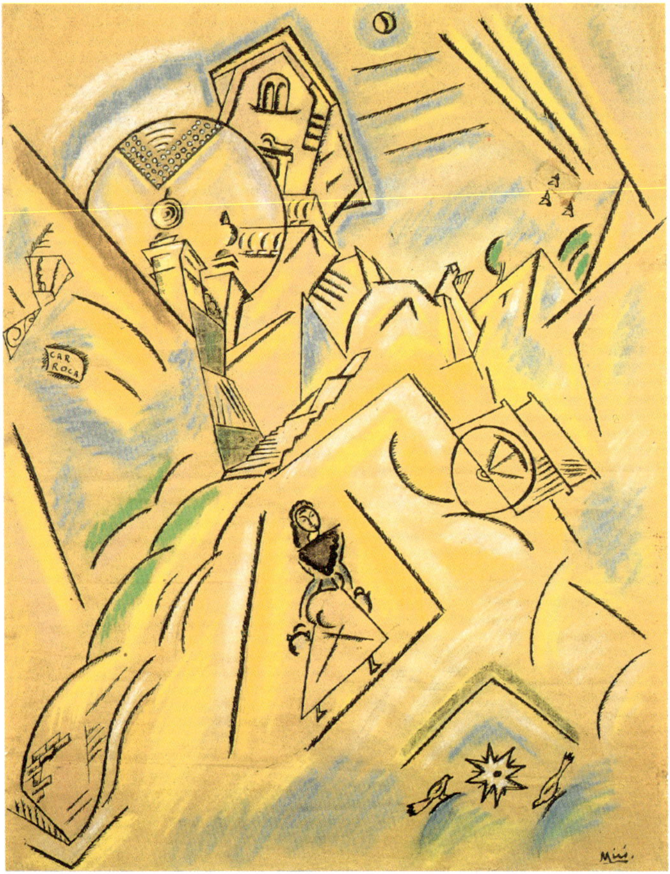

In 1917, artistic and intellectual life in Barcelona experienced a brief but intense period of effervescence with the arrival of artists and intellectuals fleeing from the scene of the First World War. Among them was Francis Picabia, a strong stimulus for those who wanted to keep abreast of the latest developments in avant-garde art. It was thanks to him that the Dada movement reached Barcelona, where he began publication of the review *391.*

Miró was not indifferent to these events, though he took a passive rather than active part in them. His style had yet to be defined and his artistic persona was as yet unformed when Dada made its impact on the city.

Miro's work at that time was basically influenced by Fauvism on the one hand, and by Cubism and even more so by Cézanne on the other. Thus, the rich and in many cases unrealistic colours, the thick brush strokes and a discreet distortion of forms – the principal features of Fauvism – can be seen in *Chapel of Sant Joan d'Horta.* The alteration of the classical values of painting brought about by the Cubist concept of space is timidly reflected in *Street in Pedralbes.*

Except for the paintings, most of which are now in private collections and foreign museums, the works by Miró that have survived from the period between his leaving the Cercle Artístic de Sant Lluc and 1923 are not many in number. Nevertheless, we know that during those years certain events took place that were of major importance to the artist and to the development of his work.

In 1918, the Barcelona gallery owner Josep Dalmau organised Miró's first solo exhibition, which contained most of the canvases painted between 1914 and 1917: landscapes, still-lifes and portraits.

After passing the test of showing his work outside his studio, Miró, now fully freed from the Fauve influence, embarked on a slowly and meticulously executed style of painting, and in the following year produced *Portrait of a young girl* and *Village and church of Mont-roig.*

In March 1920, he visited Paris for the first time, but did not move there until 1921. He took up residence in number 45 Rue

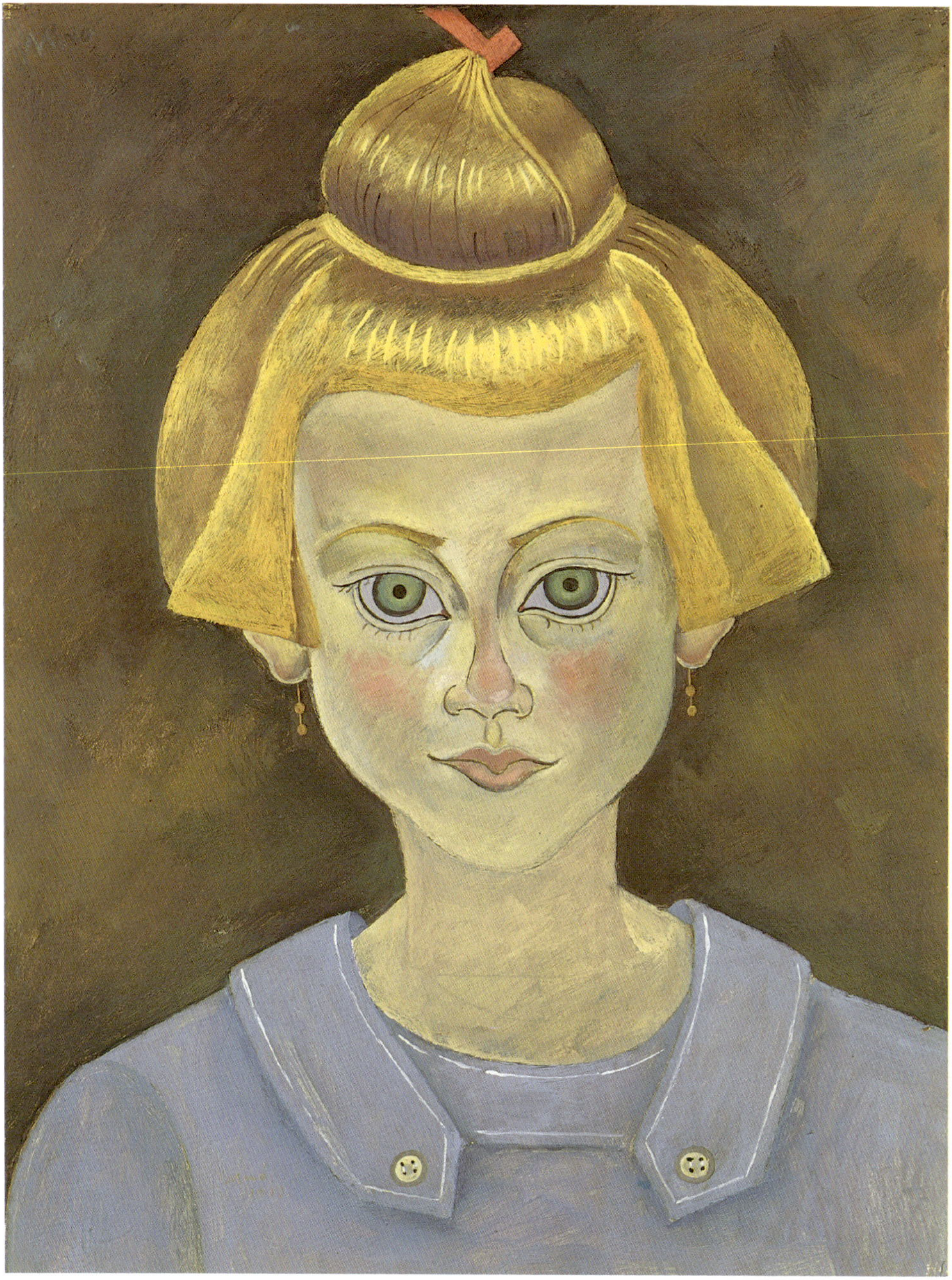

Portrait of a young girl, 1919.
Gift of Joan Prats

Blomet, in the studio used in the summers by the sculptor Pablo Gargallo, a teacher at the Escola de Belles Arts in Barcelona, but empty during the rest of the academic year.

In Paris, Miró continued painting in the minutely detailed style that had defined his work during the years immediately before leaving Spain and that he was to keep up until 1922, when he finished painting *The farm.* This masterpiece from his *détailliste* period is a milestone in Miró's career, for it contains the germs of his subsequent output: his love of the stars, respect for agricultural work, fascination with everyday objects, interest in insects, pets and farm animals, etc.

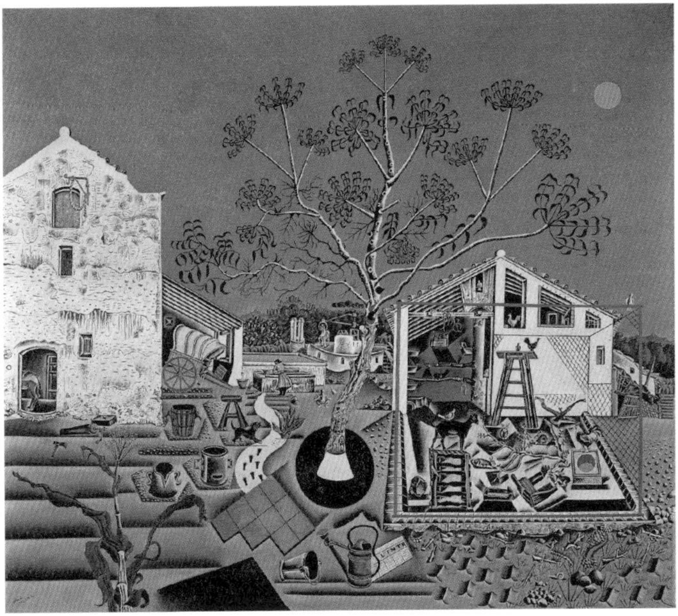

The farm, 1921-22. National Gallery of Art, Washington. Mary Hemingway Bequest

The wine bottle, 1924.
On permanent loan from Dolors Fernández

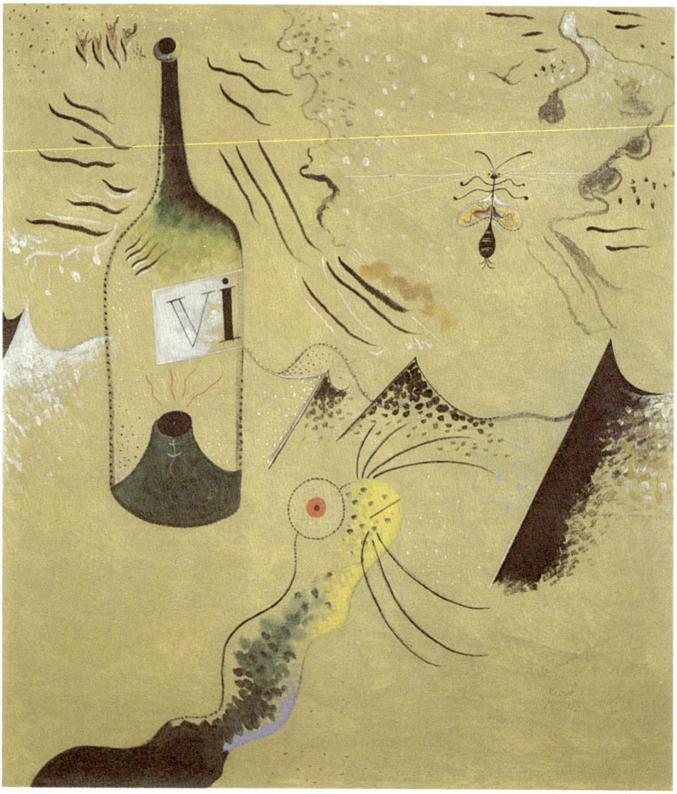

Paris

In the middle of 1924, Miró returned to Paris having spent the summer in Mont-roig, where he had started *Tilled field* and *Catalan landscape (The hunter).* His forms of expression as regards figurative representation were exhausted and he looked for new ways of transmitting his experiences through painting. These he found by distancing himself from his immediate surroundings. This restlessness coincided with the period of intellectual ferment in Paris, resulting in the first Surrealist Manifesto, published on 15th October that year.

Gradually realism gave way to suggestion and poetry in Miró's art. Form underwent a notable change as a consequence of a different approach. Instead of reproducing reality as his eyes perceived it, he let himself be invaded by what he saw and then processed it in a very subjective manner. Later on, in the studio, he painted what his feelings dictated as a consequence of the impact received.

During that time, drawing acquired a new dimension in the context of Miró's work, ceasing to be an end in itself and becoming instead a means to an end. Virtually all his sketches produced during the 1920s, and now at the Foundation, are a preliminary phase in the production of the final paintings. They enable us to compile a more than usually accurate inventory of his output during this decade, and to follow the process that preceded the execution of each painting from the moment

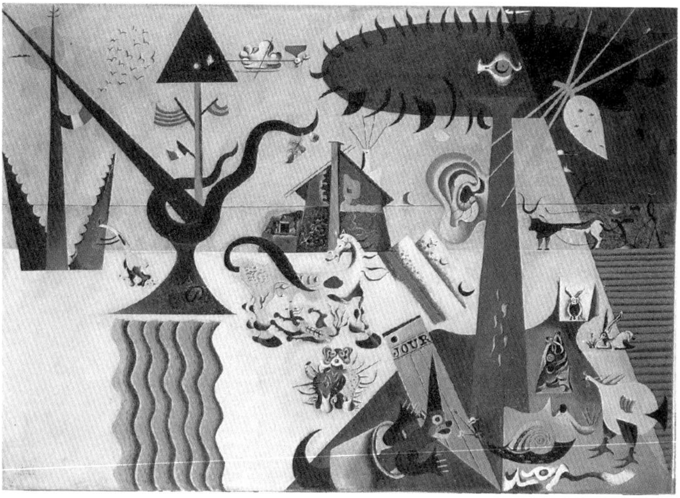

Tilled field, 1923-24. Solomon R. Guggenheim Museum, New York

when, still using reality as a point of reference, Miró ceased to portray it as an immediate experience.

This change in his approach heralded in *Tilled field* (1923-24) and consolidated in *Catalan landscape (The hunter)* (1923-24) – the preliminary sketches for which are preserved at the Foundation – can also be seen in *The wine bottle* (1924). In this small-format canvas, with its seemingly banal iconography and the inscription "To my parents" alongside the signature and date, Miró transmits a sense of vitality and of interchange between the celestial and the earthly creatures.

The possibility of following the creative process of Miró's paintings from this period, in which he faithfully followed his preliminary sketches, enables us to see very clearly his desire to refine and pare down forms in order to arrive at their essence. Furthermore, the very existence of these sketches indicates how far removed his work was from the Automatism propounded by the Surrealists.

Despite their different approaches, however, there was a certain similarity: while the Surrealist writers and artists based their explorations on the infinite possibilities offered by the world of dreams, Miró did not paint dreams but, by suggestion, provided the necessary elements to make the viewer dream.

On a monochrome ground – generally blue, ochre or brown – Miró placed indecipherable floating forms in perfect equilibrium

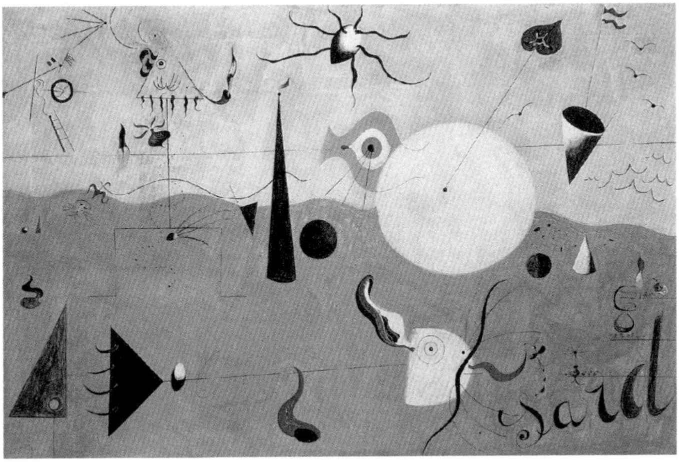

Catalan landscape (The hunter), 1923-24. The Museum of Modern Art, New York

with the empty spaces, such as can be seen in *Painting* (1925) and *Painting* (1927). At other times – as in the case of *Painting (The white glove)* (1925) and *The music-hall usher* (1925) – the object or figure on the monochrome ground, taken from real life, transmutes reality into poetry. This was a determining factor in Miró's work of the 1920s.

It was also during this decade, in 1927, that Miró produced his first book illustration, for *Gertrudis* by the Catalan poet J. V. Foix, a close friend of his. This was the start of one of the most interesting ventures in Miró's artistic career – working together with his poet and writer friends on a considerable number of special limited editions.

In the spring of 1928, Miró went to Belgium and the Netherlands, where he visited the main cities and museums. The result of this trip was the series of *Dutch interiors*.

The genre paintings of the seventeenth-century Dutch masters made a deep impression on Miró. He bought postcards of a number of pictures and used these as the basis for reworking the compositions, subjecting the figures and objects to a form of metamorphosis. The Foundation's collections enable us to follow, for example, the entire process of production of *Dutch interior II* through the set of preliminary sketches based on the postcard of *The cat's dancing lesson* by Jan Steen (1626-1679).

Preliminary sketch for *Ceci est la couleur de mes rêves*, 1925

Preliminary sketch for *Stars in snails' genitals*, 1925

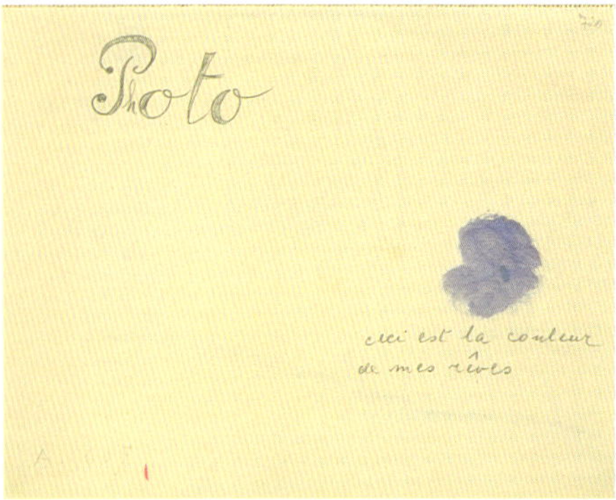

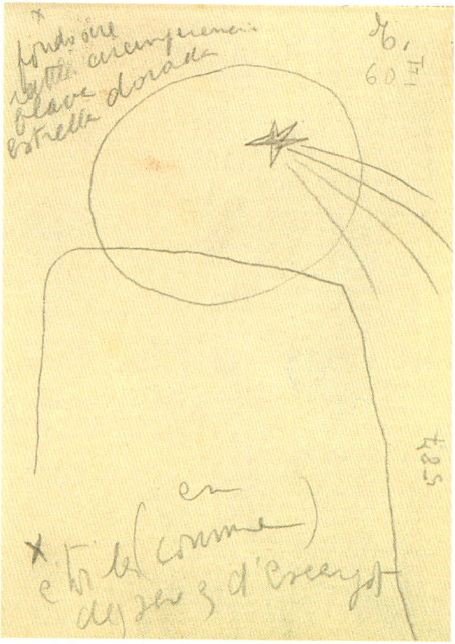

Painting, 1927.
Gift of Manuel de Muga

Painting, 1925.
Gift of Joan Prats

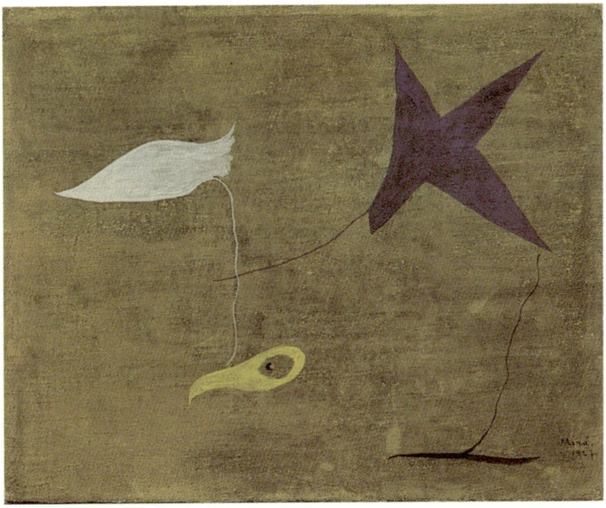

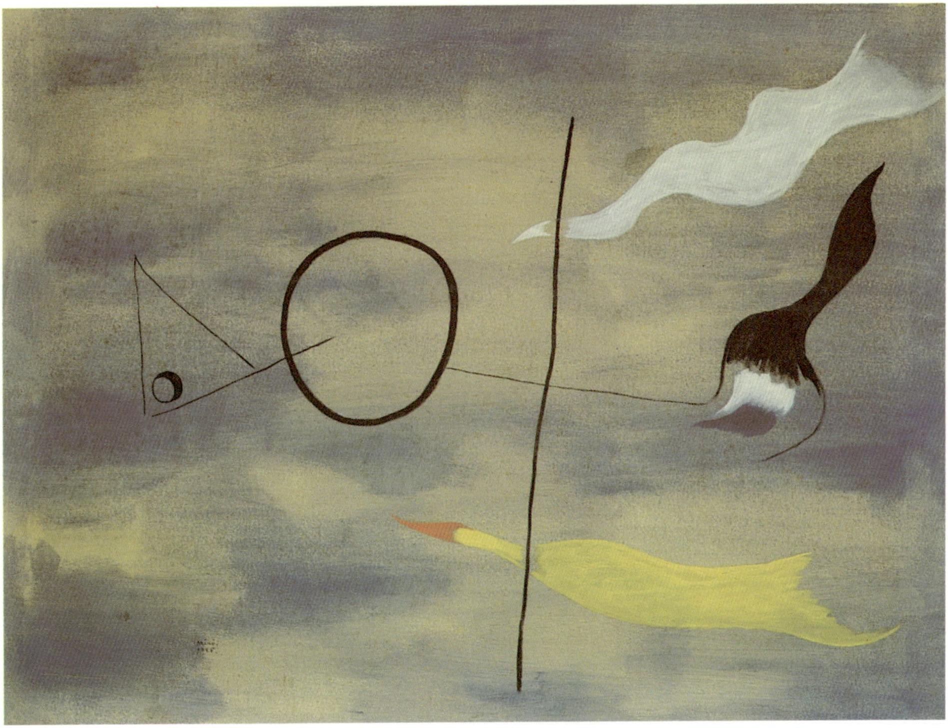

Similar approaches can be found in the series of four *Imaginary portraits*, dated 1929. On this occasion, Miró used as the starting point the *Portrait of Mrs. Mills in 1750* by George Engleheart (1752-1829), *Portrait of a lady in 1820* by Constable (1776-1837), *La Fornarina* by Raphael (1483-1520) and, finally, an advertisement for a machine cut out from a newspaper for the *Portrait of Queen Louise of Prussia*.

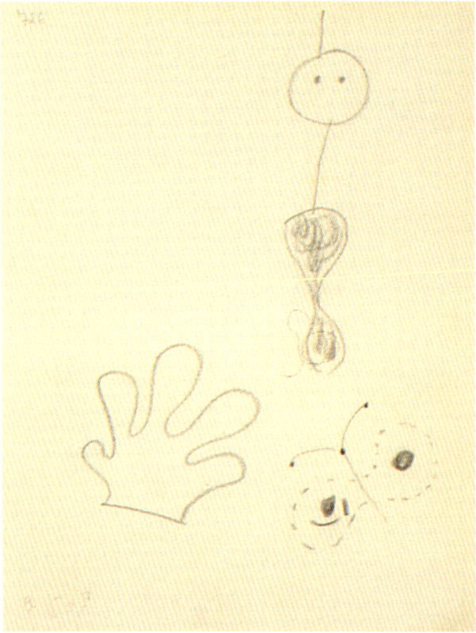

Preliminary sketch for *Painting (The white glove)*, 1925

The fact of taking the work of another artist – or, in the case of *Portrait of Queen Louise of Prussia,* simply a ready-made shape – as a reference point allowed Miró to analyse the pure form, stripping it down until he eventually produced a typically Mironian figure. This new approach required some effort, since he had to replace spontaneous creation with a painstaking process of maximum refinement. The series of preliminary sketches and notes bear witness to this.

By the late 1920s, this desire to get to the essence of things led Miró to eliminate everything he considered unnecessary and, as Michel Leiris has pointed out, to come close to the Zen aesthetic. *Untitled (Tree in the wind)* (1929) is not so very far removed from the style of oriental paintings in which the composition is determined by a single line and the different tones of the black ink.

But soon Miró again felt the need to give a new focus to his work and to search for new forms of expression. The 1930s, which at the start seemed to be a period of crisis in his painting, turned out to be one more fruitful stage in his artistic career.

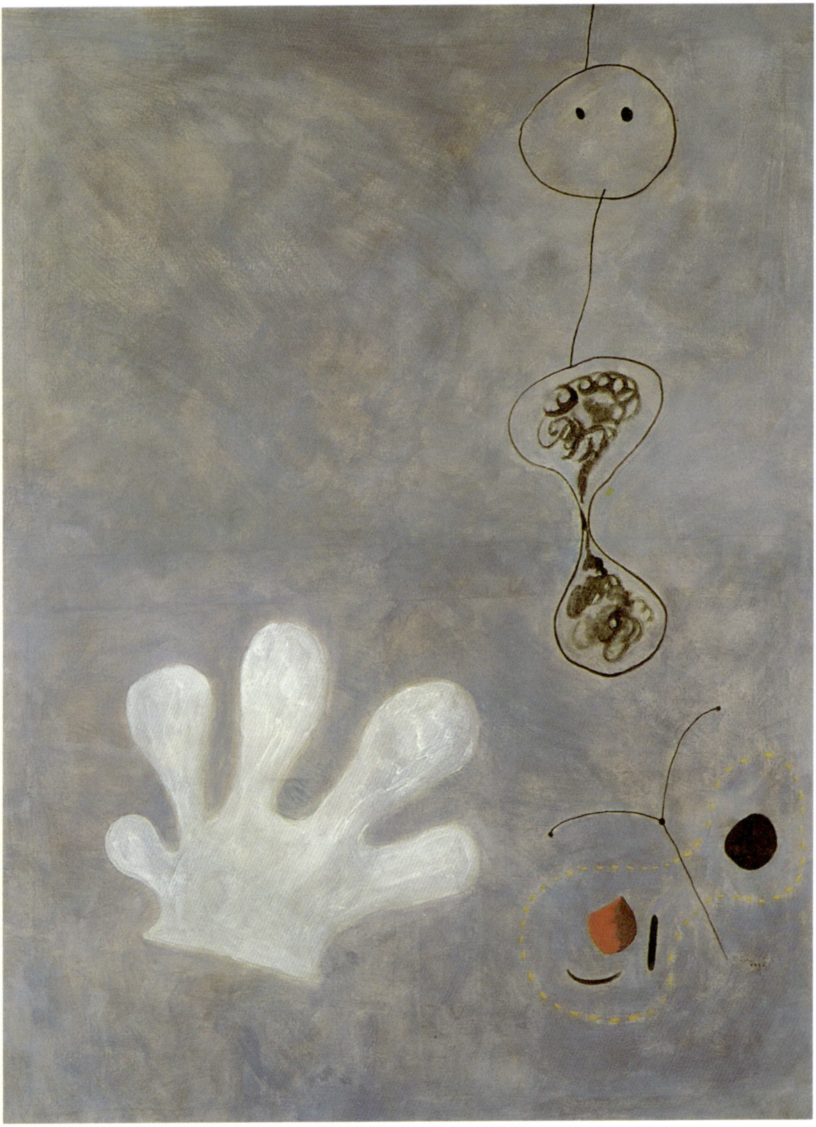

Painting (The white glove), 1925

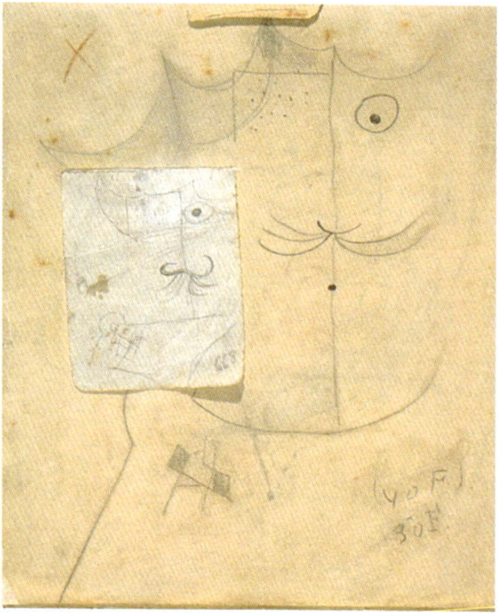

Preliminary sketch for
The music-hall usher, 1925

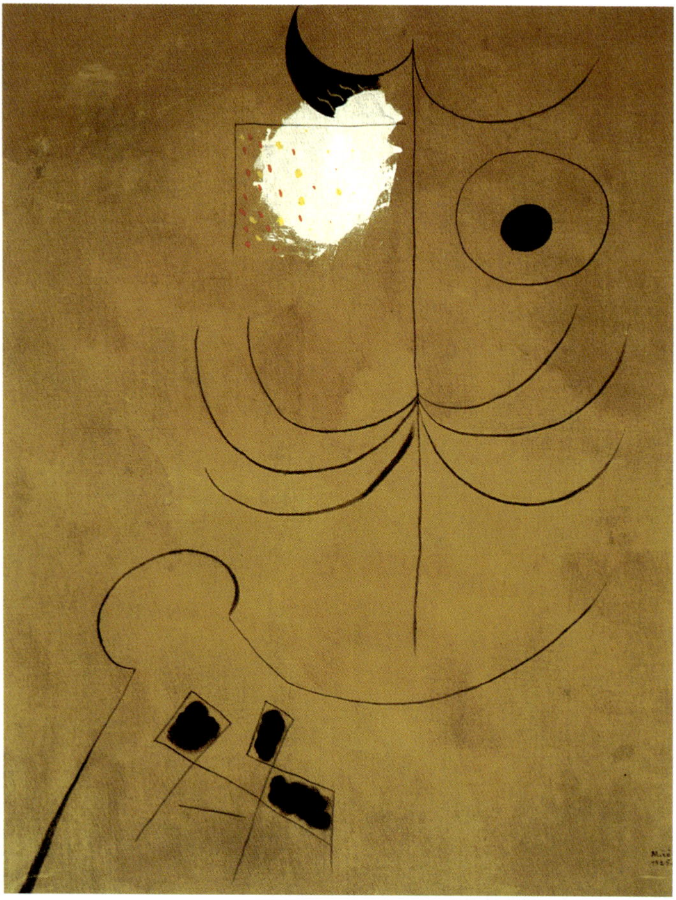

The music-hall usher, 1925.
On permanent loan from the
Generalitat de Catalunya

Dutch interior II, 1928. The Solomon R. Guggenheim Museum, New York

Postcard. The starting point for *Dutch interior II,* 1928

Preliminary sketch for *Dutch interior II,* 1928

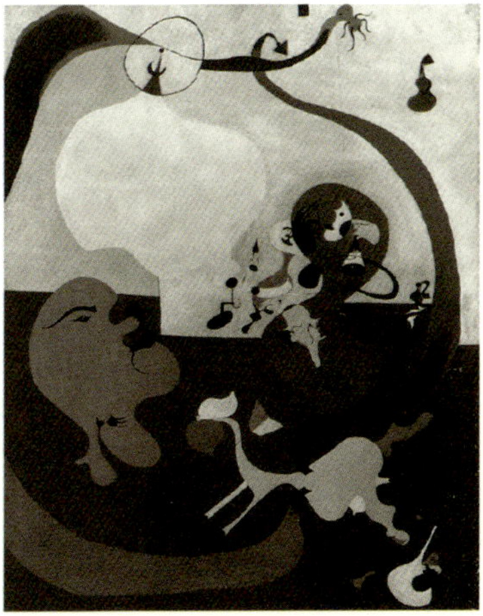

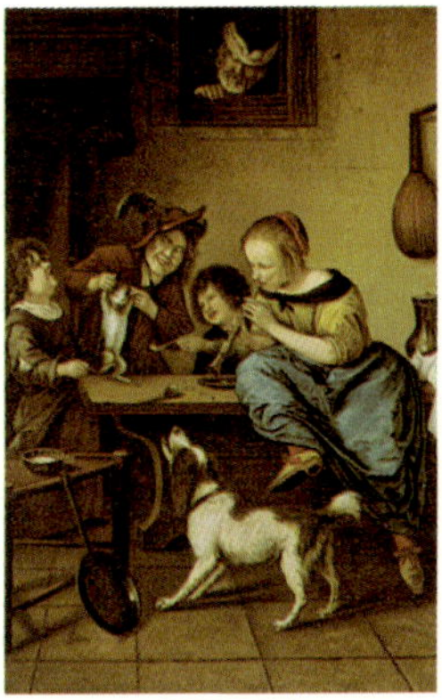

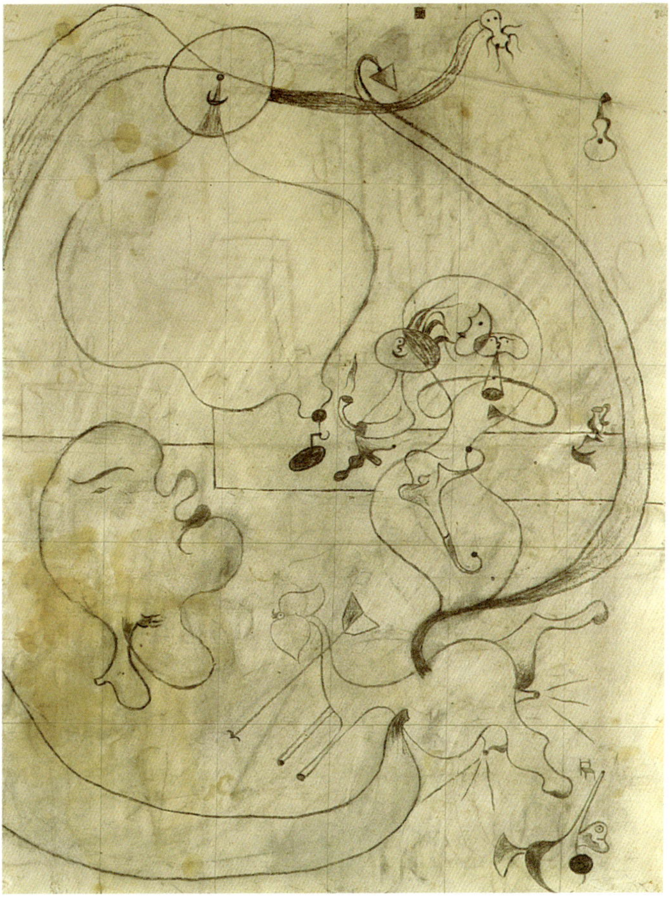

Portrait of Queen Louise of Prussia, 1929. Algur H. Meadows Collection, Southern Methodist University, Dallas, Texas

Preliminary sketch for *Portrait of Queen Louise of Prussia,* 1929

Preliminary sketch and advertisement, the starting point for *Portrait of Queen Louise of Prussia,* 1929

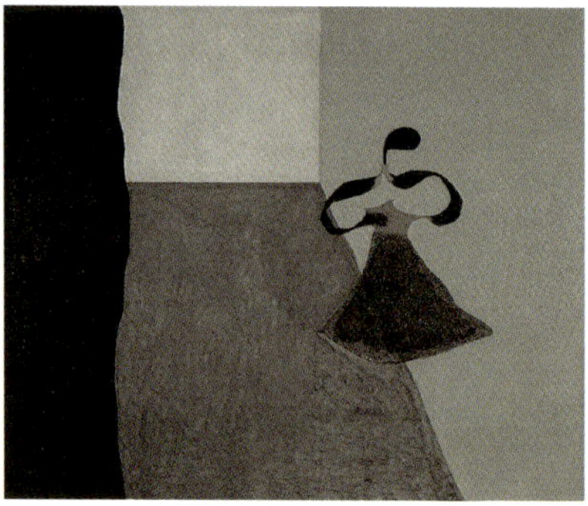

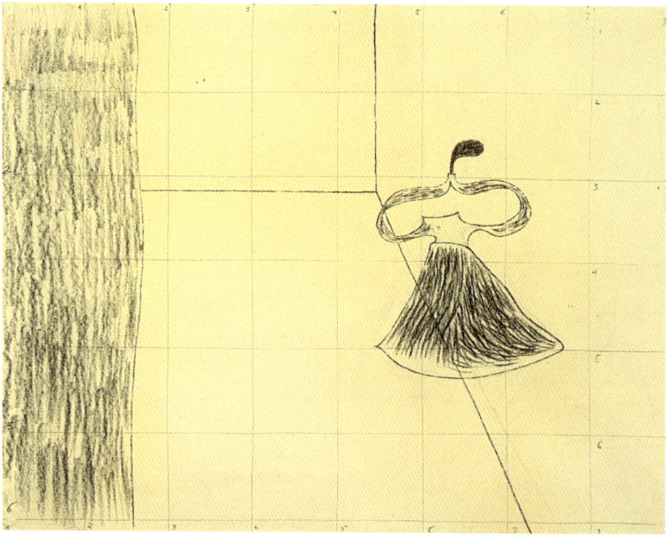

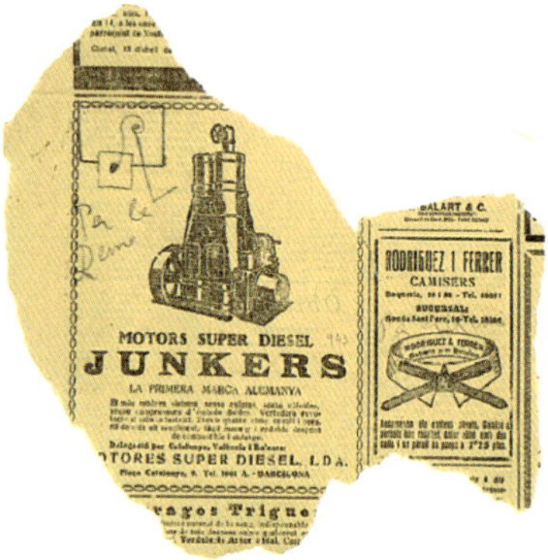

Preliminary sketch for
Untitled (Tree in the wind),
1929

Untitled (Tree in the wind),
1929

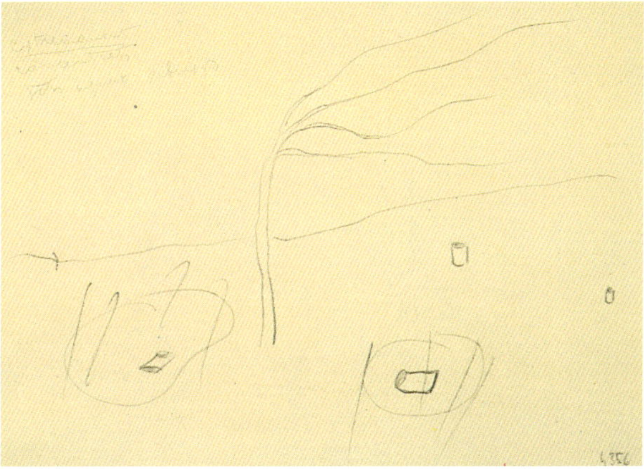

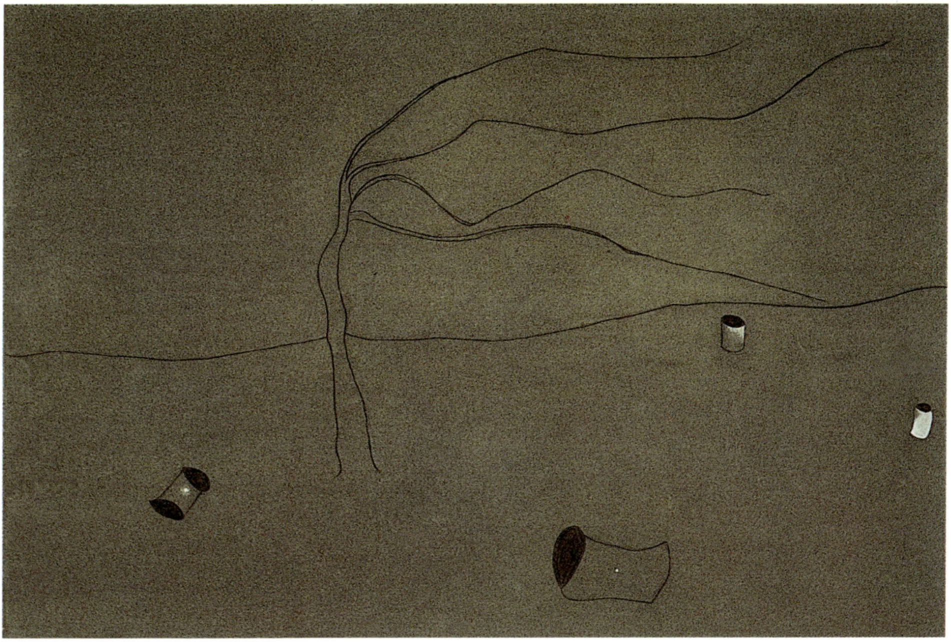

Composition with figures in a burning wood, 1931. Gift of David Fernández i Miró

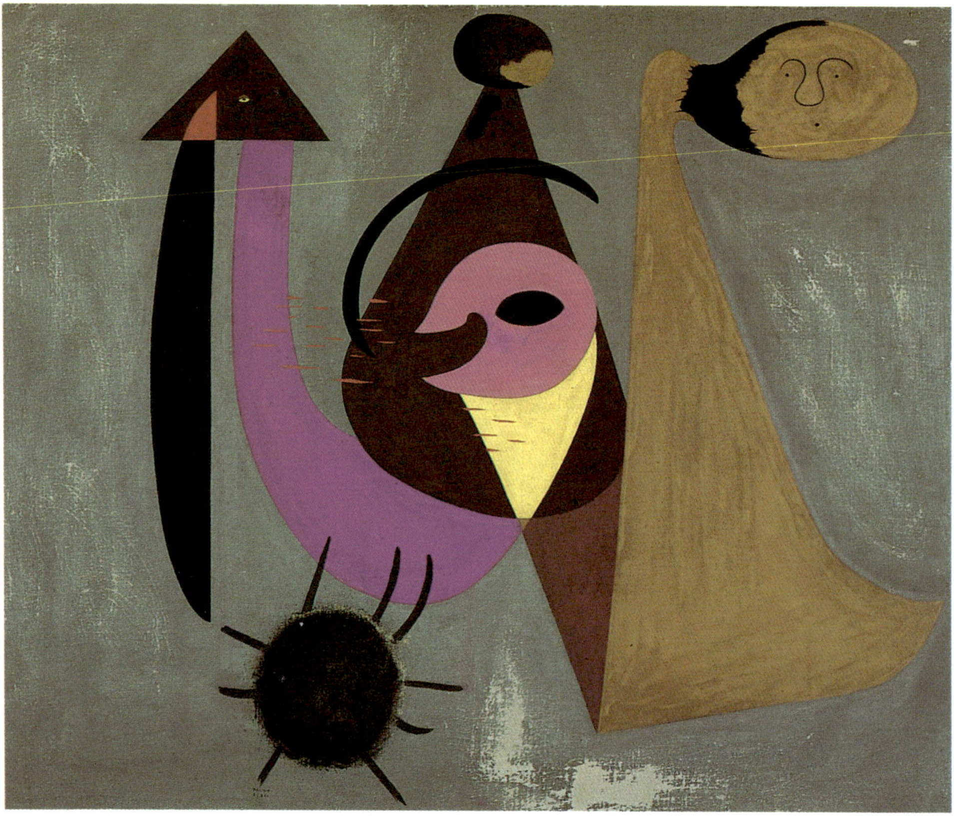

The Object in Space

For Miró, the beginning of the 1930s was a time of artistic crisis – already anticipated at the end of the 1920s – when he declared his desire to "assassinate painting". As a consequence, he sought alternative methods of expression that led to a new language and the investigation of other media such as collage, drawing, objects, etc.

The "Miró papers" also reflect this period during which the notes and jottings increased considerably as a result of the artist's reflections on his own work. On the other hand, the number of preliminary sketches for paintings fell in proportion, giving way to the drawings he produced in order to "build muscle", as he put it. Nonetheless, the ratio of preparatory sketches to finished works was still much the same.

The three-dimensional pieces that Miró produced in 1930 on the basis of objects, known as the *Constructions,* were to lead to one of his most gratifying experiences: working in the world of theatre.

In 1931, Boris Kochno, one of the artistic directors of the Ballets Russes de Montecarlo, saw Miró's *Constructions* exhibited at the Galerie Pierre in Paris. Deciding that these objects would be just right for the type of stage sets he envisaged for *Jeux d'enfants,* he immediately contacted Miró and commissioned him to design the sets and costumes for the ballet.

Miró already had some experience of working in the theatre, for in 1926, in collaboration with Max Ernst, he had painted the

Woman, 1930

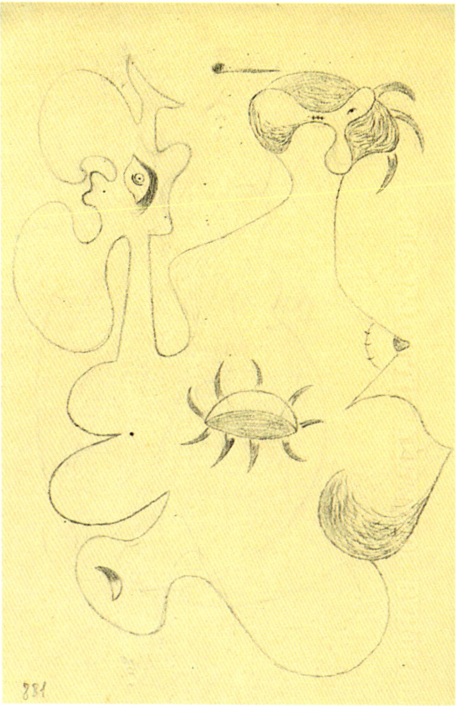

Study of costumes for the ballet
Jeux d'enfants, 1932

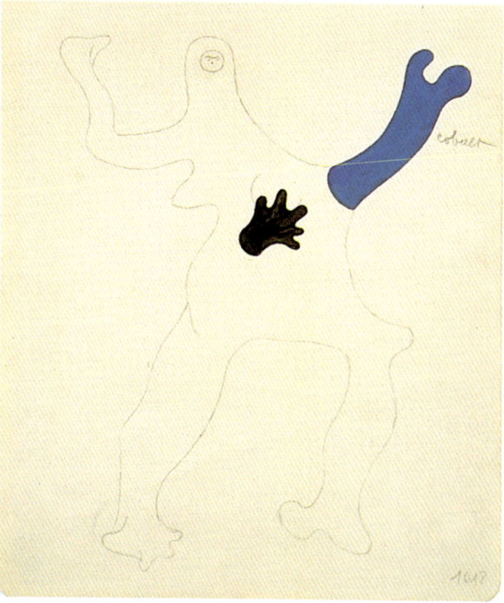

Painting on Ingres paper, 1932.
Gift of Joan Prats

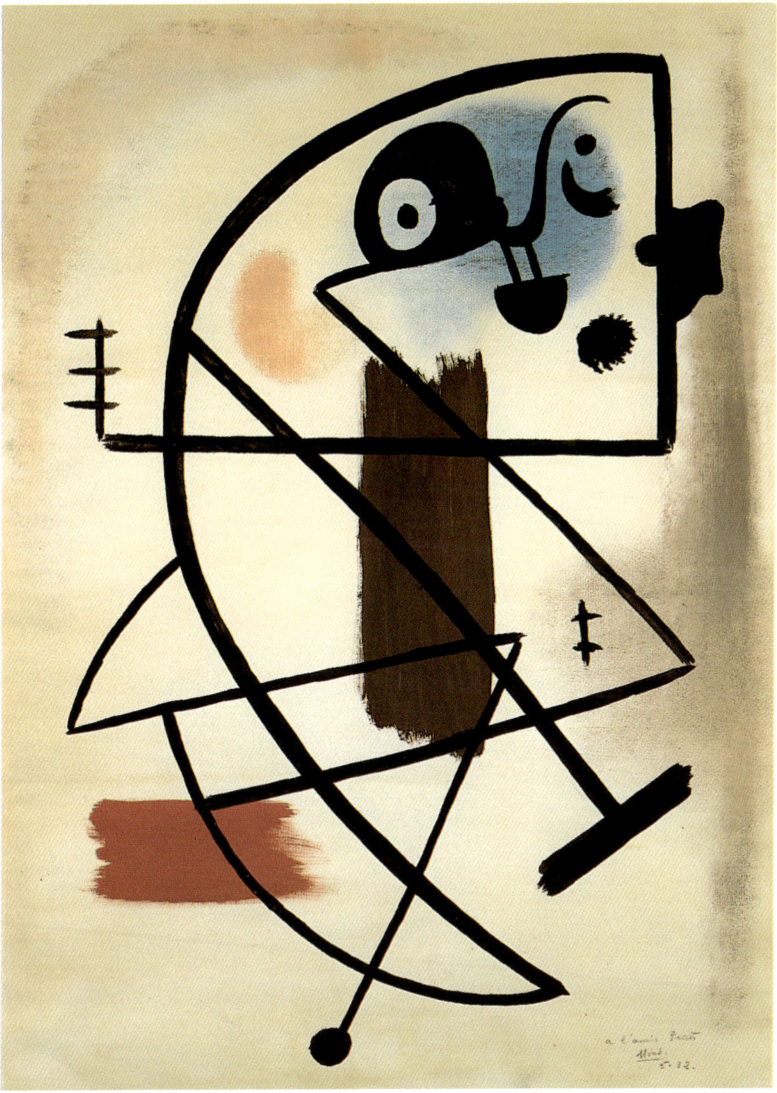

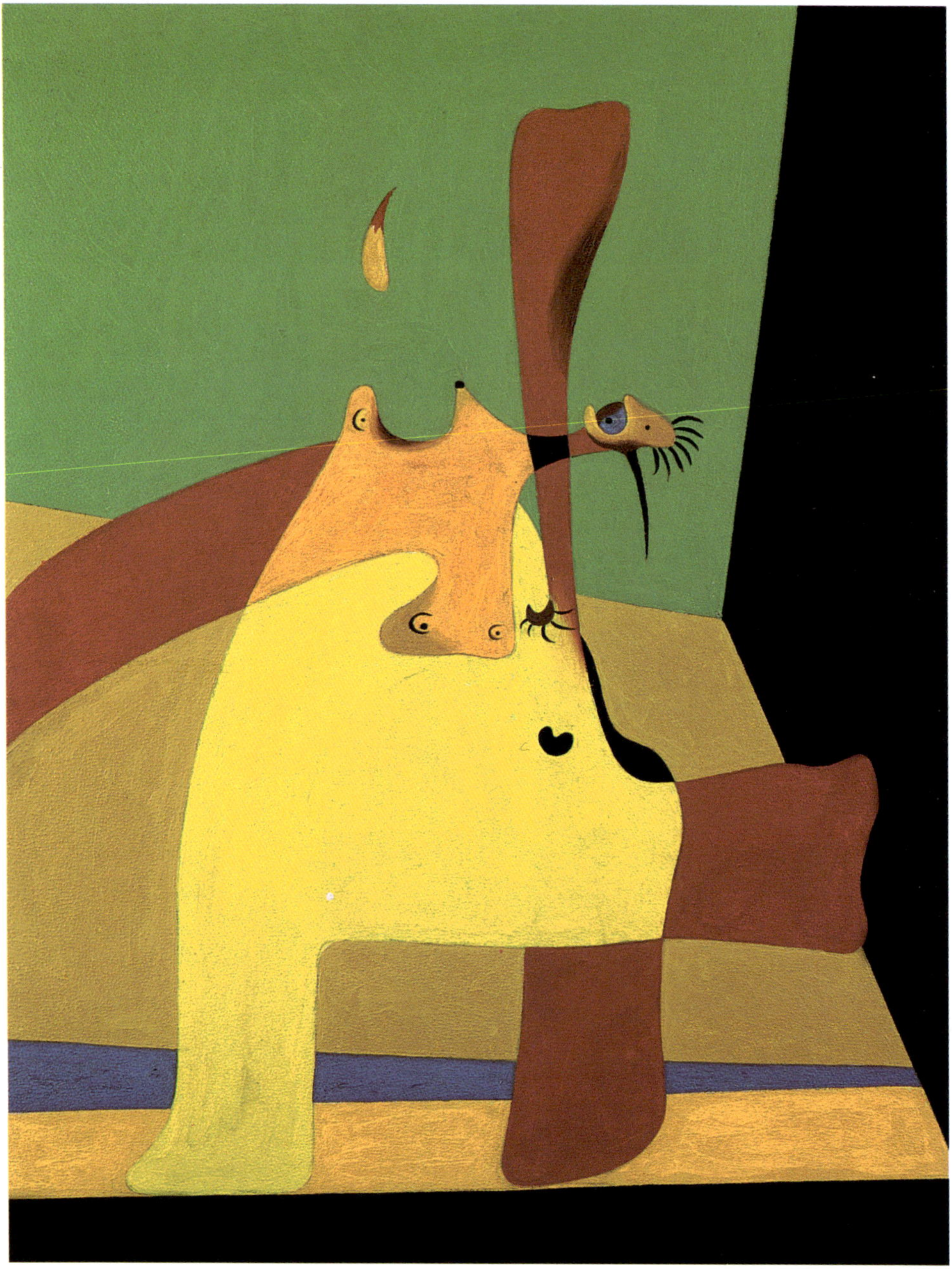

Flame in space and naked woman, 1932. Gift of Joan Prats

sets and designed the costumes and props for *Romeo and Juliet,* performed by the Ballets Russes. This time, however, the commission was a much more important one and he had to take sole responsibility for the work.

During the first three months of 1932, Miró worked hard on the ballet designs, and all this initial material – the preliminary sketches, notes and stage models – is currently held at the Foundation.

With music by Bizet, scenario by Boris Kochno, choreography by Léonide Massine and sets and costumes by Joan Miró, *Jeux d'enfants* had its highly successful premiere on 14th April 1932 at the Théâtre de Montecarlo.

The design of the proscenium curtain for this ballet is very similar to the series of paintings on Ingres paper started in 1931, one of which, from the Prats collection, is now at the Foundation.

During the time he spent in Mont-roig in 1932, Miró painted a number of small-format pictures, among them *Flame in space and naked woman.* These works are variations on the female form as seen from the artist's very individual perspective – a subject that predominated throughout his art and to which he devoted special attention during the 1930s.

Miró then changed to a larger format with the series of *Paintings based on a collage*. The preliminary stage of execution of each of these eighteen paintings, one of which is held at the Foundation, consisted in arranging the respective collages. Miró cut out newspaper advertisements and catalogue illustrations, then stuck them onto a sheet of laid paper. Using these compositions, devoid of any colour, he created a space in which to situate the forms deriving from the cut-out items, carefully establishing the relationship between each of them and the rest.

The choice of colours, the perfect balance between the forms, and the atmosphere produced by the ground, make the *Paintings based on a collage* one of the series in Miró's entire oeuvre that best demonstrates his reflective way of working.

In 1934, resorting once again to the collage technique, Miró produced a tribute to his friend Joan Prats. In an obvious reference to the latter's profession as a hatter, it consists of hats cut from an advertisement and a card reading "Prats is quality".

Preliminary collage for *Painting,* 1933

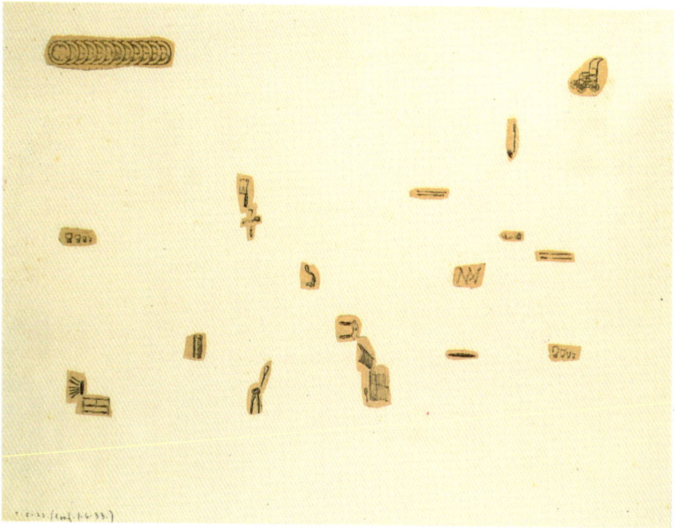

Here, the collage is not a separate item that determines the final composition but forms part of the finished picture along with the drawing.

Painting, 1933. On permanent loan from Maria Dolors Miró

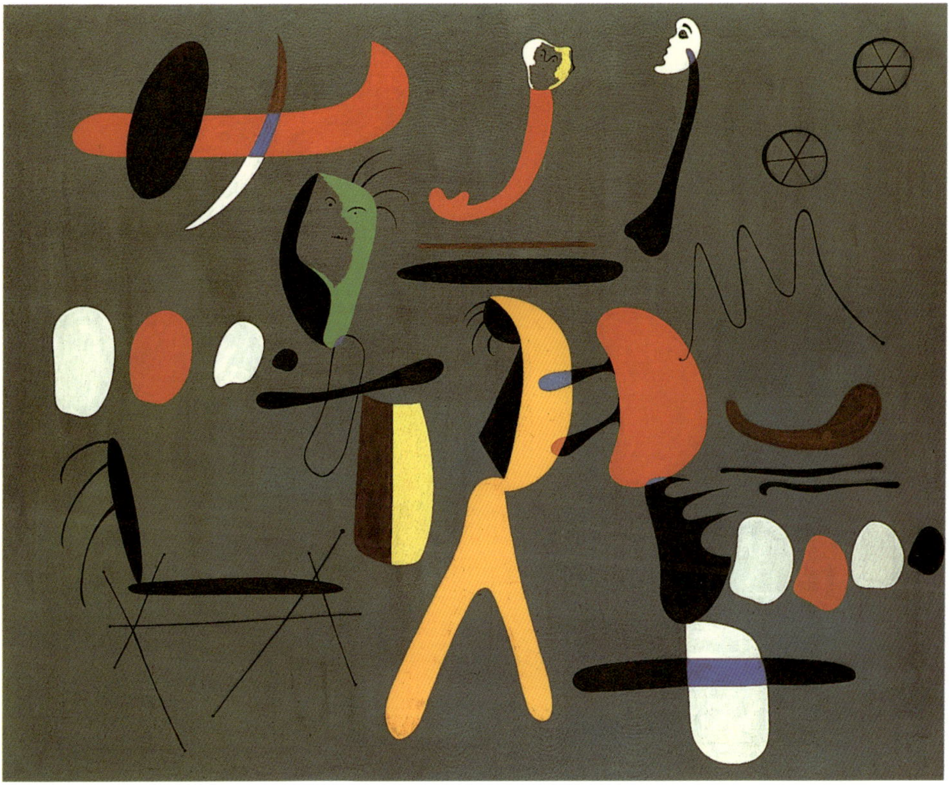

Collage-drawing (Homage to Prats), 1934. Gift of Joan Prats

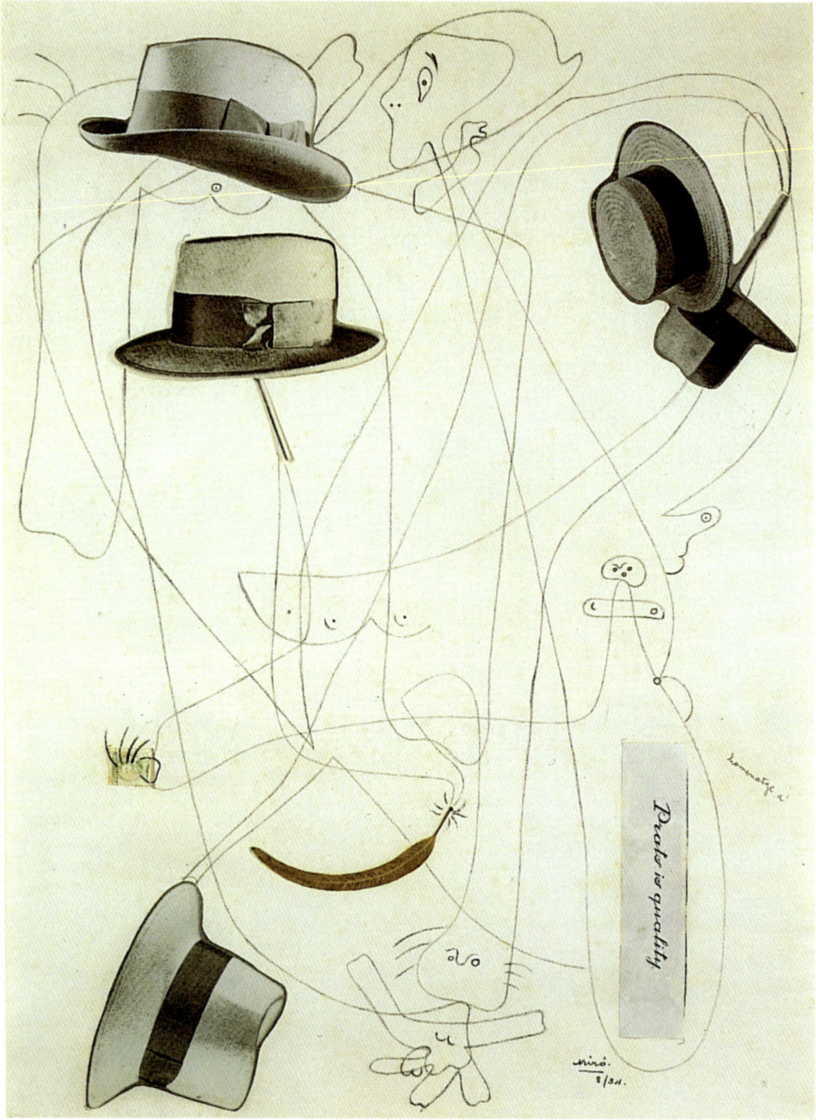

Painting, 1934. Gift of Joan Prats

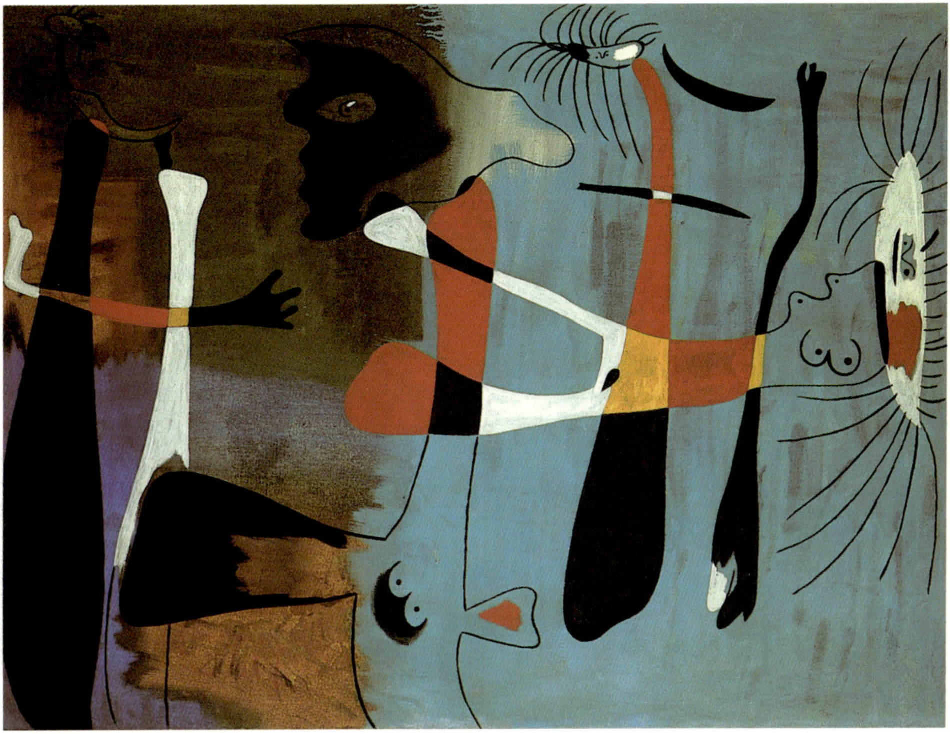

Design for a ballet curtain, 1935

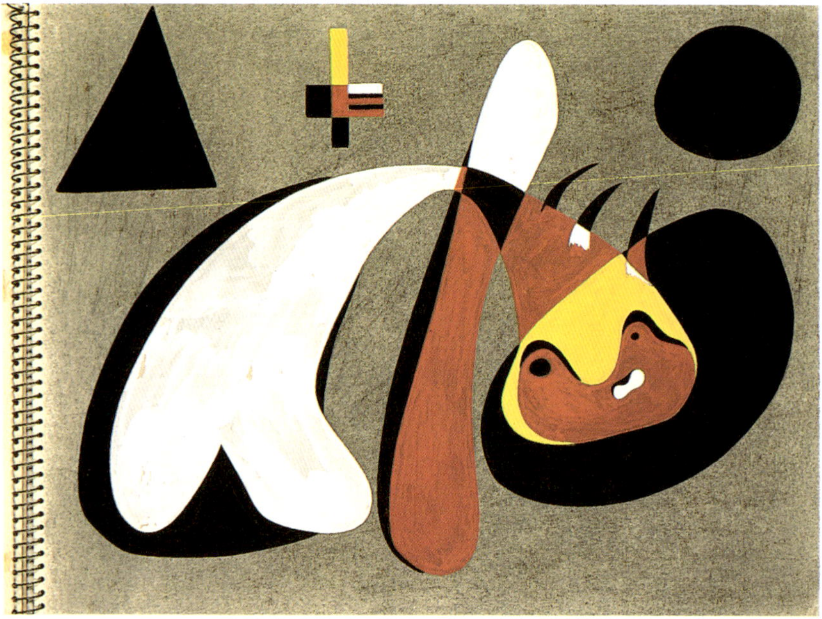

Man and woman in front of a pile of excrement, 1935. Gift of Pilar Juncosa de Miró

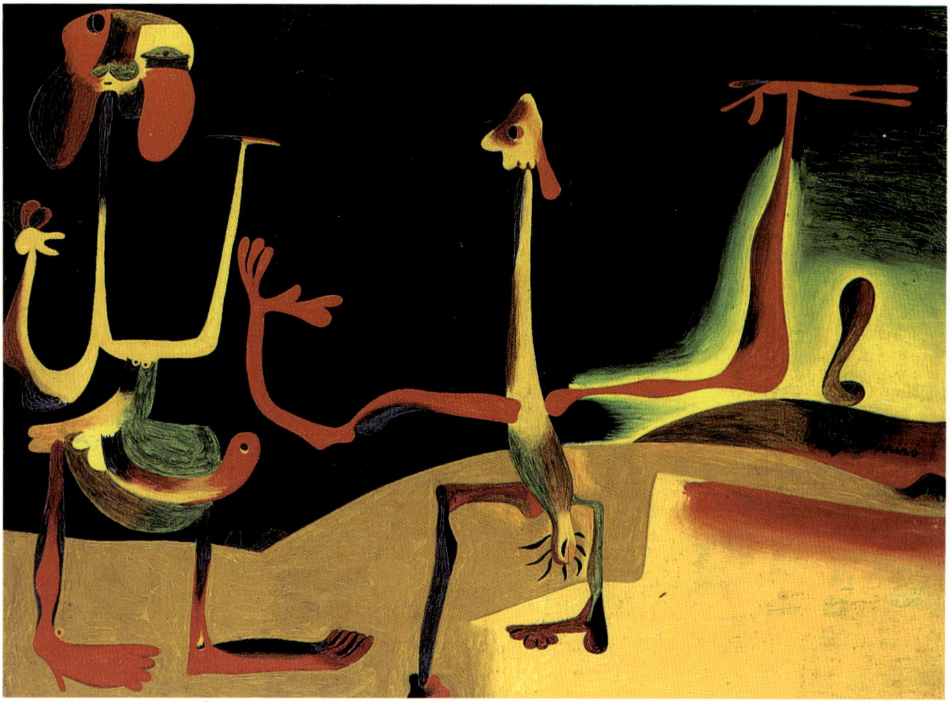

Painting on masonite, 1936. Gift of David Fernández i Miró

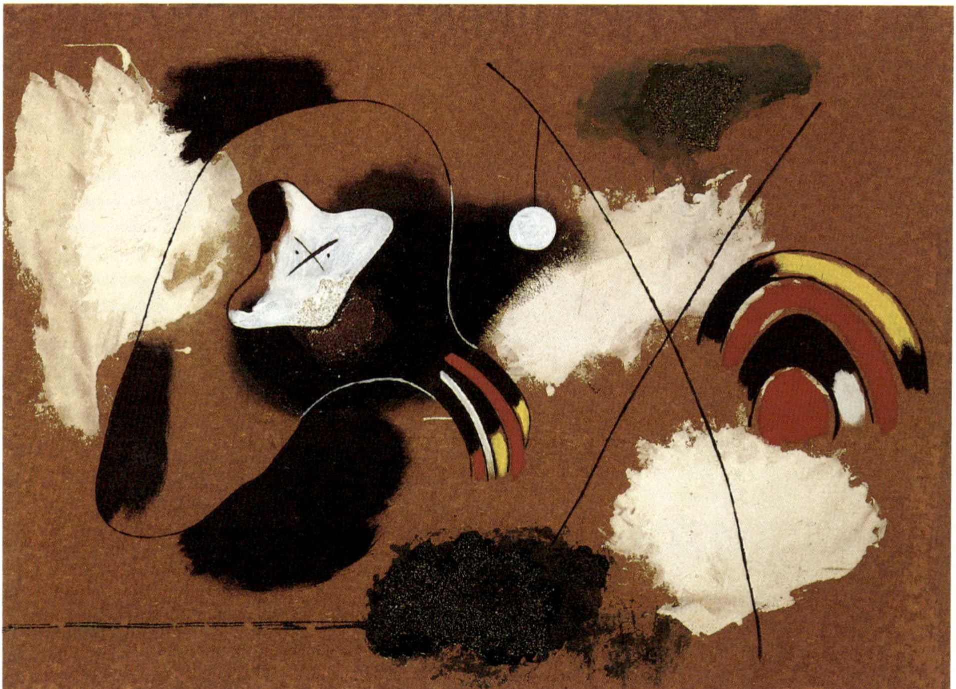

Synthesis

Following the outbreak of the Spanish Civil War, Miró expressed his opposition to it in a series of 27 paintings on masonite (a type of fibreboard). The aggressiveness is evident not only in the iconography but also in the act of painting itself: the unconventional support chosen – masonite – which is never completely covered, and the materials used in addition to oils, such as tar, sand, casein and bitumen. The forms – which are unusual though identifiable within Miró's language – can be directly linked to those for *Jeux d'enfants*. The Foundation has one *Painting on masonite* as well as some of the preliminary sketches for the series.

In 1937, Miró, once again living in Paris, began attending life-drawing classes at the Académie de la Grande Chaumière.

At a time when he was suffering on account of the dramatic events in Spain, he again approached the problem of the human figure, and his feelings can be guessed in the tortured forms he drew at the Paris art school. It was in this same spirit that he produced the grotesque *Naked woman climbing a staircase.*

Coinciding with this return to figurative representation, Miró designed the stencil *Aidez l'Espagne* – the preparatory sketch for which is held by the Foundation – in order to collect funds to help the Republican side in the Civil War. At the same time he also painted *The reaper* for the Spanish Republican Government's pavilion at the Paris World Fair in 1937.

Male nude and female nude,
1937

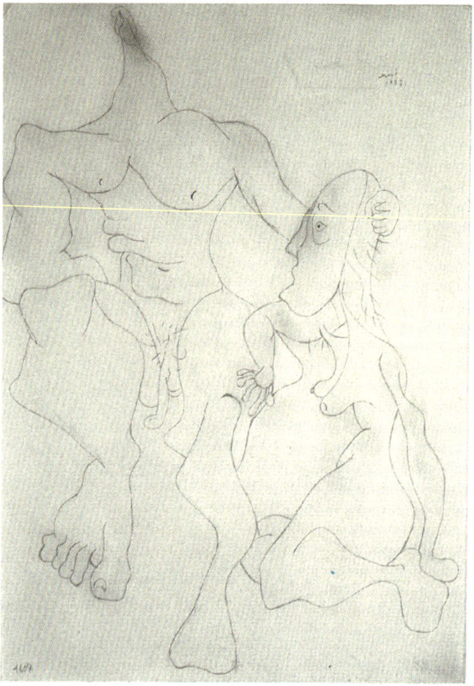

Naked woman climbing a staircase,
1937

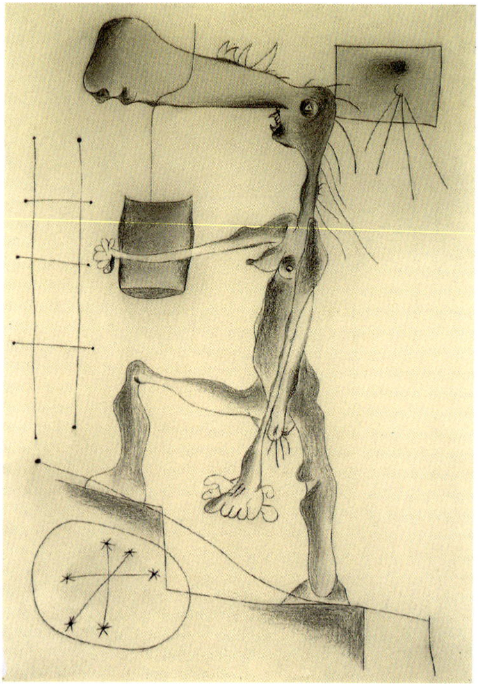

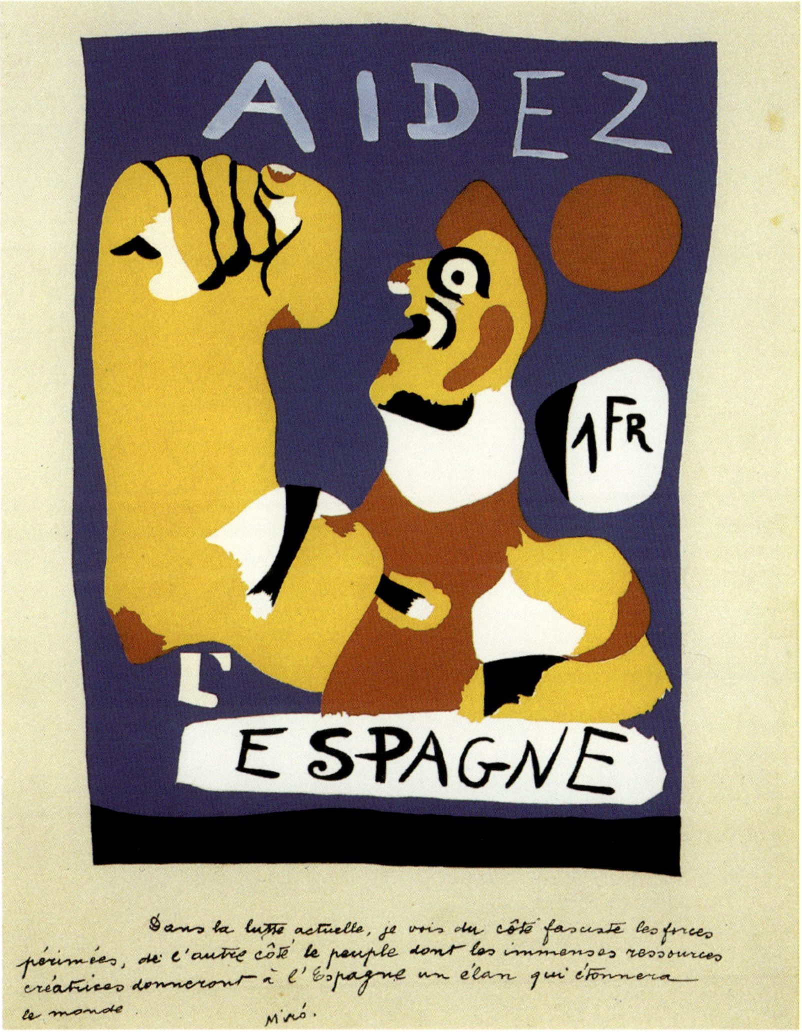
AIDEZ
1FR
L'
ESPAGNE
Dans la lutte actuelle, je vois du côté fasciste les forces périmées, de l'autre côté le peuple dont les immenses ressources créatrices donneront à l'Espagne un élan qui étonnera le monde.
Miró.

Luis Lacasa and Josep Lluís Sert were the architects commissioned to design the pavilion, and the artists involved in it worked in close conjunction with them. Picasso painted *Guernica,* Calder designed the *Mercury fountain* – now at the Foundation – Julio González produced the sculpture *Montserrat* and Alberto presented *The Spanish people have a path that leads to a star.*

Miró painted *The reaper* on six panels of celotex – the material covering the inside of the pavilion – measuring a total of 5.50 x 3.65 metres. This was his first monumental work, but unfortunately it disappeared when it was dismantled along with the pavilion and no trace of it remains other than a few photographs.

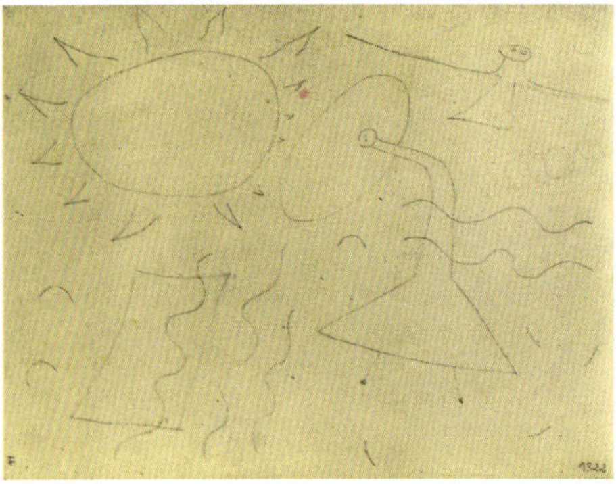

Preliminary sketch for *Flight of a bird over the plain IV,* 1939

In contrast to this piece, Miró then painted a series of seven pictures, also on celotex, of exceptional delicacy and in a spirit that could be described as profoundly poetic. He soon returned, however, to an aggressive style with *Head,* painted on the same support. Here, Miró added a strange item – a piece of towelling stiffened with glue, stuck to the surface of the fibreboard. The vibrant texture of the piece emphasises its brutal appearance.

Little by little Miró again abandoned figurative representation for signs and symbols and concentrated his attention on the sky rather than on his immediate surroundings. Thus, from notes made in the margins of a sheet of newspaper during a train journey in 1939 from Paris to Varengeville-sur-Mer on the Normandy coast, he painted the series of *Flight of a bird over the plain.*

As a result of the start of the Second World War, Miró decided to remain in Normandy with his family, and it was there that he began the *Constellations* series. The first piece, titled *Sunrise*, is dated in Varengeville on 20th January 1940. The twenty-third and final one, *The passage of the divine bird*, was painted in Mont-roig on 12th September 1941.

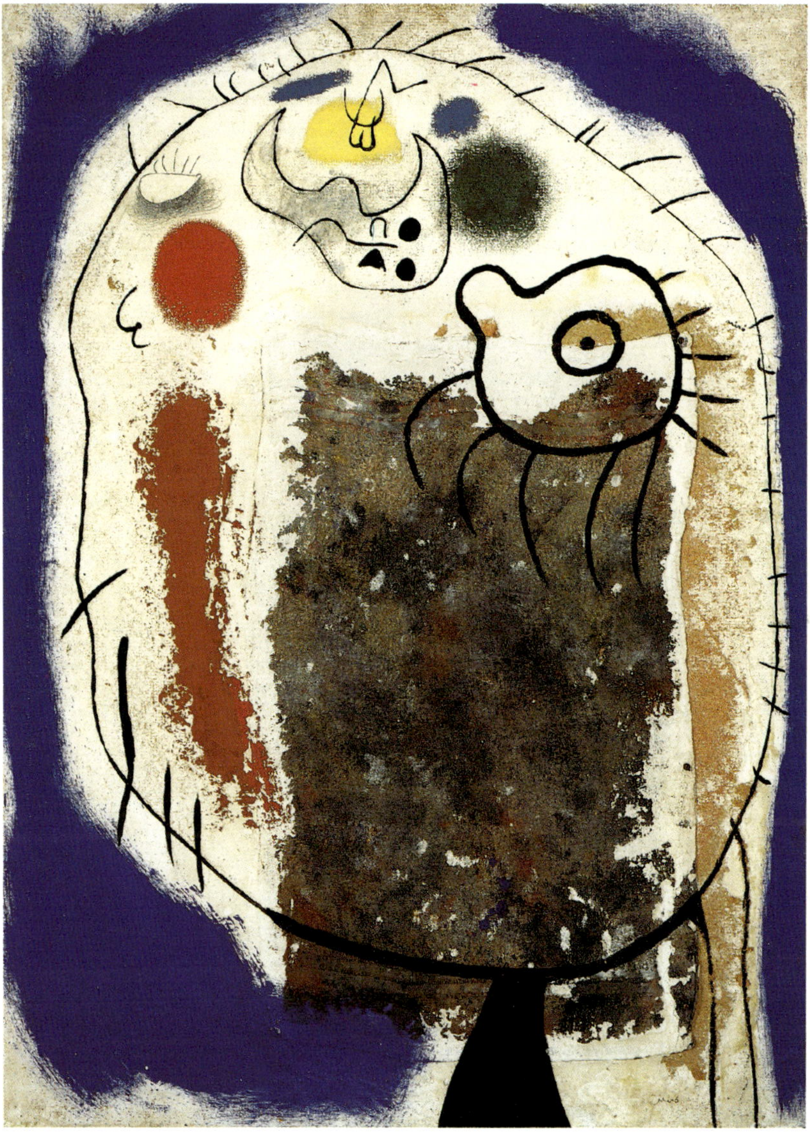

Head, 1937

The *Constellations,* all of which were painted on paper, occupy a key place in Miró's oeuvre, for they signify a new challenge in resolving the pictorial problems he faced, namely the definition of forms and the consolidation of a particular subject matter.

The initial operation consisted in wetting the paper and rubbing it in order to roughen the surface. He then applied the ground colour, which graduates gently from one tone to another, while maintaining a transparent effect that creates a delicate, subtle atmosphere.

The forms come from the preceding years but are less aggressive. The figures are no longer cruel and isolated but linked by a kind of network of lines that gives shape to the composition and removes any trace of violence.

In this complexity of forms, colour plays a fundamental role. The range used by Miró is extremely limited: often just three or four pure colours alongside the various tones of black. The colour is systematically subordinated to the form, while the superimposition of forms brings about a change of colour in overlapping areas. This particular distribution of colour is one of the typical features of Miró's work and resulted in his highly personal chequered effects.

The iconography of the *Constellations* seems to represent the entire cosmic order. The figures symbolise the earth, and the stars refer to the infinite world of the heavens, of which we have only a visual or tactile experience. The birds and the ladder of escape act as the link between the terrestrial world and the celestial world, the source of imagination.

The Foundation holds one of the *Constellations* series, *Morning star,* which Joan Miró gave as a present to his wife, Pilar Juncosa, and which after his death she generously donated to the Foundation.

Miró made no preparatory sketches for the *Constellations,* but let each composition suggest itself from a minute flaw in the paper or from the presence of one element that naturally seemed to call for another.

This method of working directly on to the paper in a unpremeditated way was employed by Miró in parallel with

Morning star, 1940. Gift of Pilar Juncosa de Miró

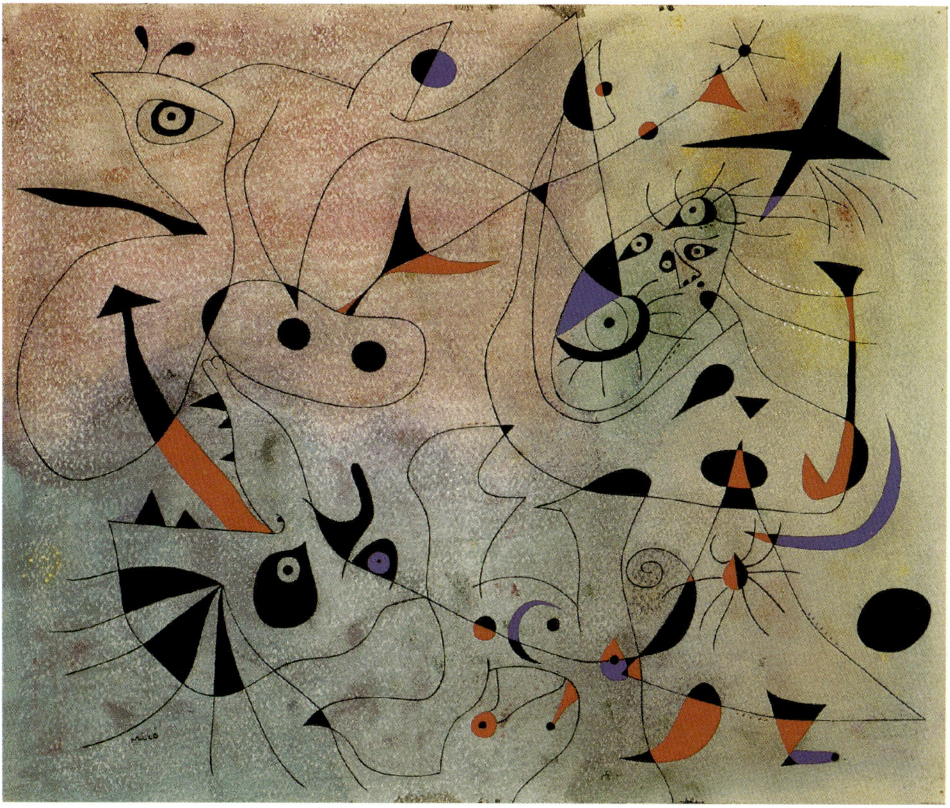

another more systematic and disciplined method reflected in the sketchbooks of the time, produced in Varengeville and Palma, with the date and time meticulously recorded.

Woman, whom the artist treats in a generic rather than an individualised manner, is the subject of most of the drawings in these sketchbooks. She is also the central theme of another exceptional set of works from the same period – the *Barcelona series.*

While Miró was working "overtly" on the *Constellations*, with their lyrical, open spirit and bright colours – he often mentioned them in his correspondence at that time with Pierre Matisse – he was "covertly" producing the *Barcelona series,* of an epic nature, with strong dramatic content and extremely austere colouring.

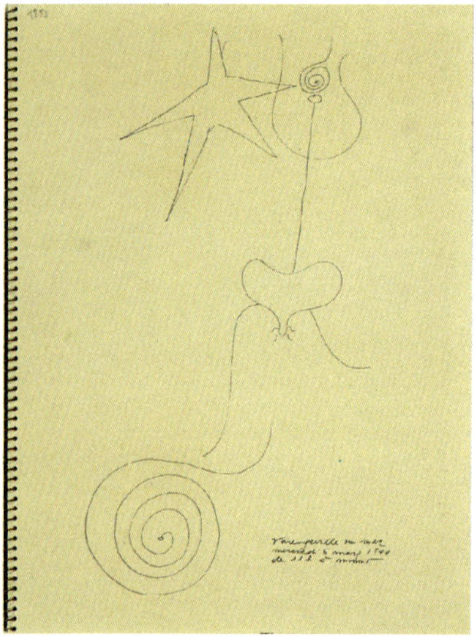

Dancer,
1940

He could never have imagined that the drawings on transfer paper, with a wide range of tones from black to grey, would one day be transferred to lithographic stone. It was thanks to the help of Joan Prats that despite the precarious post-war situation the complete series was able to be published. The edition was limited to five copies of each print, and the Foundation holds one complete set together with the various proofs and states, donated respectively by Joan Prats and Joan Miró.

The *Constellations* and the *Barcelona series,* produced simultaneously but so different in appearance, have in common the fact that they are both based on the same subjects – woman, birds and heavenly bodies – which were to be the themes of Miró's later output, from painting to ceramics.

Lithograph from the *Barcelona series,* 1944

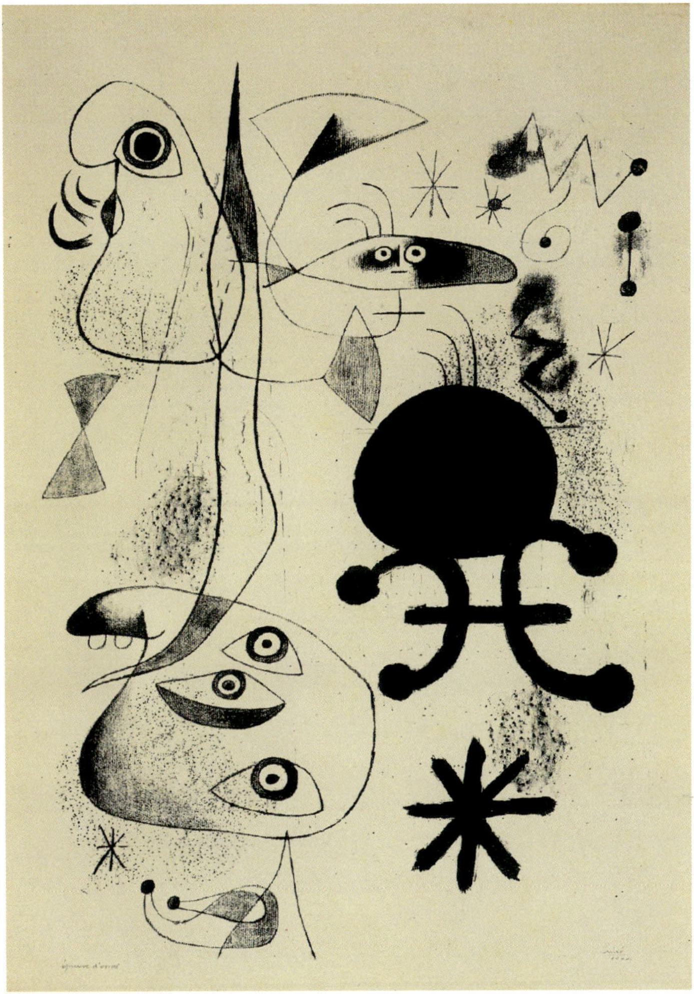

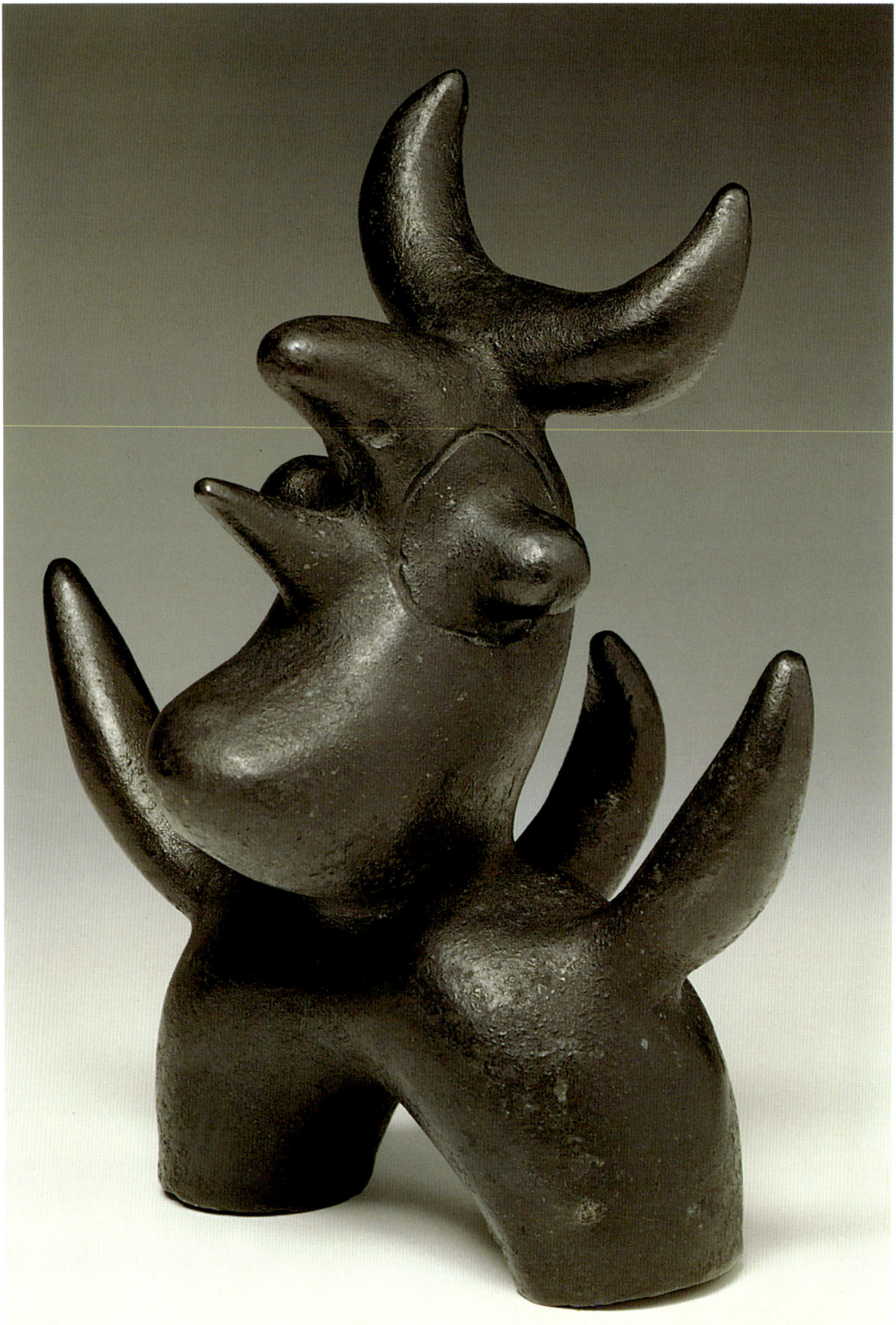

Plenitude

After completing the *Constellations* series in 1941, Miró continued using paper as the main support for the works he was to produce over the next two years. By this time he had a thorough knowledge of the secrets of painting techniques and a mastery of his own particular pictorial language.

Having reached this point in his development, he was anxious to explore the possibilities offered by other techniques and media. Thus for a period of ten years starting in 1944, when he began working on ceramics, he divided his time between painting and other forms of expression. In 1946 he produced his first sculptures in bronze.

1947 saw the appearance of Miró's first colour lithographs, at the Mourlot studio in Paris. Shortly afterwards he began the woodcuts for one of his most important illustrated books, *À toute épreuve,* containing poems by Paul Éluard and published by Gérald Cramer.

Miró's output as a result of the new paths he explored during this time continued to have close links, as regards form and content, with painting, which was always at the origin of his discoveries.

The subject matter of the works from this period was taken directly from the *Constellations.* The constant themes continued to be woman, birds and stars, which we find in *Woman and bird in the night, Woman dreaming of escape,*

Moon bird, 1946

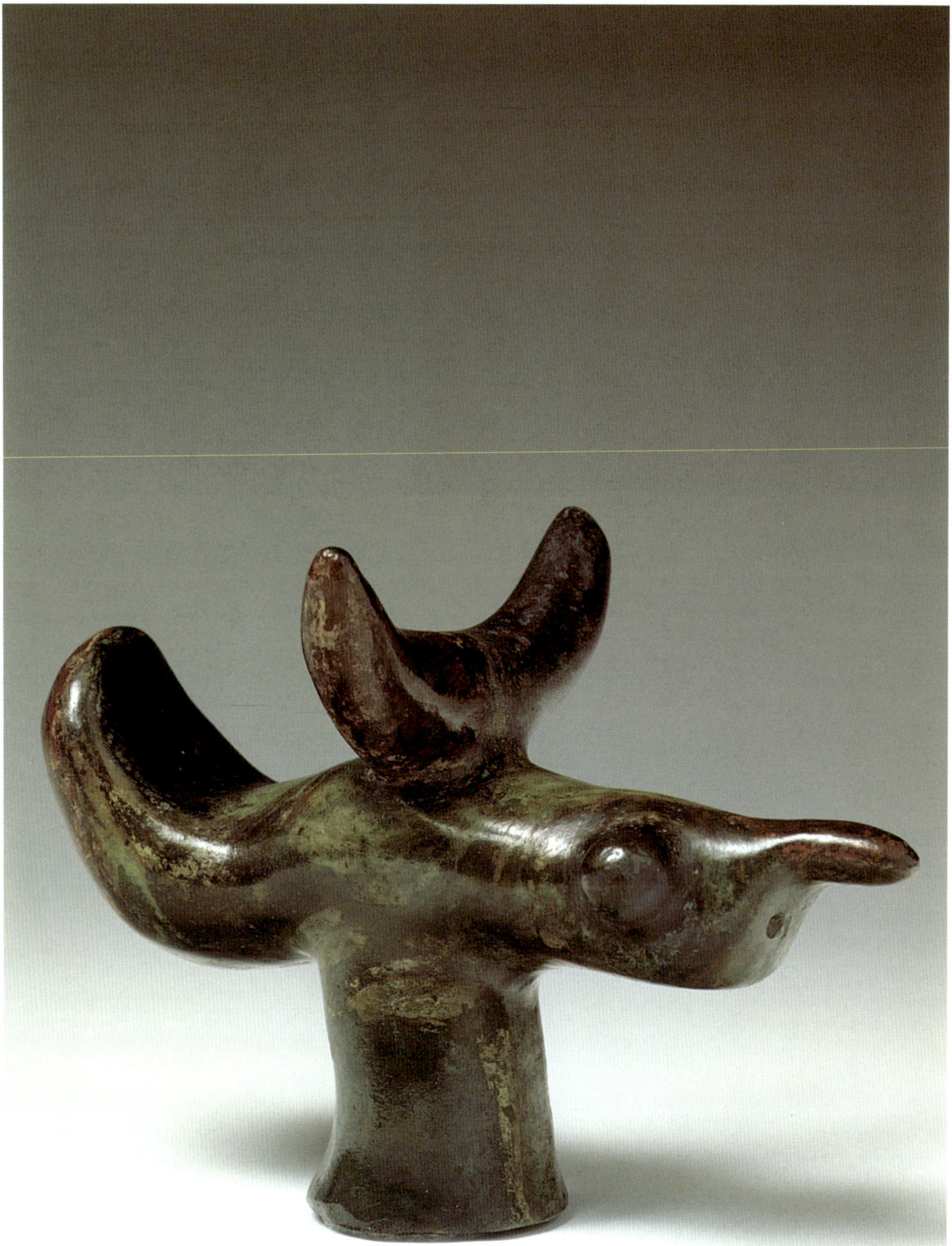

Sun bird, 1946

Woman and birds at daybreak and *Morning star.* His formal vocabulary also had its roots in the *Constellations,* but these later works were more simplified than the previous ones: forms became larger and more individualised, and the typical network of lines in the *Constellations* disappeared.

One innovation at this time was the appearance of figures on different scales, such as can be seen in *Painting in art nouveau frame.* Similarly, we find the first juxtaposition of carefully worked fine lines and almost gestural marks in thick brush strokes. Gesture becomes more apparent in paintings such as *The diamond smiles at twilight,* anticipating the predominance of the firm free-hand stroke in later works.

In 1956, Miró settled in Palma (Majorca), where he began working in the spacious studio designed for him by his friend the architect Josep Lluís Sert. He had finally realised his dream of having a large studio, which he had described in an article titled "Je rêve d'un grand atelier", published in *XXe Siècle* in 1938.

In order to create an agreeable atmosphere, he started collecting all manner of objects that might be of interest in his work, from newspaper cuttings to roots picked up during a walk along the beach, pieces of folk art, shells, old farm implements and so on. Gradually he got his new workplace together. However, his almost exclusive dedication to print-making, lithography and ceramics, which completely absorbed him for five years, left him no time to fully enjoy the new studio until 1958.

During this period Miró felt a need to branch out in new directions, so as not to remain stuck with a single image of his work, which had by then become well known. His first move was to go through all the preliminary sketches and drawings he had made throughout his life. He then produced new versions of many of them, which he kept beside the originals and which have survived as testimony to a way of working that led him to express himself plainly and directly. He would as easily be carried away by the force of a mark made in a single impulsive gesture as by the delicate lines contrasting with the matter and patches of colour.

Woman and bird in the night,
1945. On permanent loan from
Joan Punyet i Miró

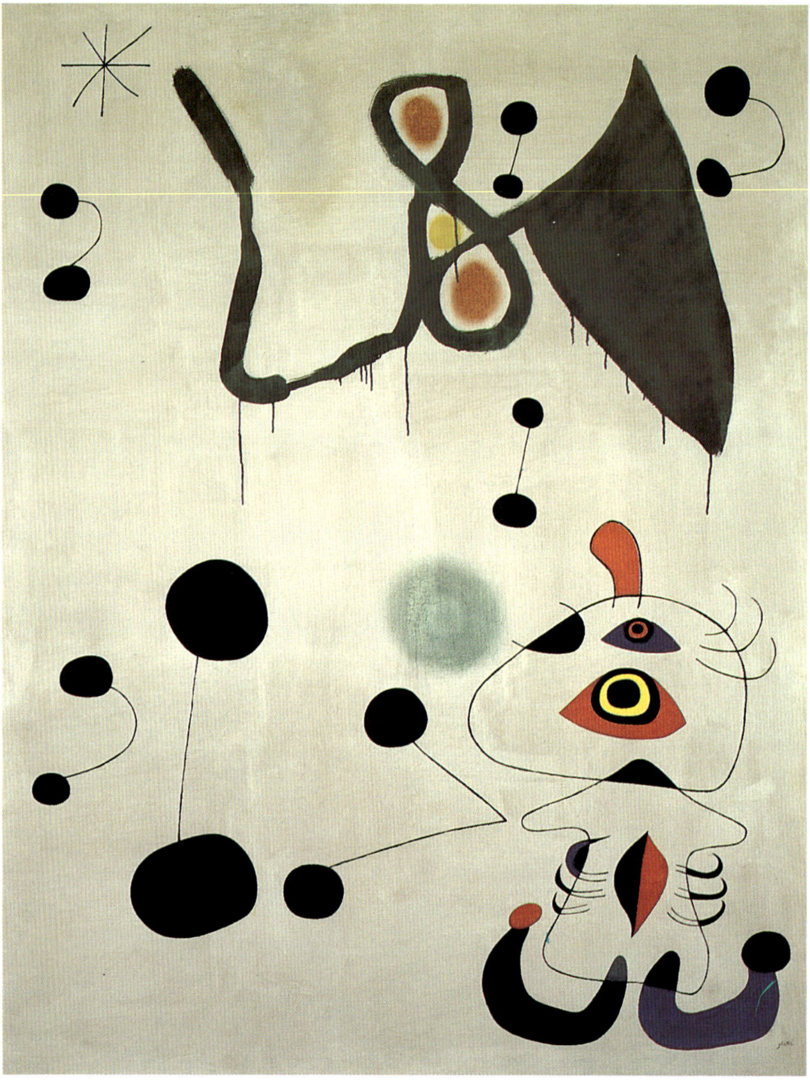

Woman dreaming of escape,
1945

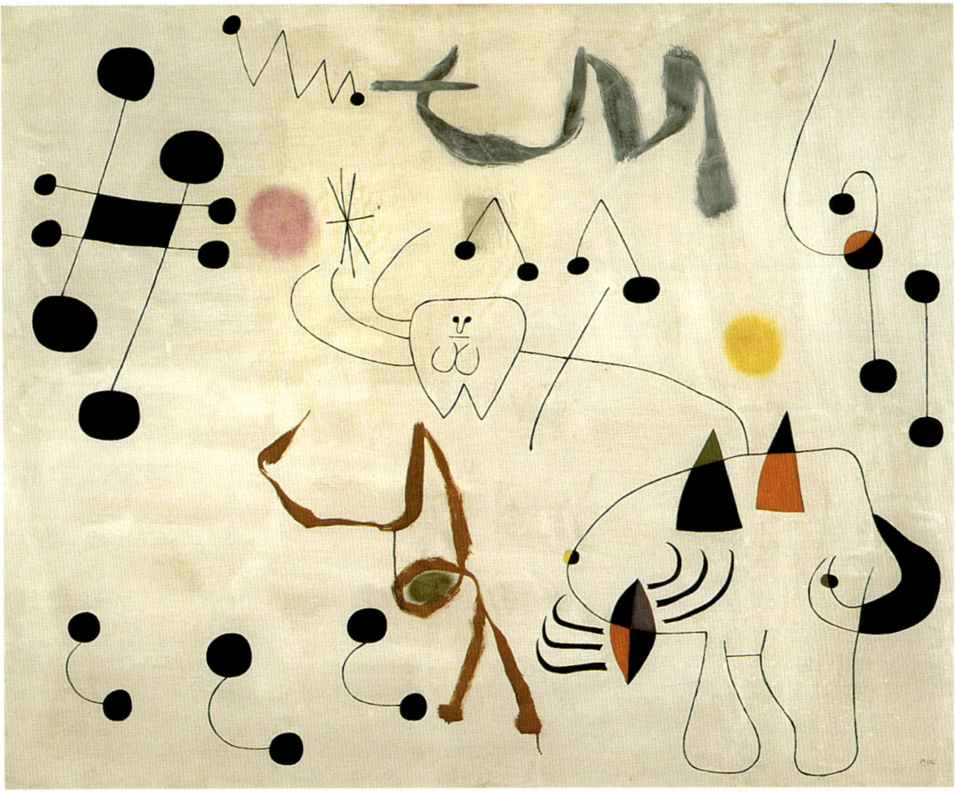

Morning star, 1946. On permanent loan from Teodor Punyet i Miró

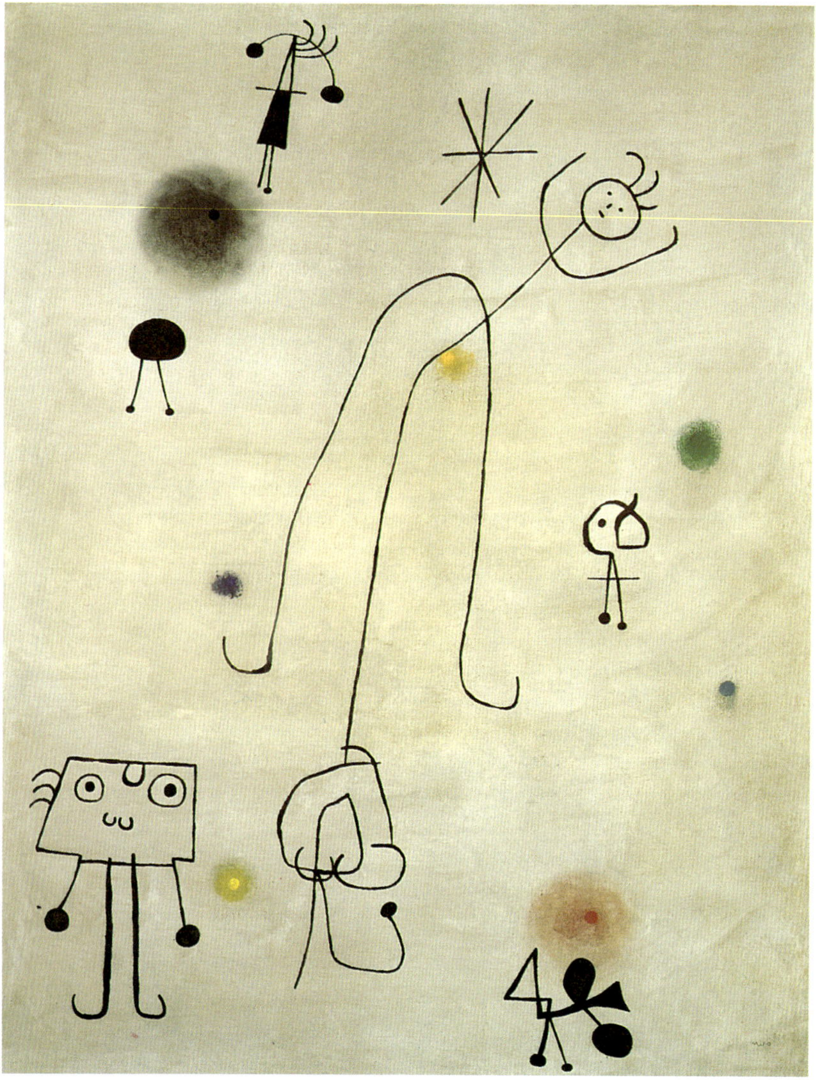

Painting in art nouveau frame,
1943. Gift of Joan Prats

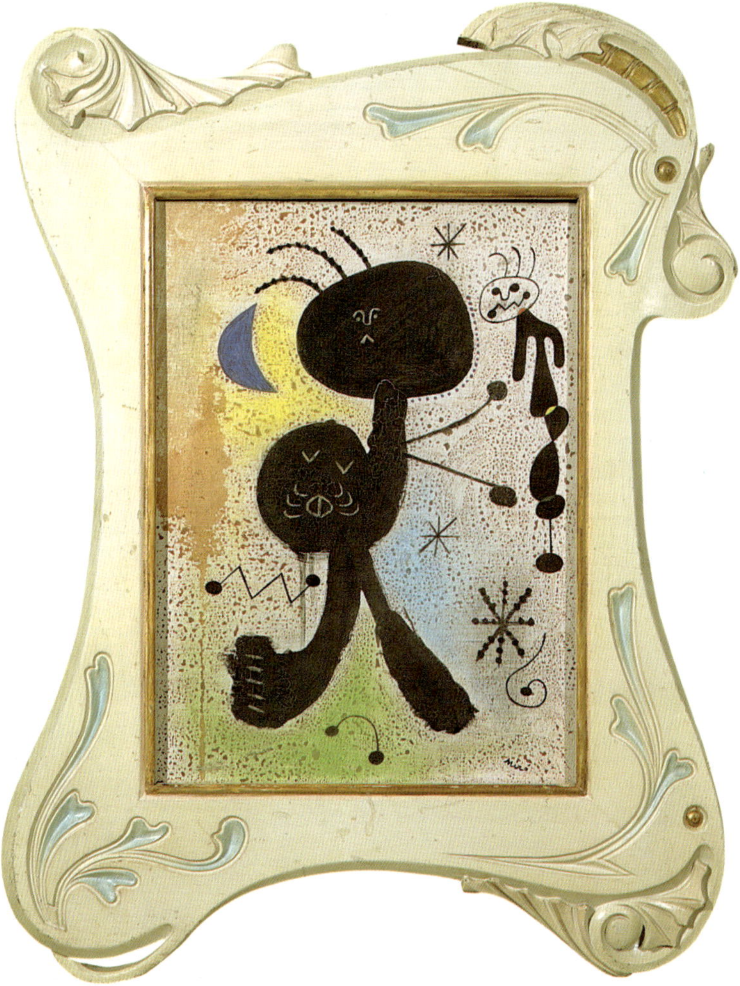

The diamond smiles at twilight,
1947. On permanent loan from
Emili Fernández i Miró

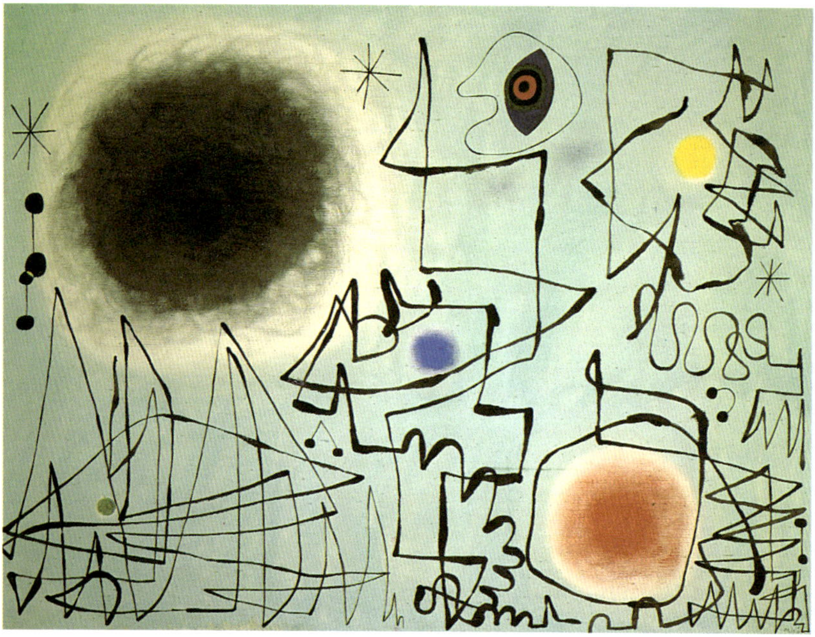

Painting, 1954. Gift of Joan Prats

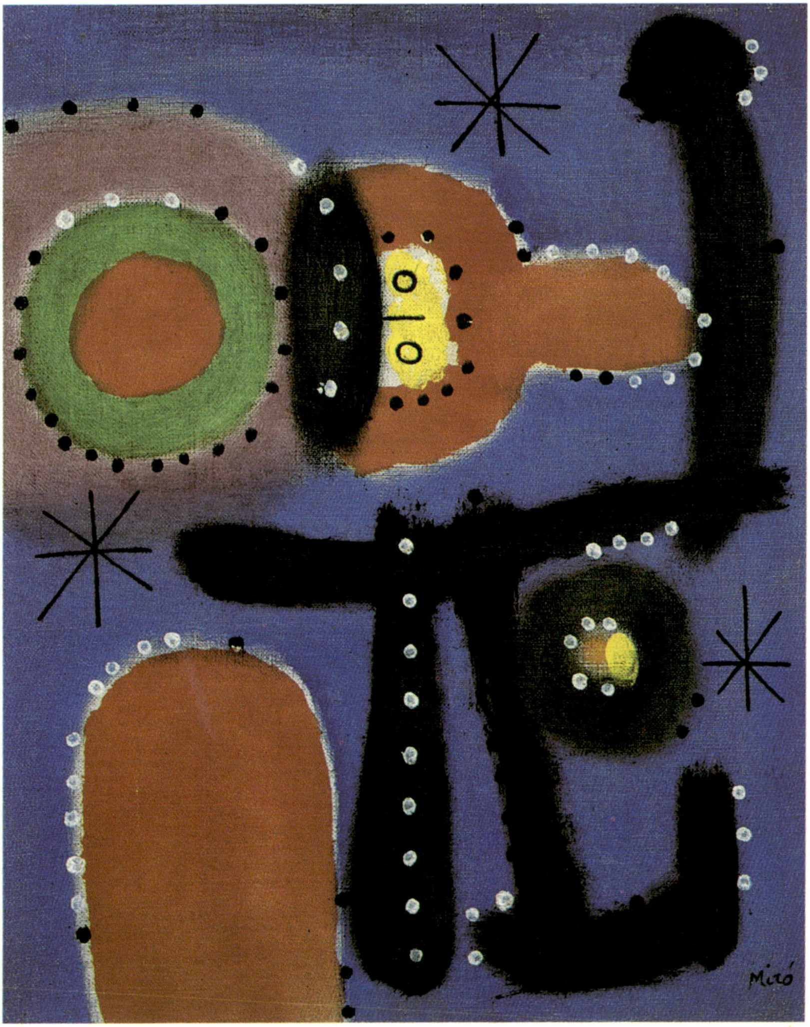

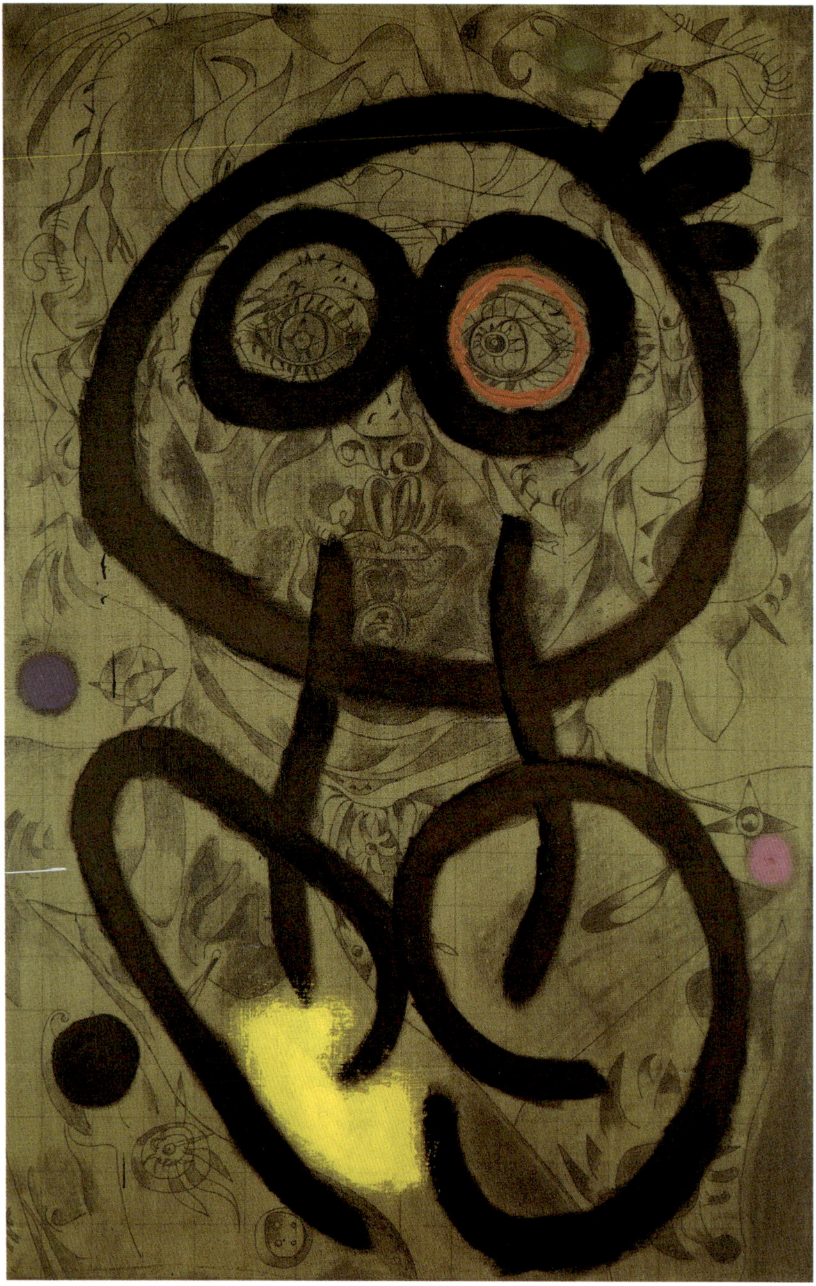

Self-portrait,
1937-38/1960.
On permanent
loan from
Maria Dolors
Miró

Woman in a pretty hat,
1960

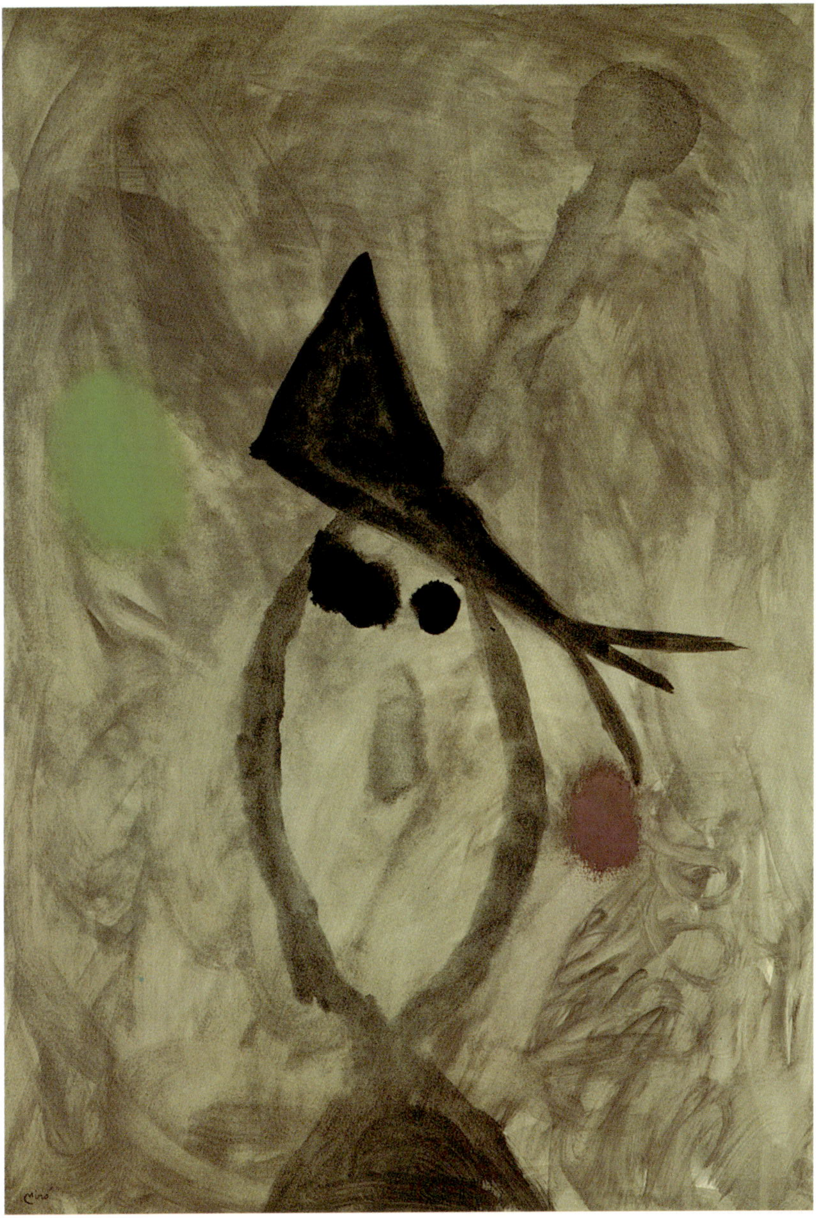

Taking Miró's work as a whole, as the product of a lifetime of exploration and experiment coupled with strict self-criticism, we can see that the early paintings are characterised by their precision and attention to detail, and those of the later period by direct, decisive strokes and a spontaneity in the act of painting: blobs of colour, dribbles of paint, brush marks and even the imprint of the hand.

During the last twenty years of his life, Miró diversified his experiments with other techniques. In 1966 he began working regularly on bronze sculpture. As in the forties, the procedure used in most instances was the *cire perdue* method, but he made less use of modelling and preferred to assemble a variety of everyday bits and pieces that, when cast in bronze, almost always coalesced into biomorphic beings. Working with different foundries (Parellada, Clémenti, Susse, Scuderi and Bonvicini) produced different patinas on the sculptures. In the mid-1960s Miró also experimented with the application of colour to a number of these pieces.

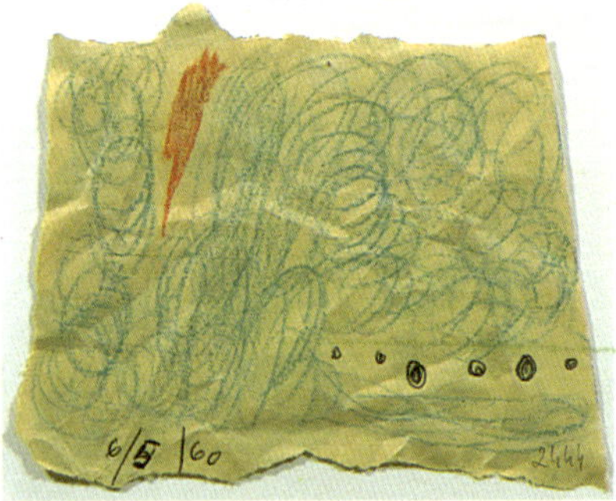

Preliminary sketch for *Blue II*, 1961

Sculpture also allowed him to produce works for different public places – in his own words, "a collective art" to be enjoyed by everyone, which always interested him. This was the case with the monumental sculptures *Couple playing with almond blossom* (1975) for the district of La Défense in Paris, and *Woman and bird* (1982) for the Parc de Joan Miró in Barcelona.

Miró began working on ceramics in 1944 with his friend the ceramicist Josep Llorens i Artigas. After an initial phase from 1944 to 1947, when he learned the techniques of firing and glazing, his so-called ceramic period commenced around 1954-56. The Foundation has one piece from this time, when Miró was experimenting with various types of clay and the formulae for obtaining colours: *Double-sided stele* dated 1956.

Two years later, in 1958, Miró and Artigas embarked on large ceramic murals, producing the *Wall of the sun* and *Wall of the moon* for the UNESCO headquarters in Paris. In 1960 they made a mural for Harvard University, and between 1964 and 1972 received commissions for five more: for the Handelshochschule in St. Gallen, Switzerland (1964), the Solomon R. Guggenheim Museum, New York (1966), Barcelona Airport (1970), the Kunsthaus in Zurich (1971) and the Cinémathèque in Paris (1972). The Foundation holds the documentation relating to two of these – the Guggenheim Museum and Barcelona Airport – the former consisting of maquettes and notes that Miró used for the mural *Alicia,* and the latter consisting of the initial maquette.

After the death of Josep Llorens i Artigas, his son Joan Gardy Artigas continued working with Miró. Together they made the ceramic paving for the Pla de l'Os in the Rambla in Barcelona, and the maquette for this is also held at the Foundation.

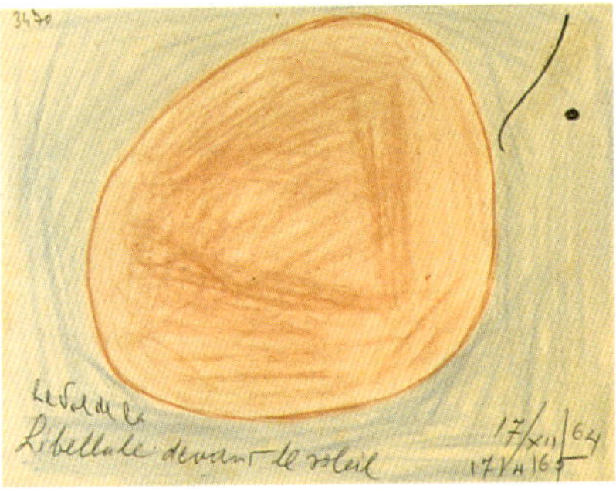

Preliminary sketch for *Flight of the dragonfly in front of the sun,* 1968

In 1972, Miró produced his first textiles – which can be placed somewhere between painting, collage and tapestry – in the form of *sobreteixims* and sacks.

The starting point for the *sobreteixims* was the neutral tapestry base prepared by Josep Royo with rustic materials such as jute, hemp, esparto grass and twine. Onto this, Miró poured petrol and let the flames take over, so that chance played its part. He then applied the colour, either with paint, appliquéd felt or skeins of wool.

Miró also used fire again in 1973 to produce the series of "burnt canvases" (three of which are held by the Foundation) that seem an attempt to show his scepticism for the concept of works of art.

In 1974, his work with textiles took a new turn after he received a commission to make a large-format tapestry for the foyer of a New York skyscraper. In 1977, the National Gallery of Art in Washington D.C. asked him for one of much the same type, measuring 11 x 7 metres. On completing it, Miró decided to produce a large tapestry very similar in concept to the Washington one, which he donated to the Foundation in 1979.

For Emili, 1963. On permanent loan from Emili Fernández i Miró

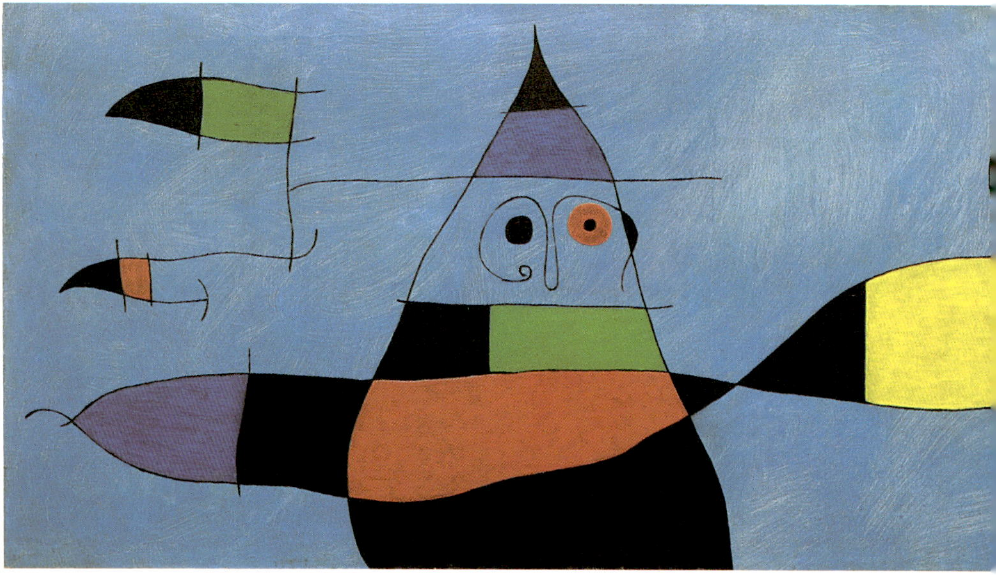

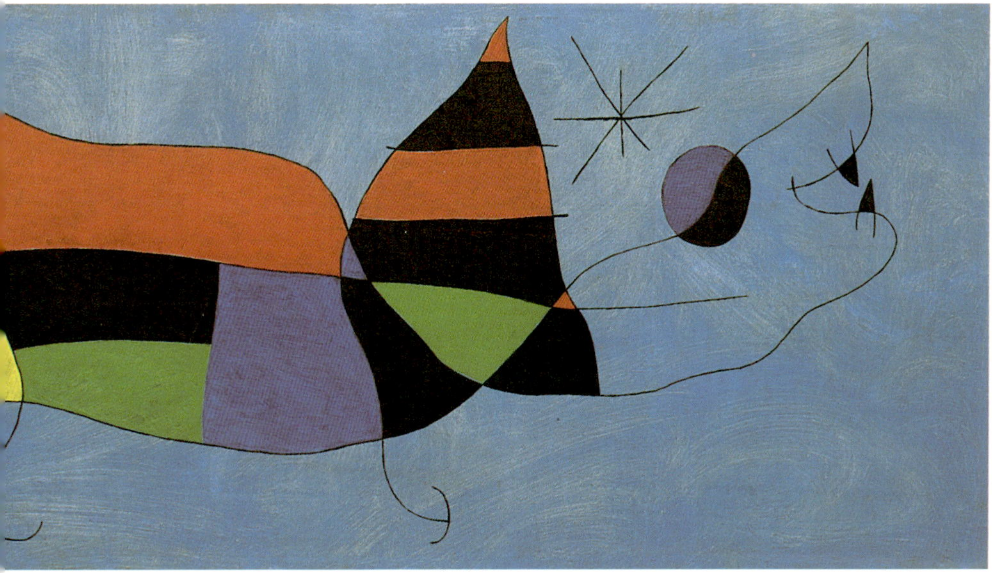

Figure in front of the sun, 1968

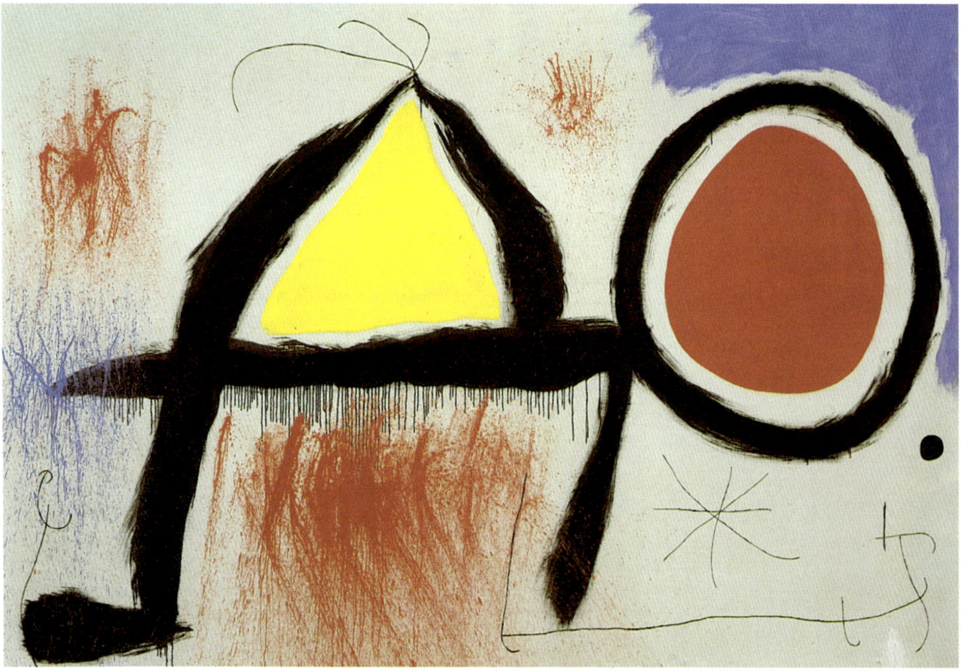

Catalan peasant in the moonlight, 1968

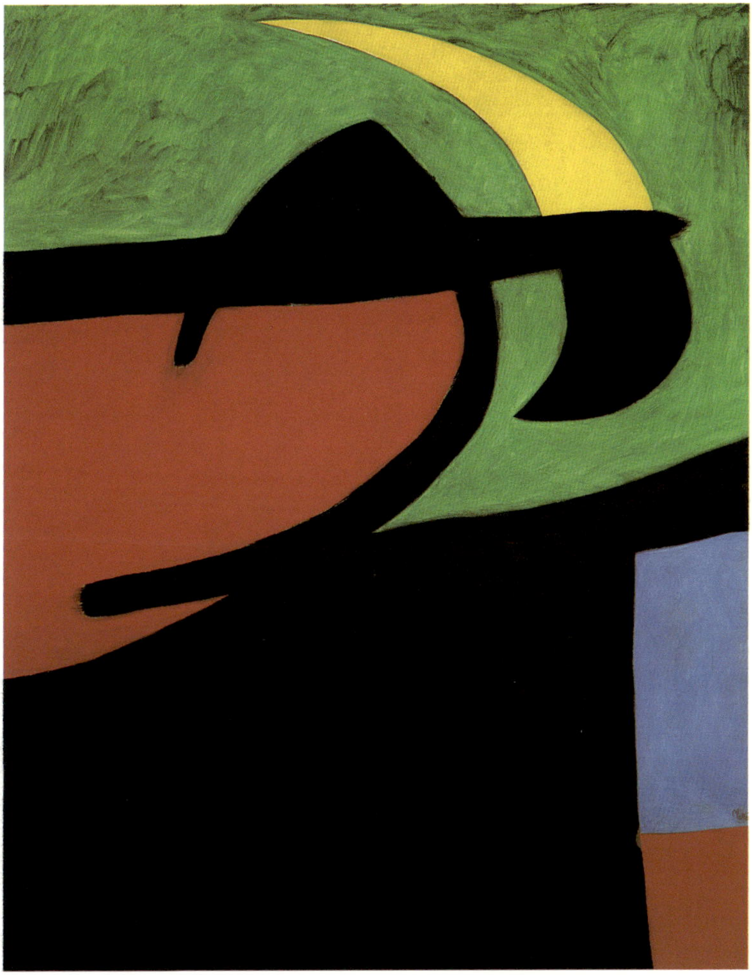

Among the "Miró papers", the Foundation has a copy of Alfred Jarry's *Ubu Roi*, published in Paris in 1921. In the margins and on small scraps of paper originally placed inside the book are a number of drawings by Miró closely connected with the text. From the nature of these drawings they can be presumed to pre-date the publication in 1966 of a special limited edition of *Ubu Roi* for which Miró produced thirteen lithographs. Other related pieces that have survived from the same period are detailed illustrations for *Ubu Roi*, which were never published but which show a faithful relationship between text and image that can almost be read like a story in pictures.

Miró was fascinated with Ubu, a grotesque figure whose bodily functions predominate over his intellectual ones, and kept the subject constantly in mind. This creature that was a caricature of all that is despicable in the human being appeared in two further limited-edition books, *Ubu aux Baléares*, 1973 and *L'enfance d'Ubu*, 1975 – the first with illustrations and text by Miró, the second with illustrations by Miró and texts taken from somewhat vulgar Majorcan and Catalan sayings.

It was this material, donated by Miró to the Foundation, that was used by the members of the Teatre de la Claca group in order to give shape and volume to the giant puppet figures for the spectacle *Mori el Merma* performed in 1978. Miró brought life to the figures by painting them. These puppets, Miró's last great creative work, now form part of the Foundation's collections.

In June 1975, as already mentioned, the Joan Miró Foundation was opened to the public. Miró made a major donation of works at that time, and the following year he gave the Foundation practically the entire collection of "Miró papers". He subsequently made further donations of paintings on various supports as well as sketchbooks.

Thanks to the existence of all these items, to the orderly way in which Miró worked and to his immense generosity, we have been able to make this documentary material accessible to students, academics and anyone else interested in following Miró's artistic career from its early beginnings to his last years. It is one of the most exciting adventures in twentieth-century art.

Lovers playing with almond blossom, 1975. Maquette for the sculptural group at La Défense (Paris)

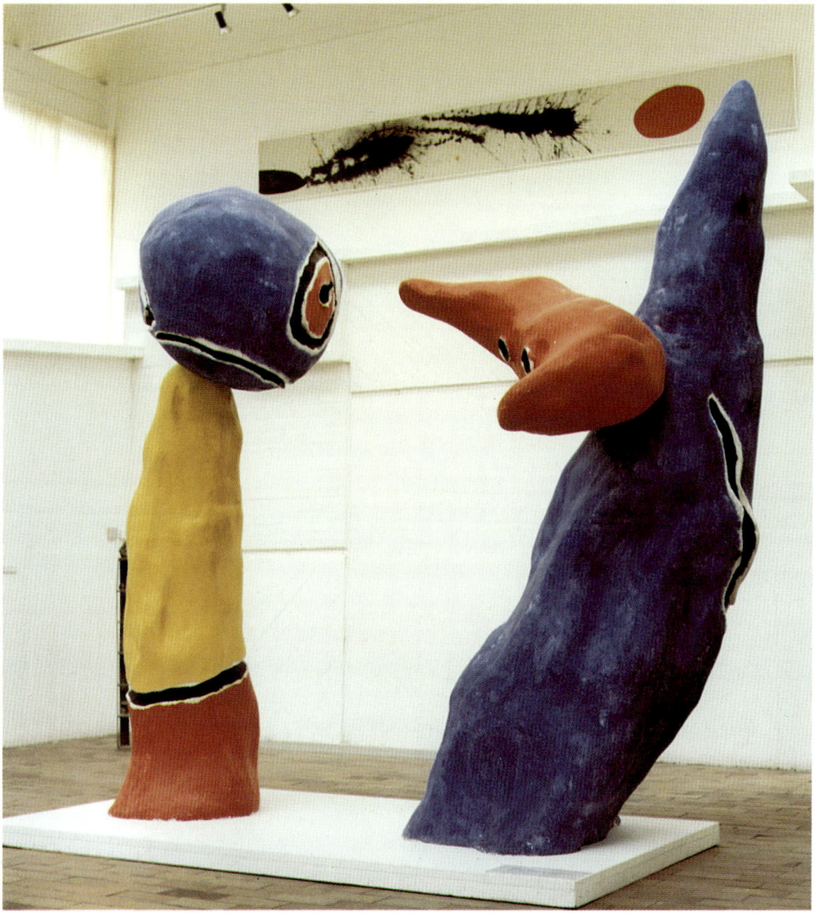

The bird makes its nest in the fingers in flower, 1969

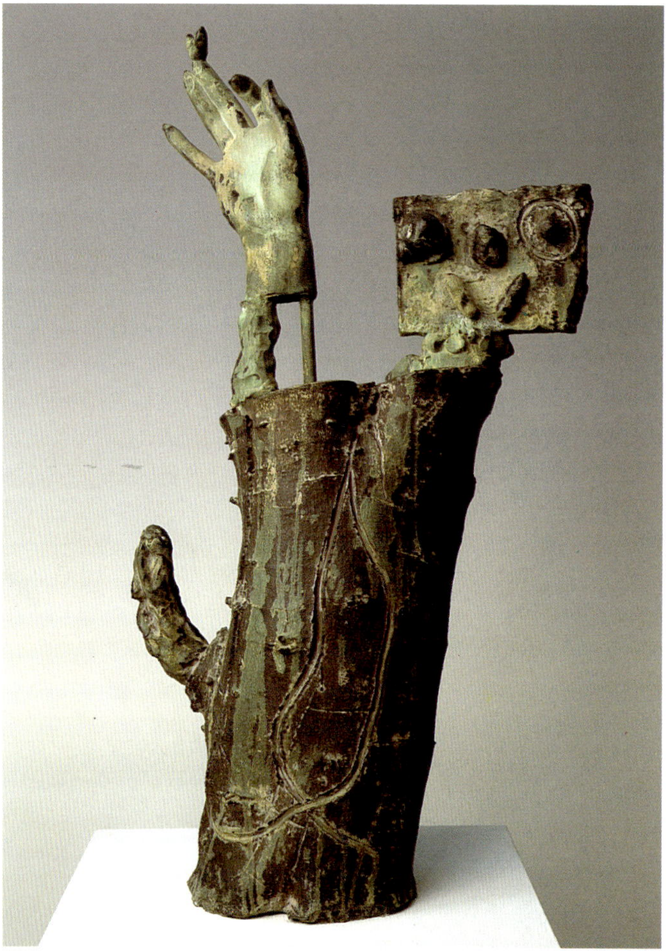

Maquette for the ceramic mural
at Barcelona Airport, 1970

Ubu Roi, undated

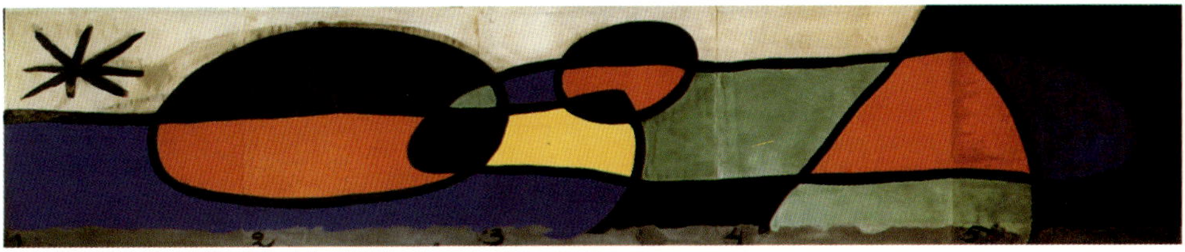

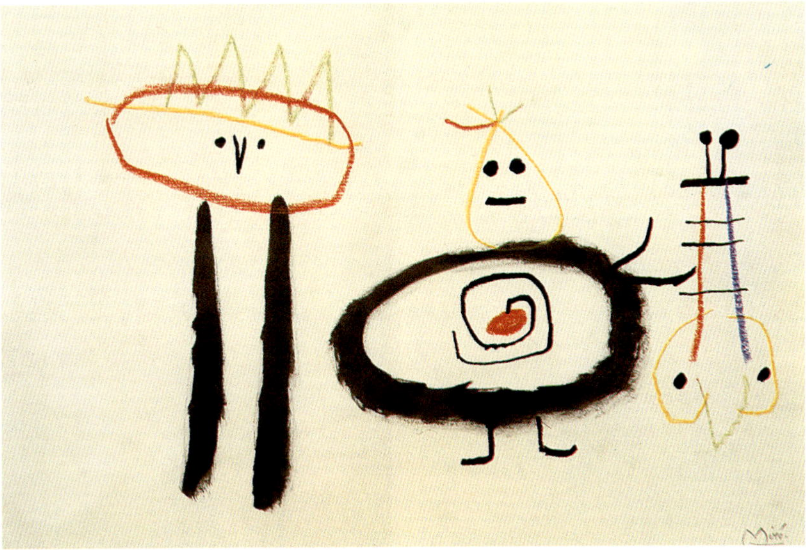

Double-sided stele, 1956.
Gift of the Galerie Lelong

Tapestry of the Foundation,
1979

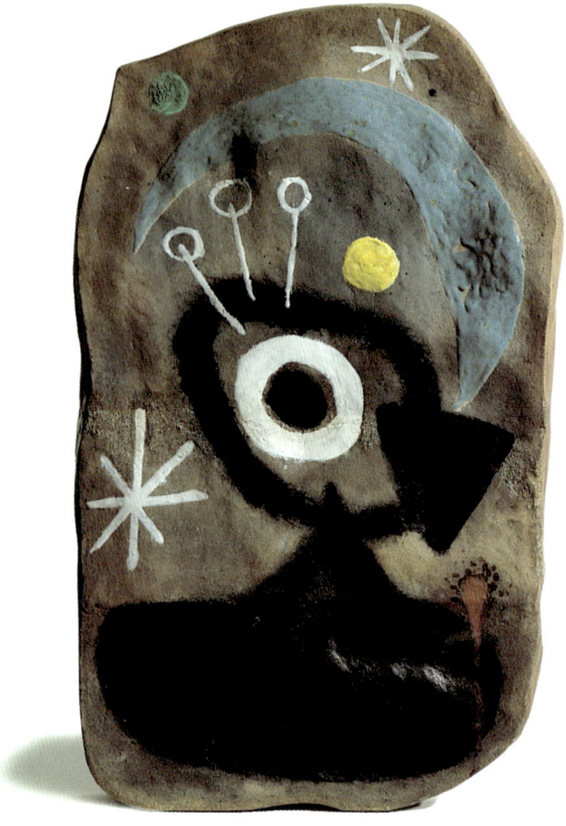

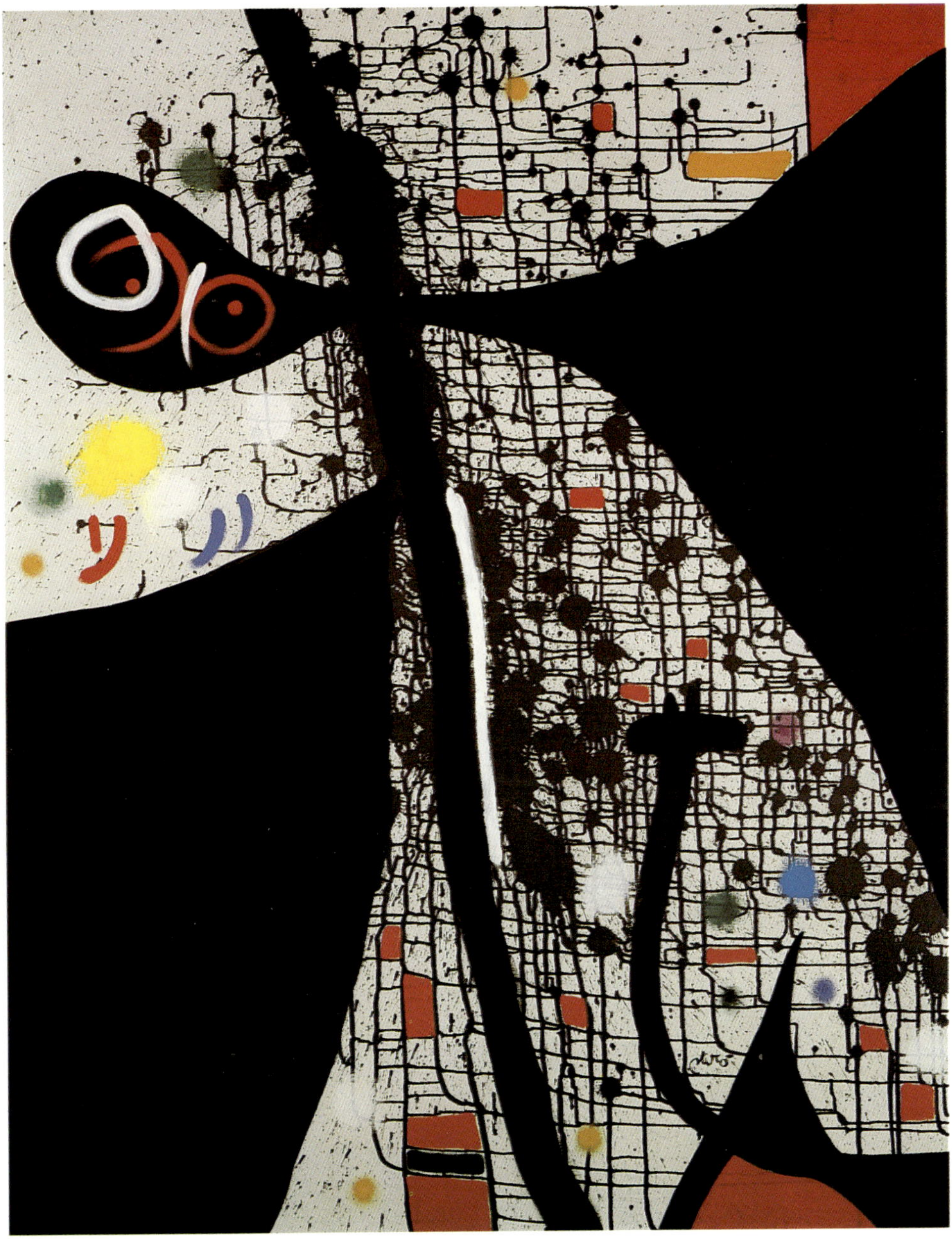

The hope of the man condemned to death I, II, III,
1974

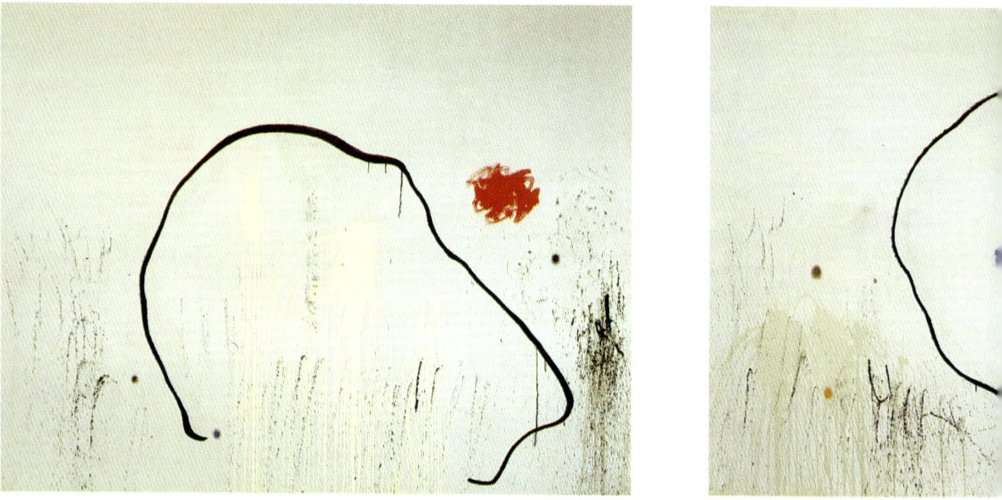

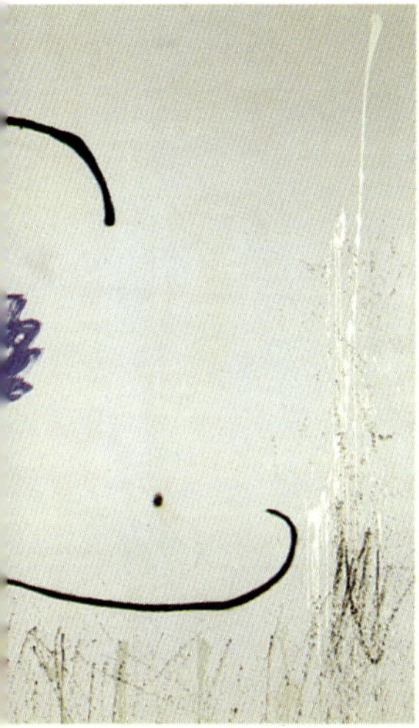

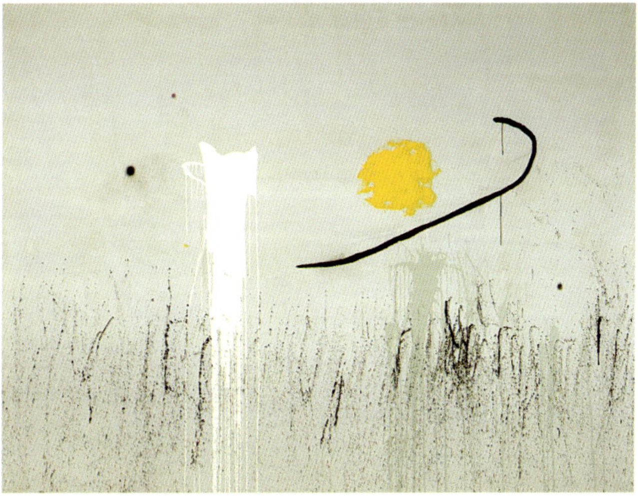

Mont-roig landscape, 1914.
On long-term loan from
Gallery K. AG

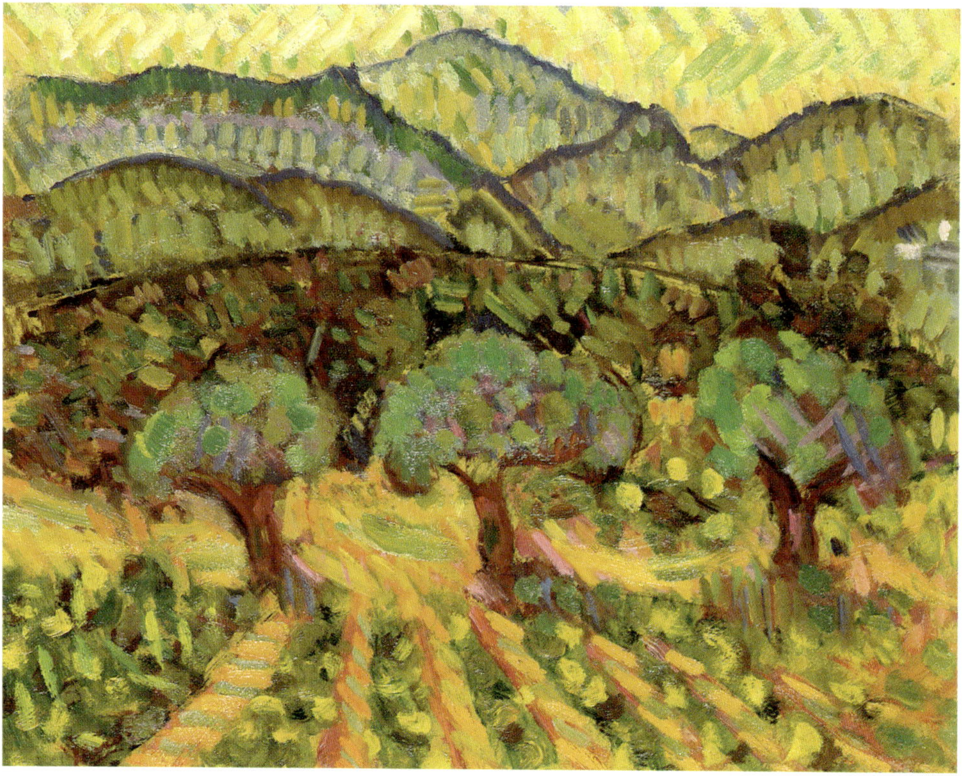

Epilogue

The celebrations to mark the twenty-fifth anniversary of the opening of the Foundation began in June 2000 and culminated a year later in the new extension to the building. This signified a substantial improvement to the installations and an increase in the exhibition area in order to house the long-term loan of 23 works by Miró from the Gallery K. AG, founded by Kazumasa Katsuta.

Relations between the Foundation and this Japanese collector – owner of the largest private collection of Miró's art – began with the preparations for the exhibition "Joan Miró 1893-1993" to mark the centenary of the artist's birth. There was further collaboration later on in connection with the exhibitions "Joan Miró. Equilibrium in space" and "Klee, Tanguy, Miró. Three approaches to landscape".

This collection of 23 pieces, produced between 1914 and 1973 and displayed at the end of the tour of the permanent collection, can be considered a synthesis of Miró's stylistic development and offers an overall reading of his creative output. *Mont-roig landscape,* dated 1914, recalls his early work marked by the freedom of expression and alteration of colours that was the result of his fascination with Van Gogh and the Fauves. In contrast, the strong, confident lines of *Untitled (Seated Nude),* a drawing produced at the Cercle Artístic de Sant Lluc, shows a desire to establish the volume of the figure.

Untitled (Seated nude), 1916.
On long-term loan from
Gallery K. AG

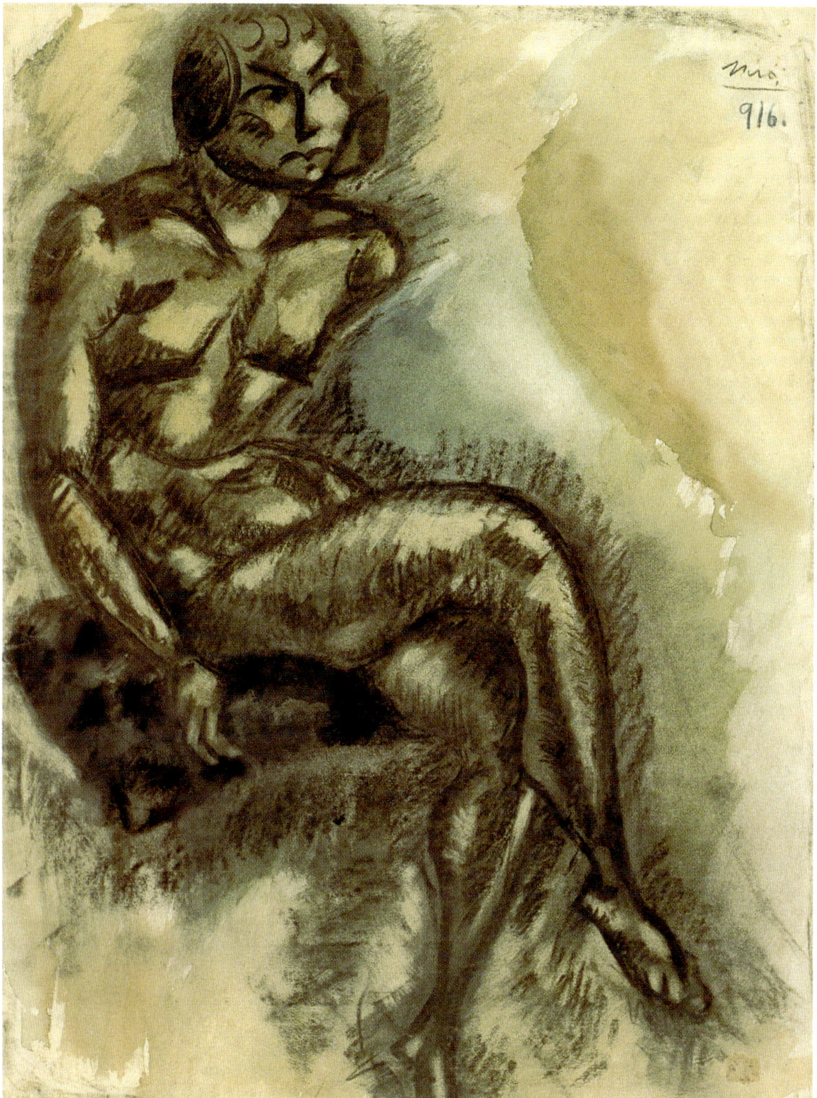

Painting, dated 1927, is a typical example of the artist's "dream paintings", characterised by the reduction of the components to their essence, floating in an undefined space.

Miró's interest in the visual possibilities of collage and the humorous combination of images and line drawings was the origin of a series of *Collage-drawings* produced in 1933-34. Nevertheless, the tone and treatment of a large part of his output in 1934 reveals other concerns, linked to specific events at the time. Vivid colouring makes a reappearance, often with darker tones that emphasise the light and shade and the illusion of mass; and the empty space is peopled with outlandish, cruelly deformed figures. The medium used – pastel – makes them soft, unreal and extraordinarily disturbing.

The fact that the outbreak of the Spanish Civil War coincided with the start of a series of paintings on "masonite" – a dark, rough surface and not a normal artist's material – would seem to point to a connection between these works and their context. However, remarks by Miró himself indicate that the appreciation of certain poetic qualities in the materials employed encouraged him to experiment with them in a decided way. At any rate, the contrast between the neutral base of the masonite and the extremely varied materials applied to it gives an overall effect of physical harshness.

In 1942-43, Miró produced around a hundred paintings on paper. He painted straight onto the paper, without any preparatory drawings, in fluid, confident strokes. *Woman, bird, stars* is dynamic in its execution, with a close association between the touches of velvety, phosphorescent pastel and the delicately modulated lines. Women, birds and stars – the basis of Miró's iconography – were thereafter to become constant reference points.

The red of the swallows and the iridescent pink, 1947, shows a natural combination of soft brush strokes, vibrant colouring and sharp, resolute draughtsmanship, together with the ever-present familiar signs.

A break in the sky gives us hope, more immediate and spontaneous in its execution, is a circular composition, the result of the artist having repeatedly changed its position while painting it. The background is covered in dribbles, washes, scratches made with the handle of the brush and negative imprints, reminiscent of the gestural creations of American Abstract Expressionism.

Landscape, whether referred to directly or obliquely, constitutes the conceptual setting for much of Miró's art, including the richly worked cosmic visions of the period of the *Constellations* and the later derivations with their harmonious figures and stars floating in an undefined setting. At times, although the allusion is direct, the pictorial definition emerges as much from the identifiable details as from the technical execution. For instance, in *Landscape at night* there are unequivocal motifs, such as the moon or the stars, situated at the top, and the wavy lines denoting the mountains, but perhaps they would not be so clearly identifiable if Miró had not prepared such a contrasting background, with whirls of transparent brush strokes in the upper part and a more dense, opaque colour lower down.

On another level, few pictures give a better idea of Miró's desire "to achieve the maximum intensity with the minimum means" than the *The lark's wing ringed in the blue of gold meets the heart of the poppy asleep on the field adorned with diamonds.* This is not only because of the contrast between the extreme austerity of the painting and the length of its title, which seems to call for the depiction of a large number of elements, but also because of the way in which the artist offsets and balances the extent and location of the strongly contrasting colours.

Finally, two pictures, *Drop of water on pink snow* and *Hair pursued by two planets,* the former on permanent loan to the Foundation by Joan Punyet Miró, the artist's grandson and a member of the Board of Trustees, and the second from the Gallery K. AG, are testimony to Miró's highly personal way of working, often based on reworkings of an original form or, as in this case, on the intrinsic relationship between the two paintings. The canvases were designed as a pair, although they were painted a month apart. The visible motifs in each of them are not exactly similar, although the communication, based on a play of equivalences, is evident.

Painting, 1927. On long-term loan from Gallery K. AG

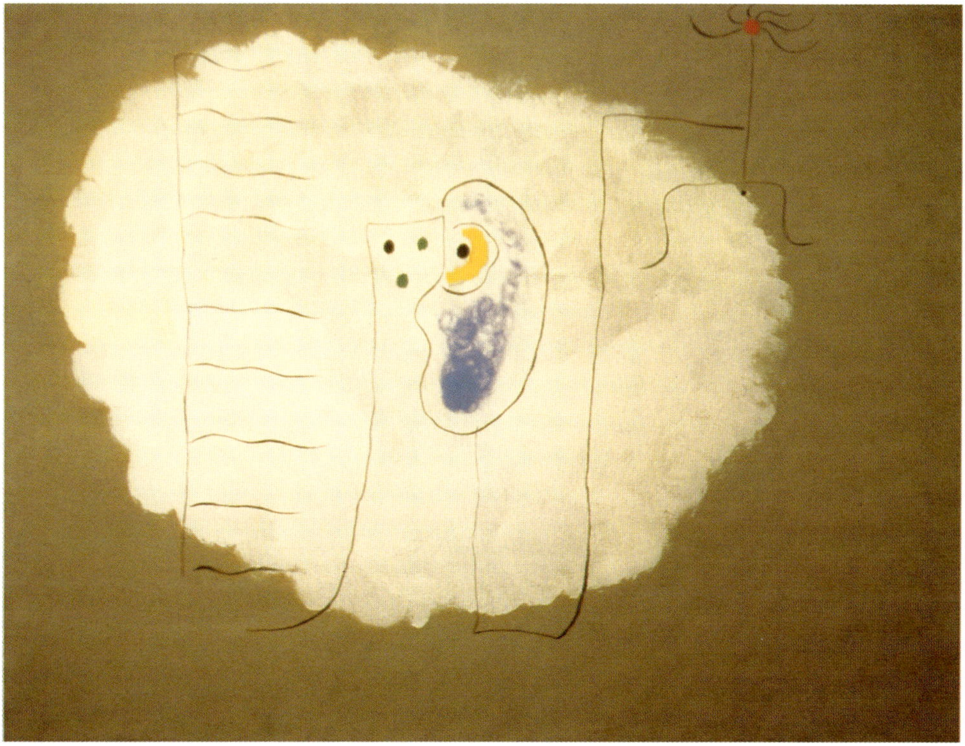

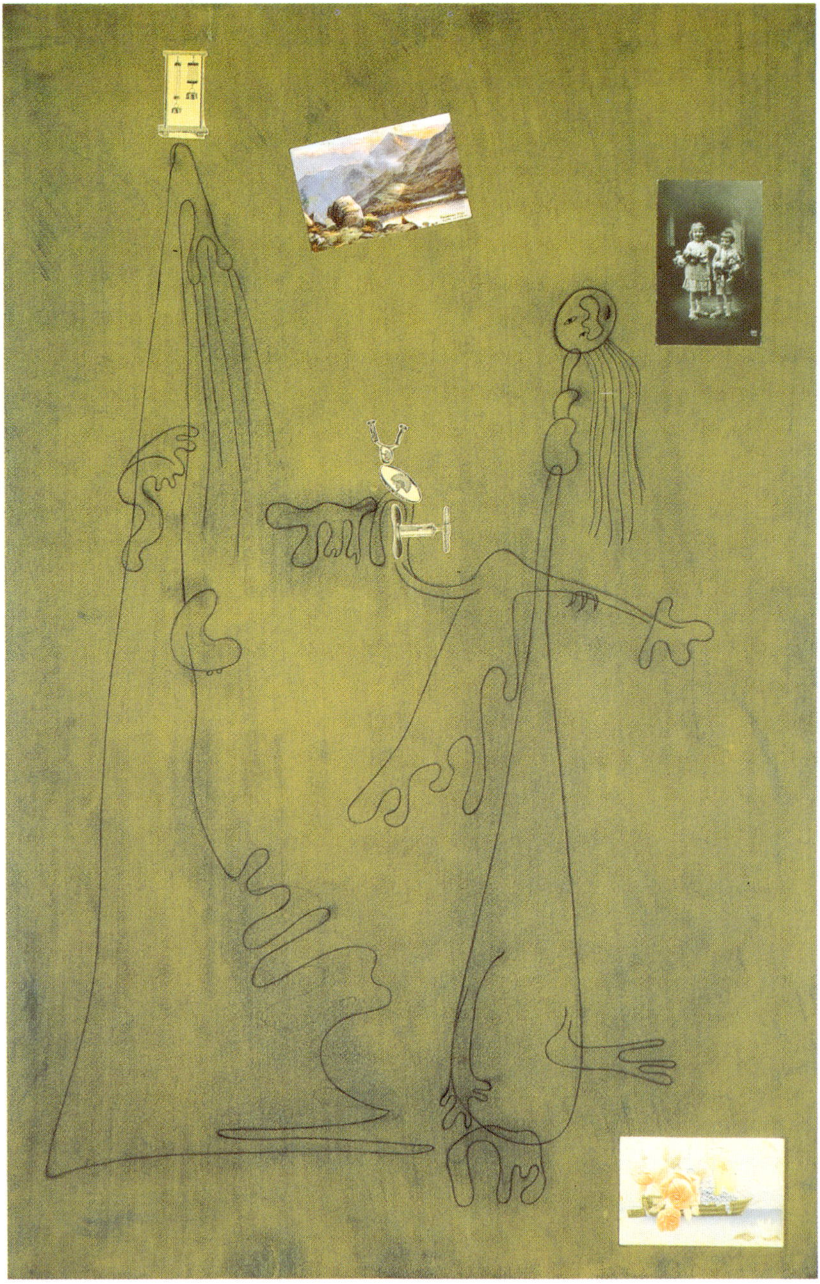

Collage-drawing, 1933. On long-term loan from Gallery K. AG

Figure, 1934.
On long-term
loan from
Gallery K. AG

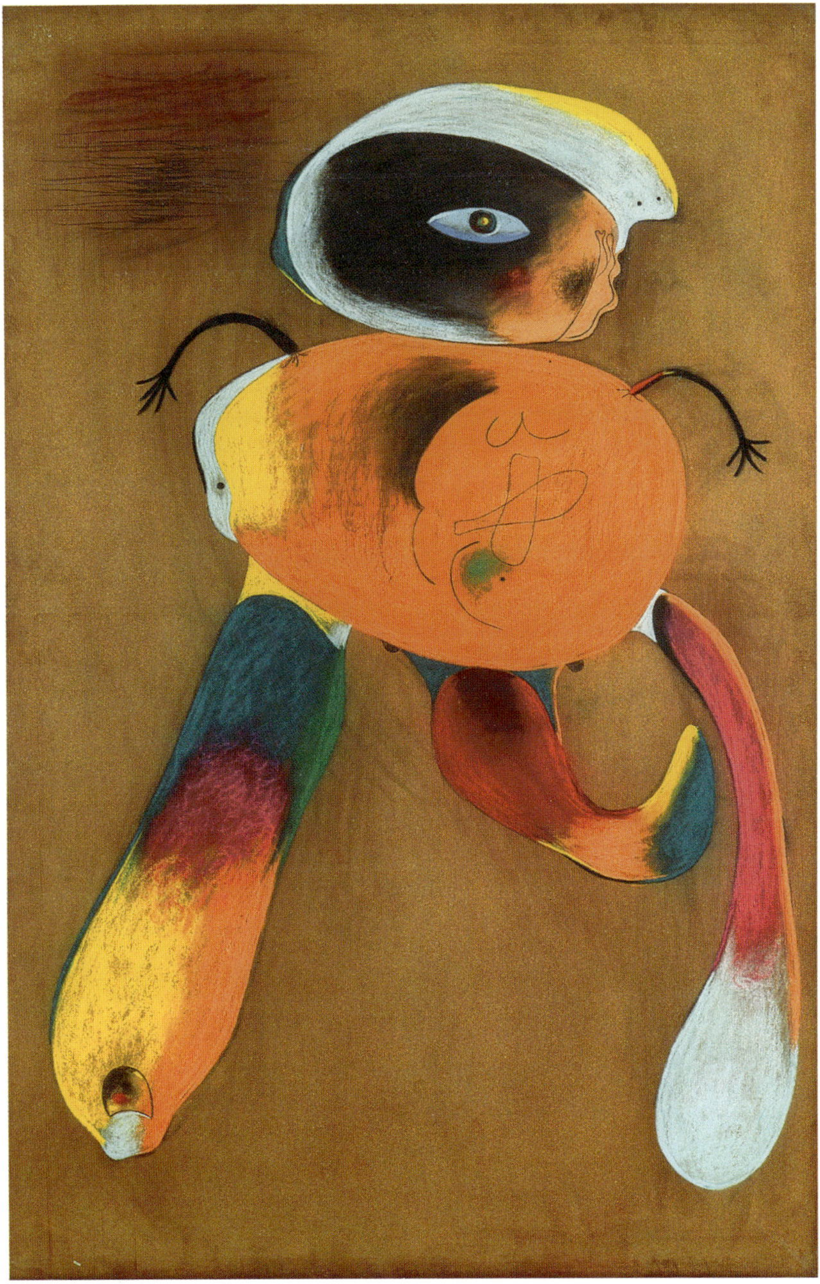

Painting, 1936. On long-term loan from Gallery K. AG

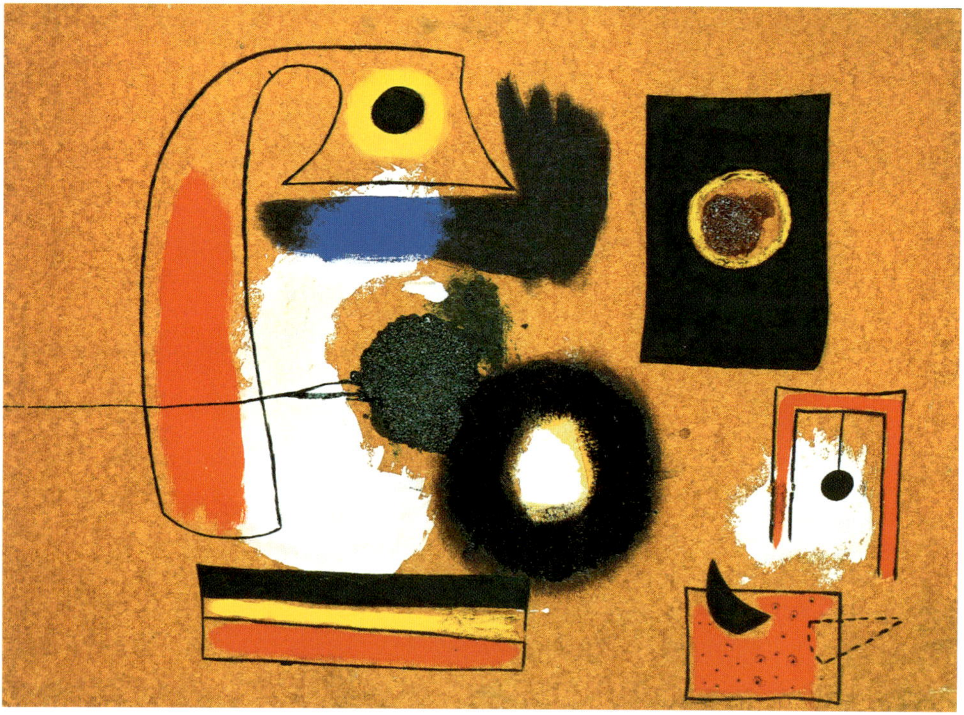

Woman, bird, stars, 1942.
On long-term loan from
Gallery K. AG

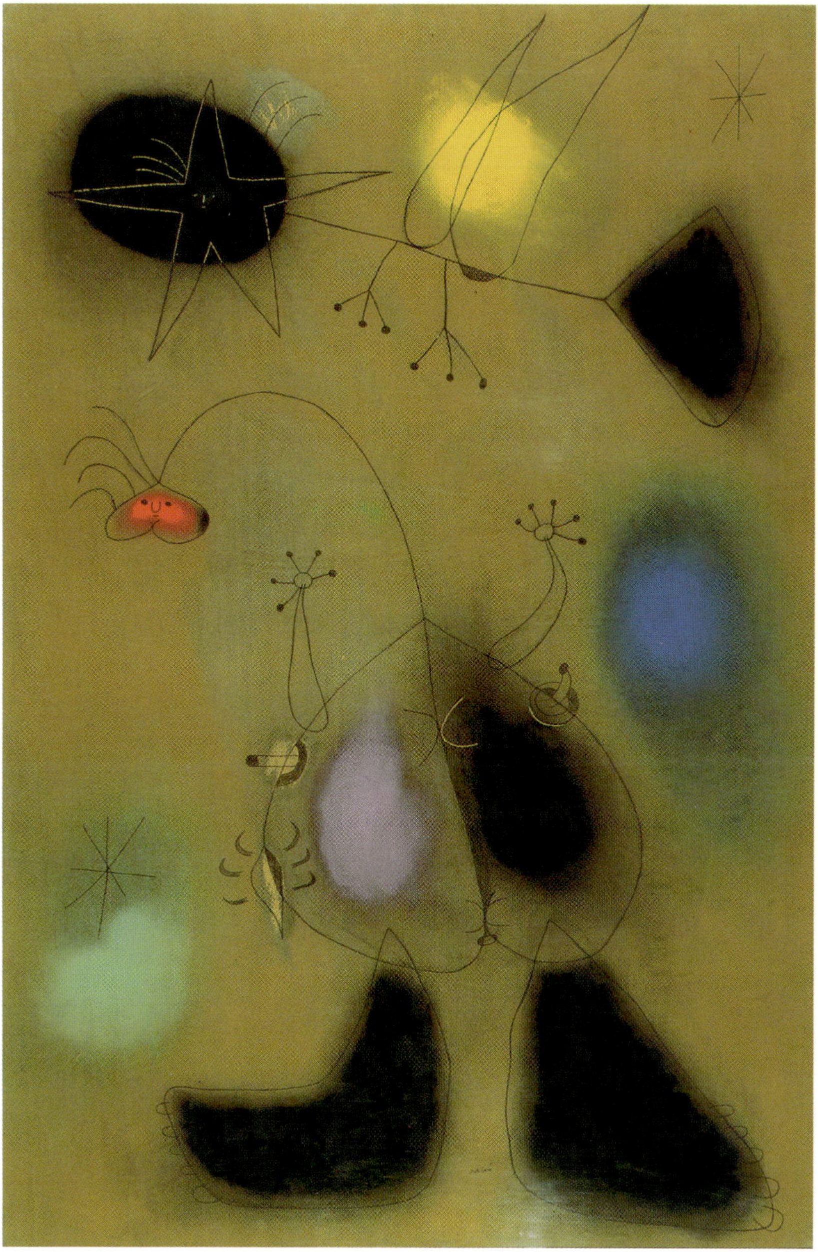

The red of the swallows and the iridescent pink, 1947.
On long-term loan from
Gallery K. AG

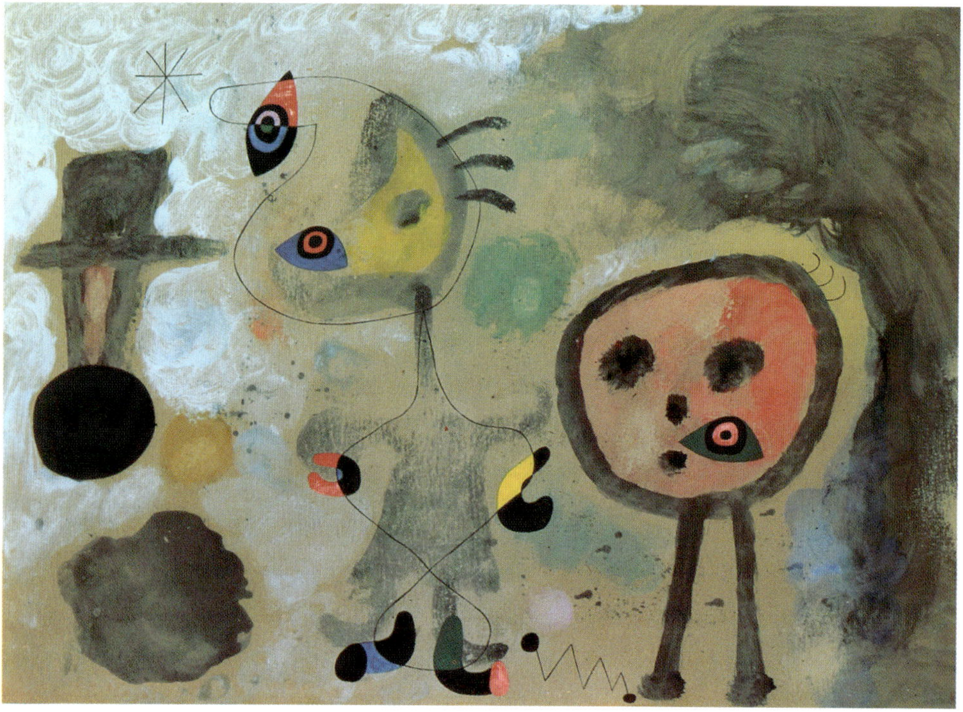

A break in the sky gives us hope, 1954. On long-term loan from Gallery K. AG

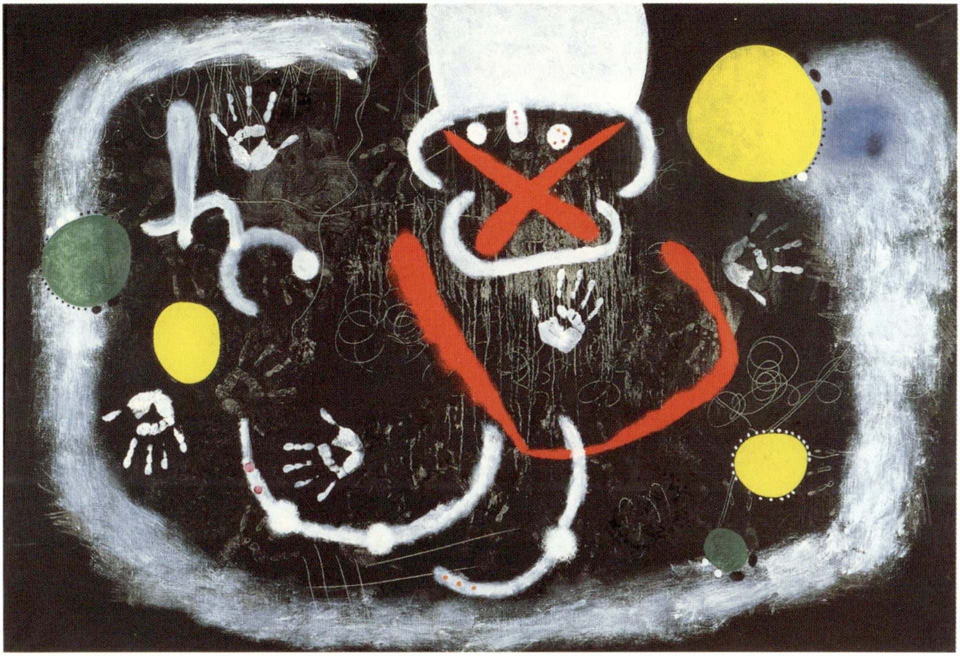

Landscape at night, 1966/1974.
On long-term loan from
Gallery K. AG

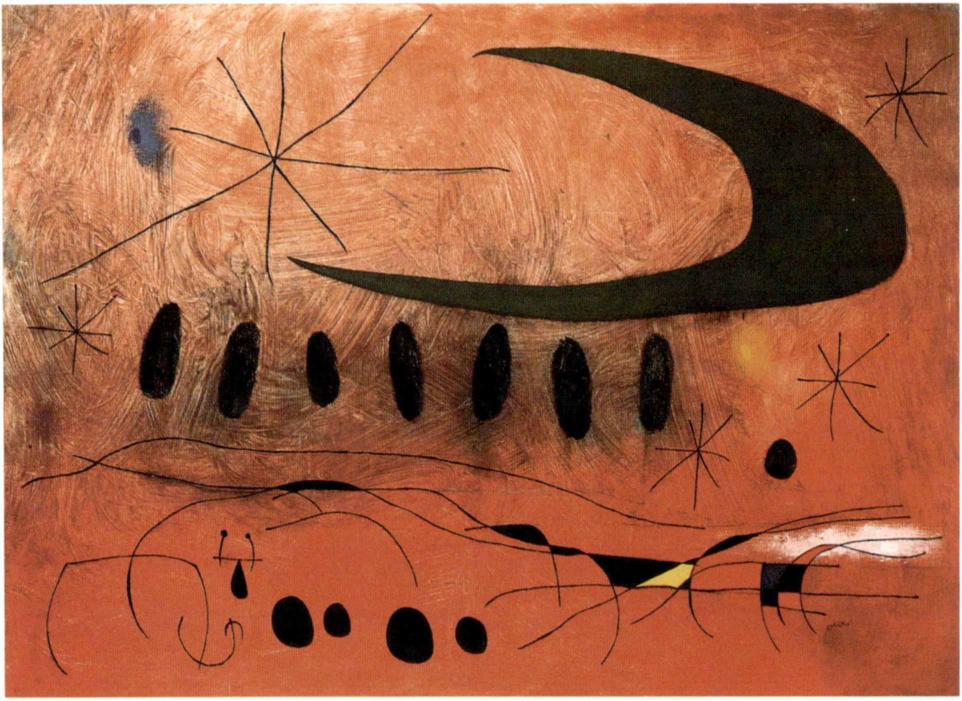

The lark's wing ringed in the blue of gold meets the heart of the poppy asleep on the field adorned with diamonds, 1967. On long-term loan from Gallery K. AG

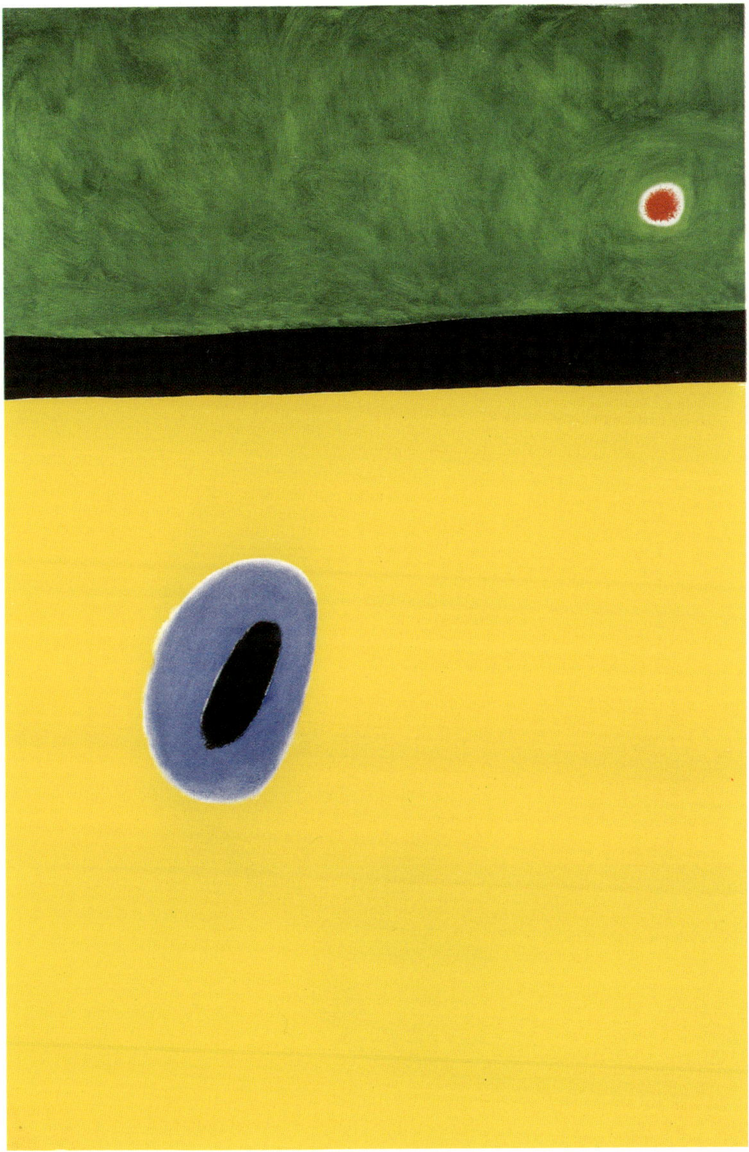

Drop of water on pink snow,
1968. On permanent loan from
Joan Punyet Miró

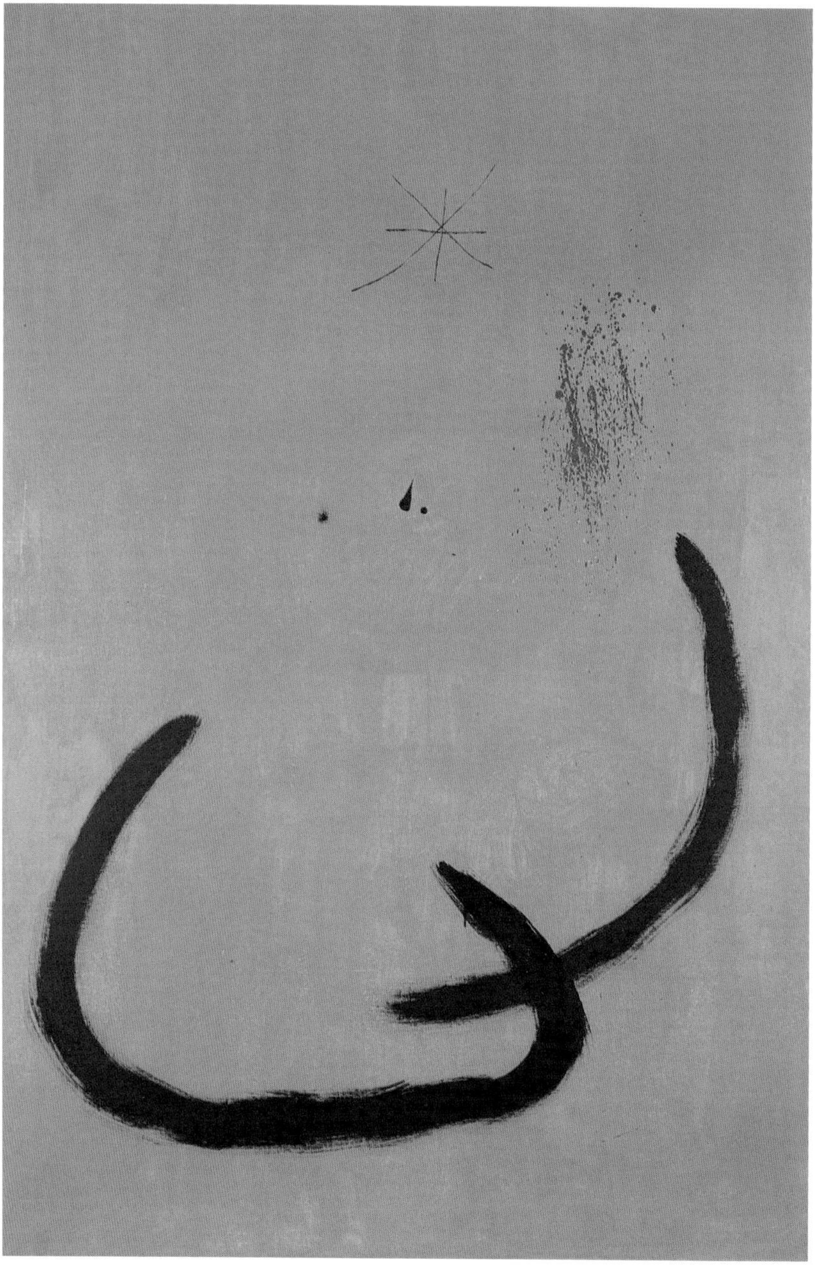

Hair pursued by two planets,
1968. On long-term loan from
Gallery K. AG

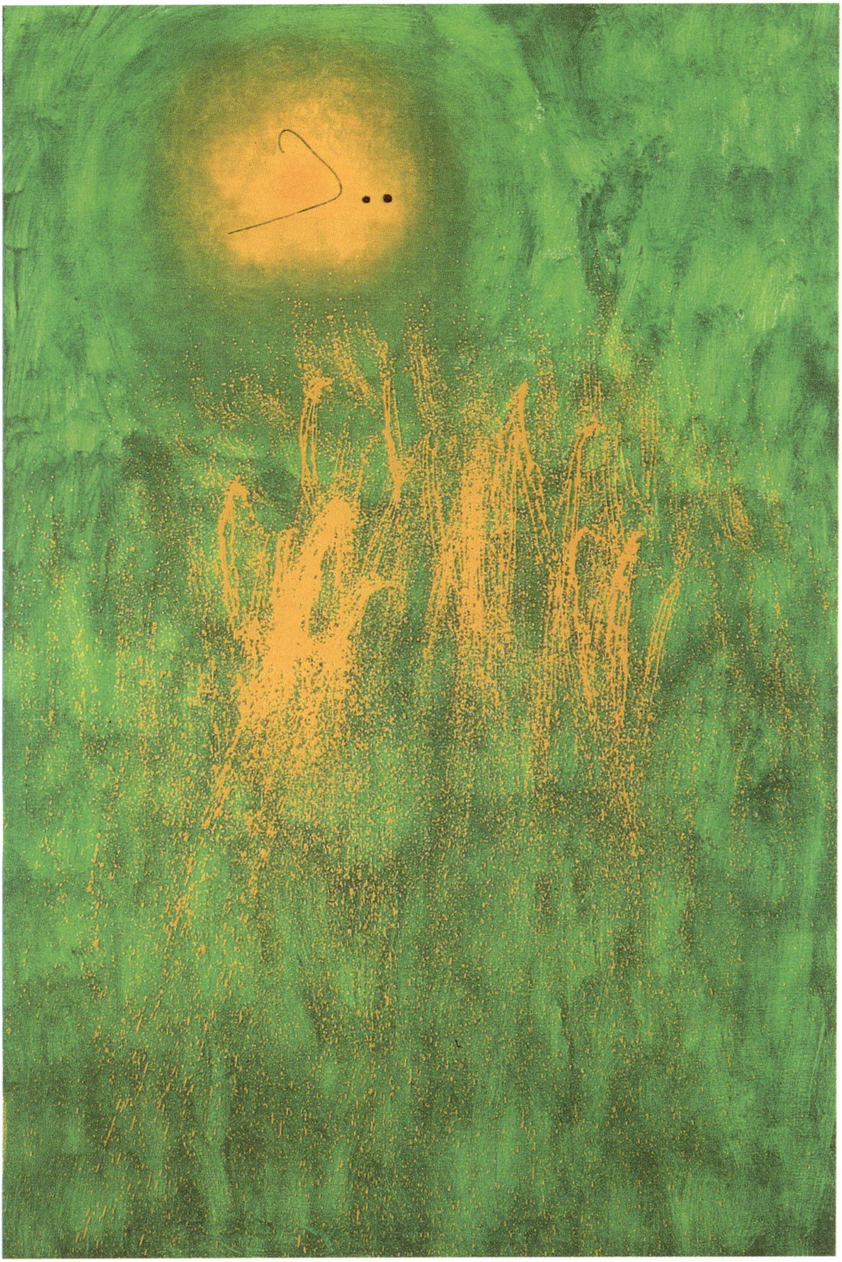

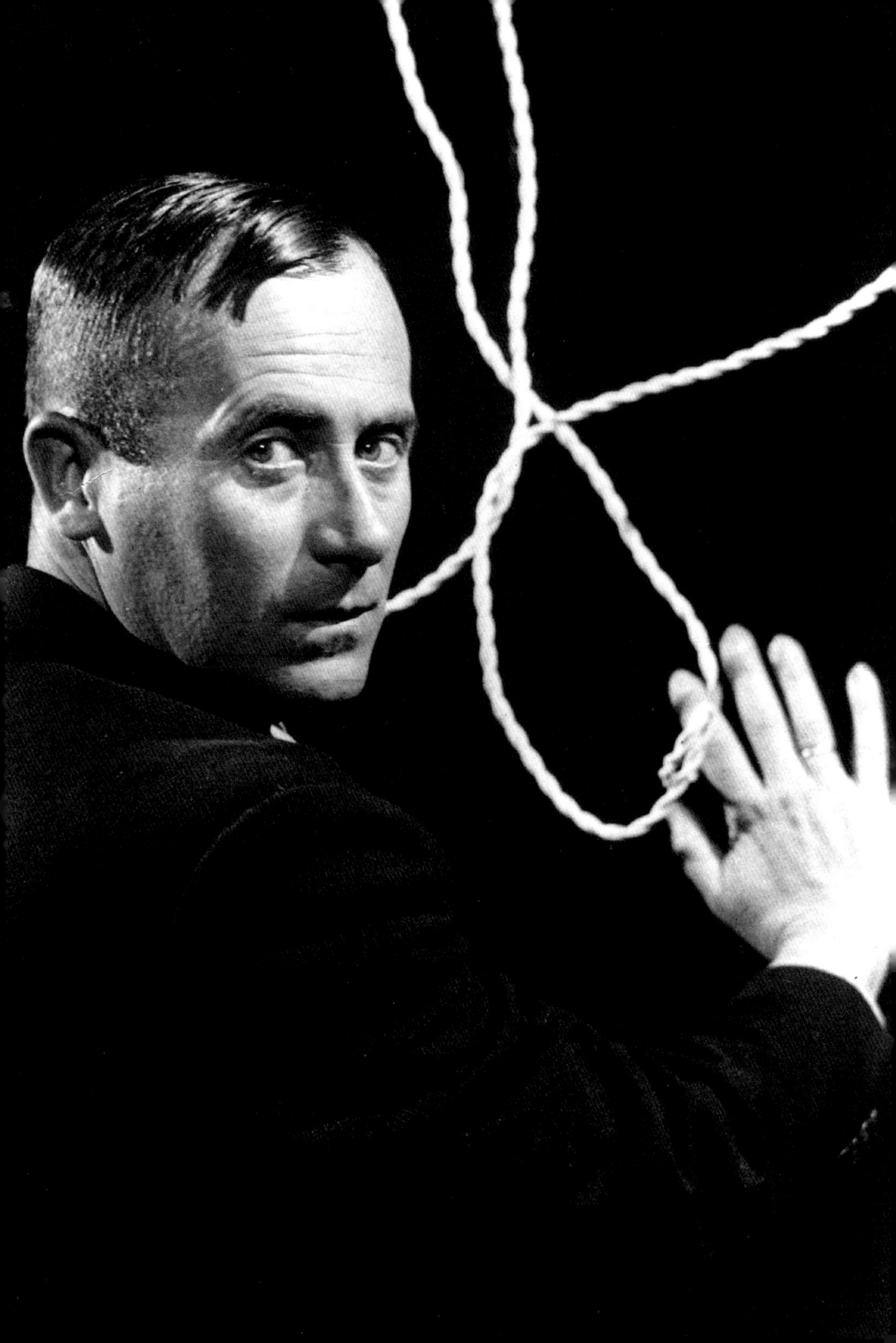

Chronology

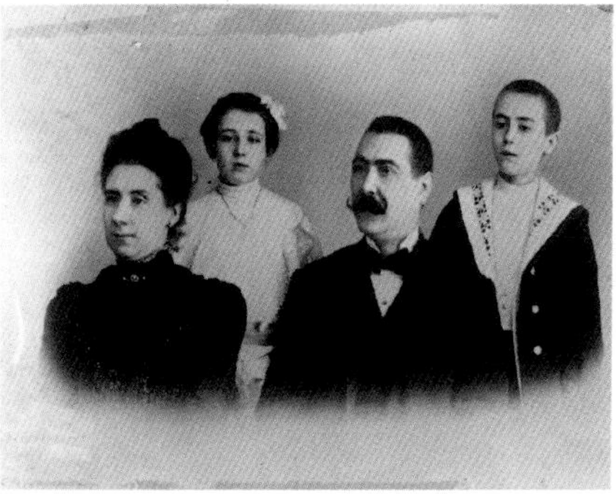

Joan Miró with his parents and sister Dolors

1893
20 April: Birth of Joan Miró i Ferrà at 9.00 p.m. at number 4 Passatge del Crèdit, Barcelona. His father, Miquel Miró i Adzerias, son of a blacksmith in Cornudella, was a watchmaker and silversmith. His mother, Dolors Ferrà i Oromí, was the daughter of a cabinet-maker in Palma, Majorca.

1900
Begins primary school at Carrer del Regomir 13, Barcelona, where he attends drawing classes given by Sr. Civil.

1901
The earliest preserved drawings, now at the Joan Miró Foundation in Barcelona, date from this year.

1907
Enrols at the School of Commerce in Barcelona. At the same time he attends classes at the School of Industrial and Fine Arts (the Llotja) until 1910, where his teachers are Modest Urgell and Josep Pascó.

1910
Works as an accounts clerk at Dalmau i Oliveres drugstore in Barcelona.
Participates for the first time at an exhibition of old and modern portraits and drawings organised by the City Council.

1911
His inability to adapt to the job at Dalmau i Oliveres affects his health. He catches typhoid fever and spends time convalescing in Mont-roig (province of Tarragona) at the farm recently bought by his parents.

1912
Decides to devote himself entirely to painting and enrols in the school of art run by Francesc Galí, which he attends until 1915. Among his fellow students are Joan Prats, Josep Francesc Ràfols, Enric Cristòfol Ricart and possibly Josep Llorens Artigas, among others.

1913
Enrols in the Cercle Artístic de Sant Lluc, where he attends life classes. Here he meets up again with Joan Prats, with whom he forms a close friendship.

1916
Meets the dealer Josep Dalmau, who shows an interest in his work. Rents a studio with E.C. Ricart in Carrer de Sant Pere més Baix 51,

Joan Miró photographed by Man Ray, Paris, 1933

Joan Miró and other students from Francesc Galí's art school on the beach in Barcelona, 1912-15

Joan Miró in his Barcelona studio, 1918-1920

Joan Miró and Pilar Juncosa on their wedding day. Palma, 12 October 1929

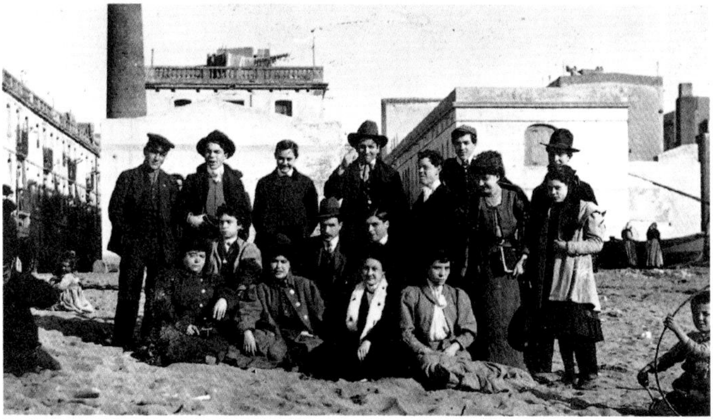

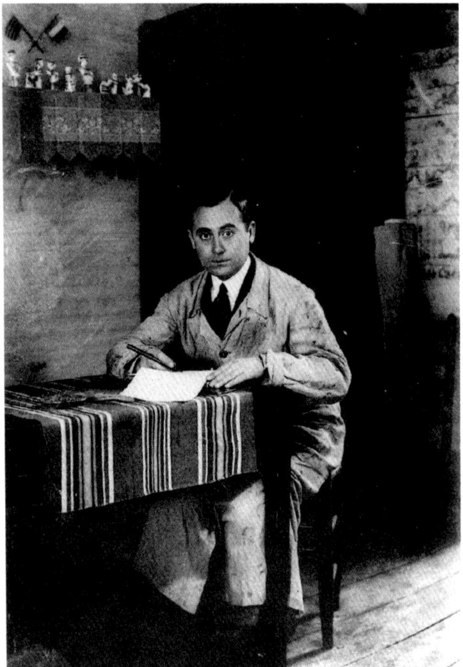

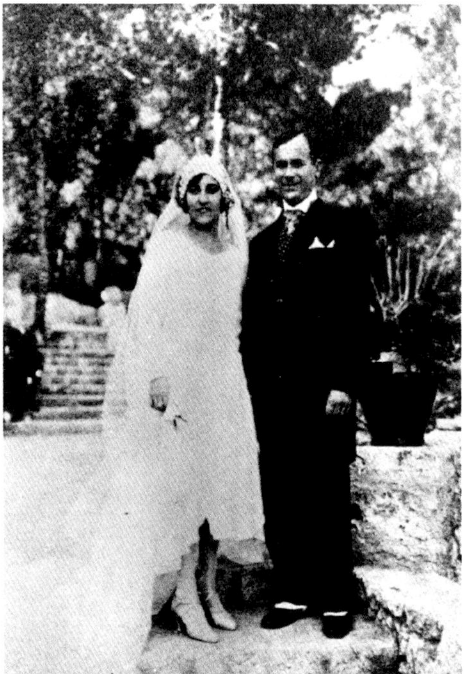

Barcelona, which they share until 1918.

1917

Through Josep Dalmau he probably meets Maurice Raynal and Francis Picabia.

Takes an interest in poetry and reads Catalan and French avant-garde reviews such as Pierre Reverdy's *Nord-Sud* and Albert Birot's *SIC*.

Visits the "Exposition d'Art Français" in Barcelona.

1918

Forms part of the Agrupació Courbet together with Josep Llorens Artigas, J.F. Ràfols, E.C. Ricart, Rafael Sala, Francesc Domingo and Marià Espinal, all students of Galí's art school and the Cercle Artístic de Sant Lluc.

First one-man show at the Galeries Dalmau, Barcelona.

1920

Travels to Paris for the first time, where Josep Dalmau tries to organise an exhibition for him. Visits Picasso in his studio.

1921

In Paris until 1925, where he has the use of Pablo Gargallo's studio at 45 Rue Blomet during the academic terms. Spends the rest of the year mainly at Mont-roig.

First solo exhibition in Paris at the Galerie La Licorne, organised by Josep Dalmau. The introduction to the catalogue is written by Maurice Raynal.

1922

In Paris, living and working at 45 Rue Blomet. Becomes friendly with André Masson, who is a neighbour, and with Roland Tual.

1923

Through Masson he meets Michel Leiris and probably Antonin Artaud, Robert Desnos, Jean Dubuffet, Paul Éluard, Marcel Jouhandeau, Georges Limbour, Raymond Queneau and Armand Salacrou. He also meets Ernest Hemingway, who purchases *The farm*, and Ezra Pound.

In Mont-roig he begins painting *Tilled field, Catalan landscape (The hunter)* and *Pastoral*, which mark a turning point in his art.

1924

Avant-garde poets and writers gather in Masson's studio at 45 Rue Blomet. Miró's friends during this period are Max Jacob, Michel Leiris, Georges Limbour, Benjamin Péret, Armand Salacrou and Roland Tual.

1925

André Breton meets Miró during a visit to the studio in the Rue Blomet.

First solo exhibition at the Galerie Pierre, Paris.

1926

Moves into a new studio at 22 Rue Tourlaque, in the Cité des Fusains. His neighbours are Max Ernst, Hans Arp and probably Paul Éluard and Camille Goemans.

Diaghilev commissions Miró and Ernst to design the sets and costumes for the ballet *Romeo and Juliet* to be performed by the Ballets Russes.

1928

Produces the first object-collages titled *Spanish dancer*.

Visits Belgium and Holland.

Paints the *Dutch interiors* in Mont-roig.

1929

Works on the series known as "Imaginary portraits".

Marries Pilar Juncosa in Palma, Majorca. They settle in Paris, in an apartment at 3 Rue François Mouton.

1930

Works on a series of paintings in very varied styles. According to Miró, they are a farewell to painting, albeit a temporary one, as he wishes to work in other media such as bas relief, sculpture, etc.

Birth of his only daughter, Maria Dolors, in Barcelona.

In Mont-roig he produces his first three-dimensional pieces.

First one-man show in the United States, at the Valentine Gallery, New York.

1931

In Mont-roig he starts a series of paintings on Ingres paper and object-paintings.

1932

Through Joan Prats he meets the architect Josep Lluís Sert.

Decides to spend more time in Barcelona. Lives and works in the family home at Passatge del Crèdit 4 until 1936.

Works on a new series of objects.

Designs the curtain, sets, costumes and objects for the ballet *Jeux d'enfants* performed by the Ballets Russes de Montecarlo, with scenario by Boris Kochno, music by Georges Bizet and choreography by Léonide Massine.

First one-man show at the Pierre Matisse Gallery, New York.

1933

Works on a series of 18 collages and then on the paintings based on them.

Publication of *Enfances* by Georges Hugnet, the first book illustrated by Miró with etchings.

1934

Signs a contract with Pierre Matisse, who represents him in the United States.

1936

Starts a series of 27 paintings on masonite.

Travels to Paris with his latest works, which are to be exhibited in New York. Due to the outbreak of the Spanish Civil War, he decides to stay in Paris. His wife and daughter join him, and they remain in France until 1940.

1937

Living and working in an apartment at 98 Boulevard Auguste Blanqui, Paris.

Attends life classes at the Académie de la Grande Chaumière, where he produces a large number of drawings.

Produces a large mural painting, *The reaper (Catalan peasant in revolt)*, for the Spanish Republican Government's pavilion, designed by Josep Lluís Sert and Luis Lacasa, at the Paris World Fair.

1938

Works on etchings and dry-point engravings with Marcoussis and prints these at the studios of Roger Lacourière and Stanley W. Hayter.

1939

Leaves Paris in the summer and rents a house in Varengeville-sur-Mer, Normandy, where the family remain until 1940.

1940

In January he starts a series of 23 gouaches, which he continues in Palma and completes in Mont-roig in September 1941. This series was later to be known as the *Constellations*.

The Germans bomb Normandy at the end of May and Miró decides to return to Spain with his family, where they settle in Palma (Majorca).

Joan Miró with the Ballets Russes de Montecarlo, 1932

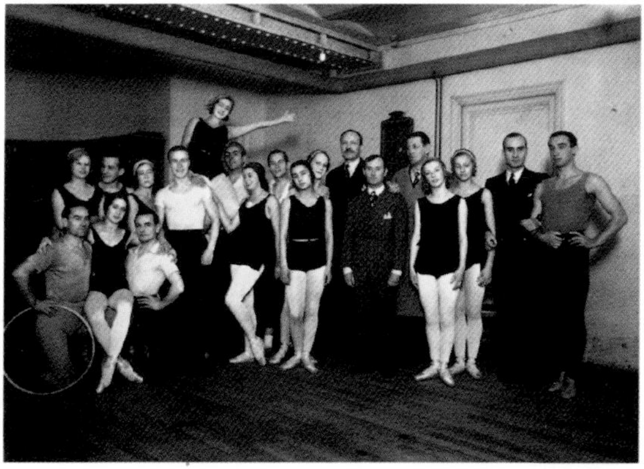

Joan Miró painting *The reaper* in the Spanish Republican Government's pavilion at the Paris World Fair, 1937

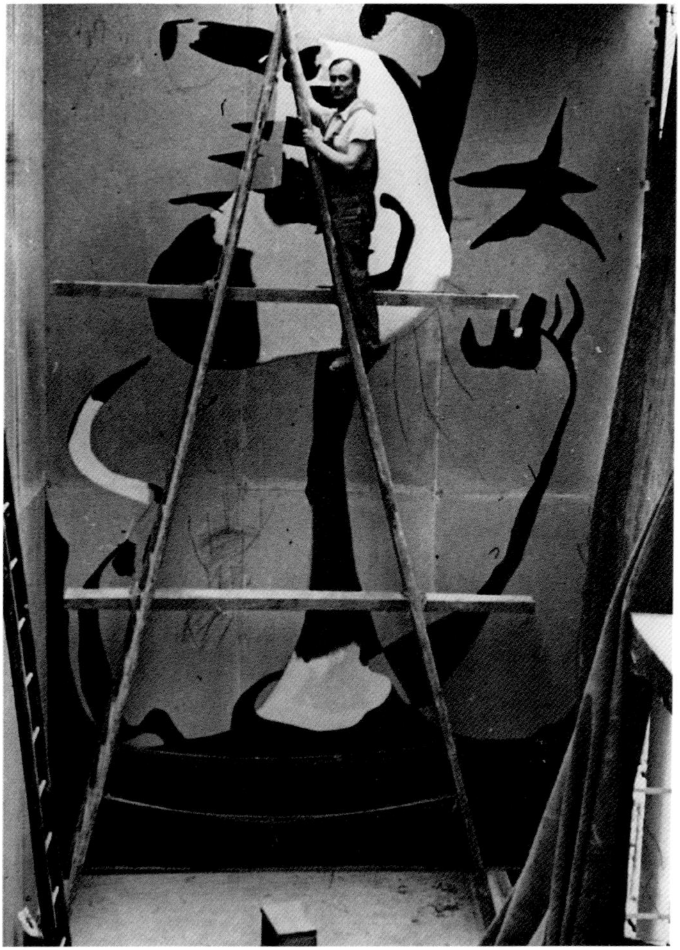

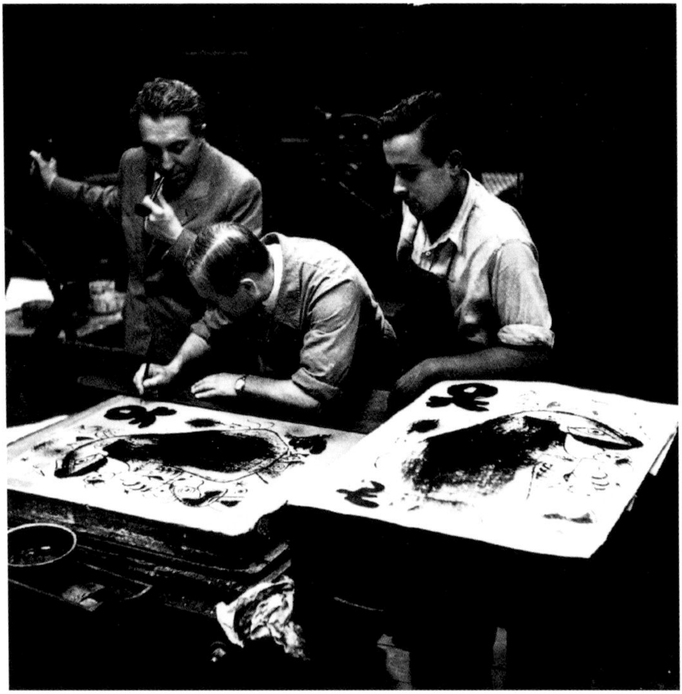

Joan Miró with Joan Prats during production of the *Barcelona series*, Barcelona, May 1944

1941
First large retrospective exhibition at the Museum of Modern Art, New York. Organisation and catalogue by James Johnson Sweeney.

1942
Continues working exclusively on paper.
Returns to Barcelona and lives at Passatge del Crèdit 4.

1943
Continues working exclusively on paper, with the sole known exception of *Painting with art nouveau frame,* from the Joan Prats collection.

1944
Produces his first ceramics, using materials from an unsuccessful firing in 1941 by Josep Llorens Artigas. This is the start of the first period of collaboration between them, which continues until 1947.
Publication of the set of 50 lithographs known as the *Barcelona series*, under the supervision of Joan Prats.
Returns to painting on canvas, which he had virtually abandoned since 1939.

1945
Works on several series of large-format paintings.

1946
Produces his first bronze sculptures.

1947
First trip to the United States, where he produces a mural painting for the Gourmet Room at the Terrace Plaza Hotel in Cincinnati.
During his stay in New York he frequents Stanley W. Hayter's studio Atelier 17, where he experiments with engraving techniques.
Takes part in "Le Surréalisme en 1947: Exposition internationale du

Joan Miró and Josep Llorens Artigas working on ceramics, Gallifa, 1954-56

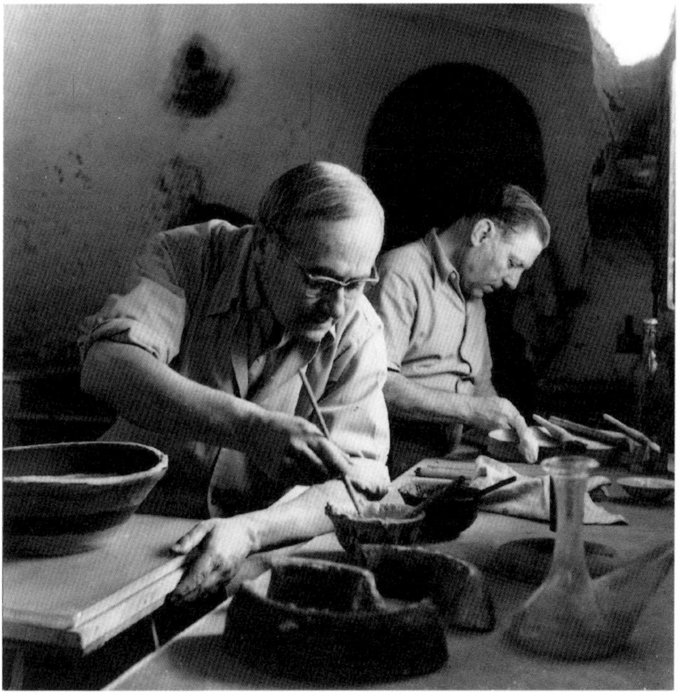

Following pages:

Joan Miró working in the studio designed for him by Josep Lluís Sert in Palma, Majorca, 1962

surréalisme" at the Galerie Maeght, Paris, organised by André Breton and Marcel Duchamp.

1948

First solo exhibition at the Galerie Maeght, Paris. Aimé Maeght becomes his new representative in France.

1949

This year and next he alternates between two types of painting: one more reflective and the other more gestural and impulsive.

Although based in Barcelona, he makes frequent visits to Paris to work on printing techniques at the Mourlot printing studio (lithographs) and at the Atelier Lacourière (engravings). His work on ceramics and sculpture becomes increasingly intensive.

Exhibition at the Galerías Layetanas, Barcelona, sponsored by Cobalto 49.

1950

In Barcelona, living and working at Passatge del Crèdit 4 until the autumn, when he moves to a flat at Carrer de Folgaroles 9, where he also works, although he keeps on the studio in the Passatge del Crèdit.

Starts work on the mural painting for the dining hall at Harkness Commons, Harvard University, commissioned by Walter Gropius, which he completes the following year.

1951

In Mont-roig, working on sculptures in a studio he had built at the farm.

1952

Second visit to the United States.

1954

Starts a new period of collaboration with Josep Llorens Artigas in Gallifa (near Barcelona). Over the next two years he produces more than 200 ceramic pieces.

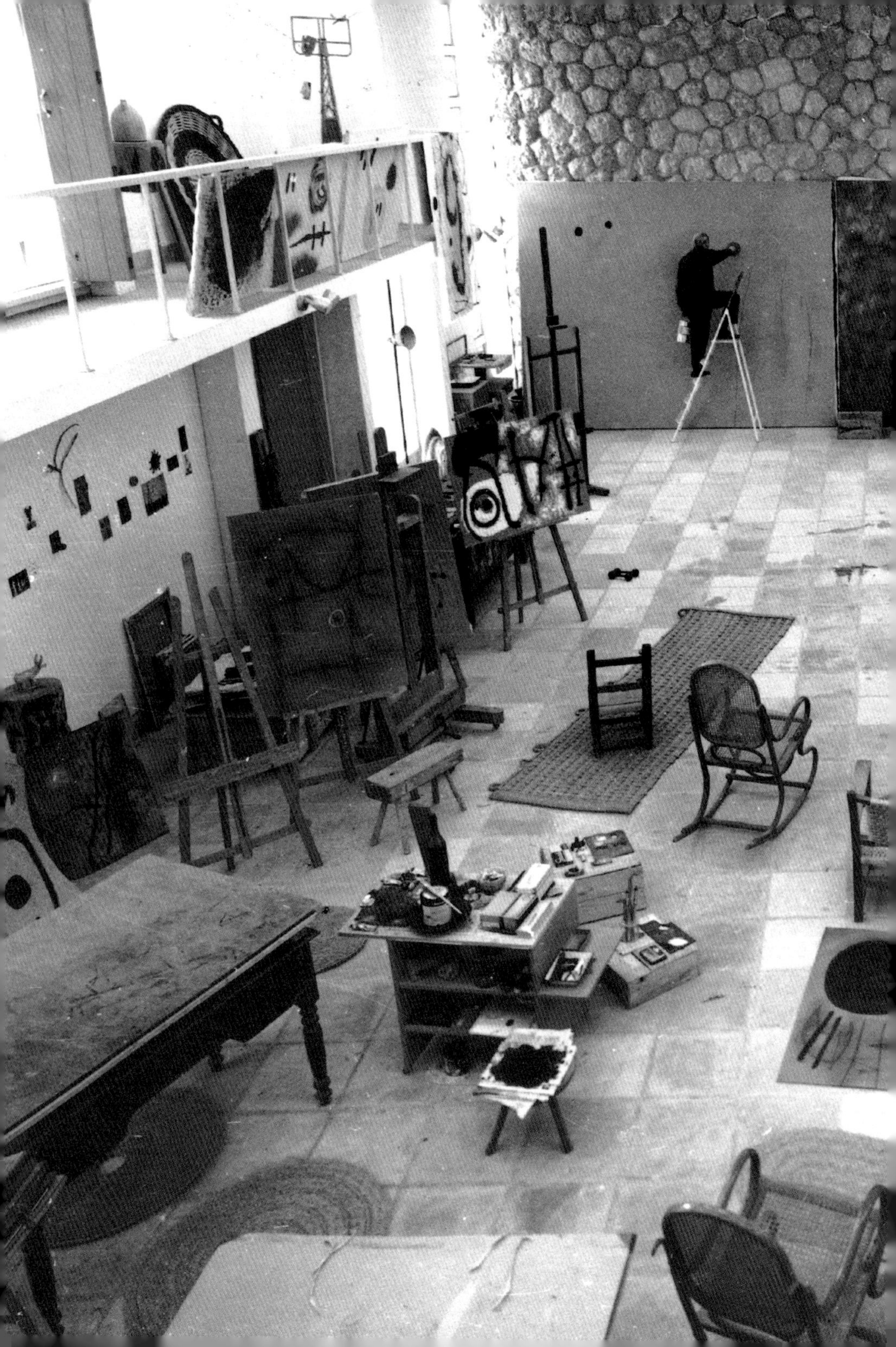

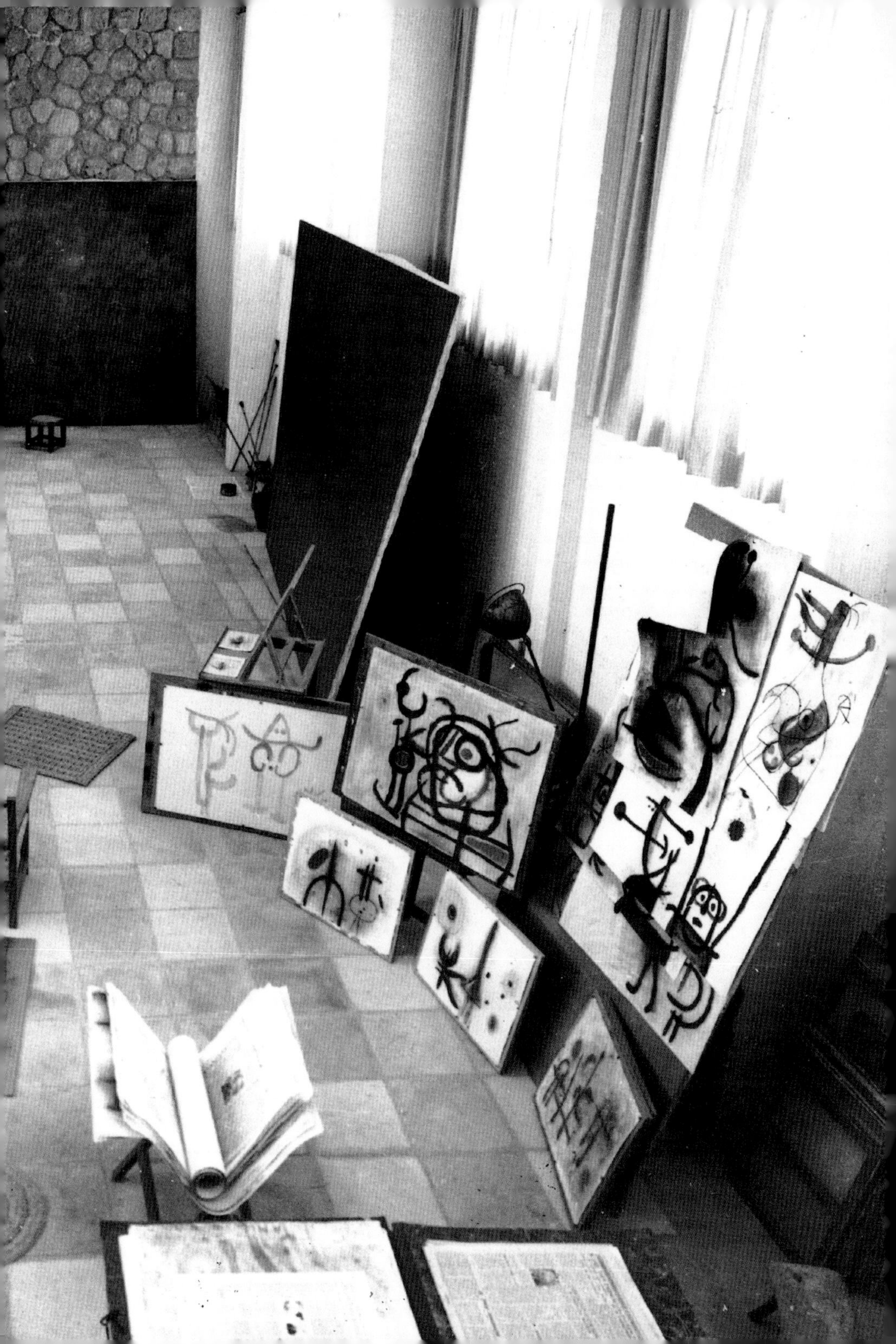

Produces a series of paintings on cardboard. He then stops painting until 1959 but continues working on ceramics and graphic arts.

1956

Sells the flat in Passatge del Crèdit and moves permanently to Palma, where he builds a house and commissions Josep Lluís Sert to design a studio for him.

1958

Inauguration of the two murals for UNESCO in Paris. The project receives the Guggenheim International Award.

1960

Works with Josep Llorens Artigas on the ceramic mural for Harkness Commons, Harvard University, to replace the mural painting.

1961

Publication of Jacques Dupin's book on Miró.

1962

Retrospective exhibition at the Musée National d'Art Moderne, Paris.

1964

Opening of the Fondation Maeght, designed by Josep Lluís Sert, and of the Labyrinth, with sculptures by Miró and Artigas, at Saint-Paul-de-Vence.

1966

Produces his first monumental sculptures in bronze, *Sun bird* and *Moon bird*.

Retrospective exhibition at the National Museum of Art, Tokyo.

Visits Japan for the first time, where he meets the poet Shuzo Takiguchi, author of the first monograph on Miró.

1967

Installation of a ceramic mural, produced in collaboration with Josep Llorens Artigas, at the Solomon R. Guggenheim Museum, New York.

Awarded the Carnegie International Grand Prize for painting.

1968

Last visit to the United States. Awarded an honorary doctorate by Harvard University.

Retrospective exhibitions at the Fondation Maeght, Saint-Paul-de-Vence, and at the Antic Hospital de la Santa Creu, Barcelona, sponsored by the City Council.

1969

"Miró otro" exhibition at the College of Architects, Barcelona. Miró paints the glass front of the building (an ephemeral action that is erased when the exhibition is over).

1970

Ceramic mural and mural painting for the Laughter Pavilion sponsored by Japanese gas companies at the Osaka World Fair.

In conjunction with Artigas, he produces a monumental ceramic mural for Barcelona Airport.

1972

The Fundació Joan Miró, Centre d'Estudis d'Art Contemporani, is legally constituted in Barcelona. Josep Lluís Sert is commissioned to design the building.

1975

The Fundació Joan Miró, Centre d'Estudis d'Art Contemporani, is opened to the public. A large selection of paintings, sculptures, textiles and prints are exhibited.

1976

Installation of the ceramic paving in the Pla de l'Os in the Rambla, Barcelona.

Official opening of the Fundació Joan Miró in Barcelona, with an exhibition of drawings from the collection donated by the artist.

Joan Miró working on the figures for the spectacle *Mori el Merma*, Sant Esteve de Palautordera (Barcelona), March 1977

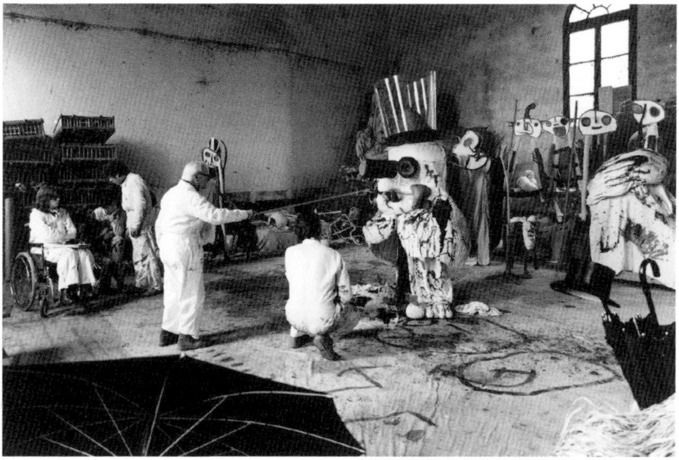

1977
Produces a large tapestry in conjunction with Josep Royo for the National Gallery, Washington D.C., and starts work on the tapestry for the Foundation.
Paints the sets and figures for *Mori el Merma* with the help of the actors in the Teatre de la Claca group.
1978
Retrospective exhibition at the Museo Español de Arte Contemporáneo, Madrid, organised in conjunction with the Fundació Joan Miró, Barcelona.
Premiere of *Mori el Merma* at the Gran Teatre del Liceu, Barcelona, performed by the Teatre de la Claca company, with giant puppets, masks and sets painted by Miró.
Unveiling of the monumental sculpture *Couple playing with almond blossom* in La Défense, Paris.
1979
Unveiling of the stained-glass windows at the Fondation Maeght, produced in collaboration with Charles Marcq, with whom Miró also made the stained-glass windows for the Chapelle Royale de Saint-Frambourg-de-Senlis, the venue for artistic and musical events held by the Cziffra Foundation.
Awarded an honorary doctorate by Barcelona University.
1980
King Juan Carlos awards him the Gold Medal for Fine Arts.
1981
Installation of the monumental sculpture known as *Miss Chicago* in Brunswick Plaza, Chicago.
1982
Installation of the monumental sculpture *Woman and bird* in the Parc de Joan Miró, Barcelona.
1983
Various events and exhibitions to celebrate Miró's ninetieth birthday.
"Joan Miró: A Ninetieth-Birthday Tribute" at the Museum of Modern Art, New York, and "Joan Miró: anys 20. Mutació de la realitat" at the Fundació Joan Miró, Barcelona.
Unveiling of a monumental sculpture in the courtyard of Barcelona City Hall.
Death of Joan Miró in Palma, Majorca, on 25 December. He is buried on 29 December in the Montjuïc cemetery, Barcelona.

Select Bibliography

1940

Takiguchi, Shûzo. *Miró,* Tokyo, Atelier.

1941

Sweeney, James Johnson. *Joan Miró,* New York, The Museum of Modern Art.

1947

Leiris, Michel. *The prints of Joan Miró,* New York, Curt Valentin.

1948

Greenberg, Clement. *Joan Miró,* New York, Quadrangle Press.

1949

Cirici, Alexandre. *Miró y la imaginación,* Barcelona, Omega.

Cirlot, Juan Eduardo. *Joan Miró,* Barcelona, Cobalto.

Queneau, Raymond. *Joan Miró ou le poète préhistorique,* Paris, Skira (Les trésors de la peinture française).

1954

Elgar, Frank. *Miró,* Paris, Fernand Hazan.

1956

Prévert, Jacques; Georges Ribemont-Dessaignes. *Joan Miró,* Paris, Maeght Éditeur.

Verdet, André; Roger Hauert. *Joan Miró,* Geneva, Kister.

1957

Duthuit, Georges. *Joan Miró,* Zurich, Ernst Scheidegger.

Hüttinger, Eduard. *Miró,* Berne, Alfred Scherz Verlag.

Scheidegger, Ernst. *Joan Miró: Gesammelte, Schriften, Fotos, Zeichnungen,* Zurich, Arche.

Verdet, André. *Joan Miró,* Nice, Galerie Matarasso.

1958

Baljeu, Joost. *Mondrian or Miró,* Amsterdam, De Beuk.

Hunter, Sam. *Joan Miró: His graphic work,* New York, Harry N. Abrams; *Joan Miró: L'œuvre gravé,* Paris, Calmann-Lévy; *Joan Miró: Das graphische Werk,* Stuttgart, Gerd Hatje; *Joan Miró: Su obra gráfica,* Barcelona, Gustavo Gili, 1959.

1959

Cela, Camilo José. *Joan Miró: Dibujos y litografías, Papeles de Son Armadans;* Barcelona, Seix y Barral; New York, New York Graphic Society.

Erben, Walter. *Joan Miró,* Munich, Prestel Verlag; London, Lund Humphries; Montecarlo, André Sauret; Mexico City, Hermes, 1961.

Soby, James Thrall. *Joan Miró*, New York, The Museum of Modern Art; Puerto Rico, Universidad de Río Piedras, 1960.
Sweeney, James Johnson. *Atmósfera Miró,* Barcelona, RM.
Wember, Paul. *Joan Miró farbige Lithographien*, Wiesbaden, Insel.

1960

Weelen, Guy. *Miró: 1924-1940*, Paris, Fernand Hazan; Barcelona, Gustavo Gili.
Weelen, Guy. *Miró: 1940-1955,* Paris, Fernand Hazan; Barcelona, Gustavo Gili.

1961

Borchert, Bernhard. *Joan Miró*, London, Faber and Faber.
Dupin, Jacques. *Miró*, Paris, Flammarion; New York, Harry N. Abrams; Cologne, Du Mont Schauberg; Milan, Mondadori, 1962.

1962

Taillandier, Yvon. *Creación Miró 1961,* Barcelona, RM.

1963

Gasch, Sebastià. *Joan Miró,* Barcelona, Alcides (Biografies populars).
Lassaigne, Jacques. *Miró,* Lausanne, Skira (Le goût de notre temps).

1964

Bonnefoy, Yves. *Miró,* Paris, Bibliothèque des Arts; Milan, Sylvana Editoriale d'Arte; New York, Viking Press, 1967; Barcelona, Juventud, 1970.

1965

Gasser, Manuel. *Joan Miró,* New York, Barnes & Noble; Paris, Marabout Université.

1966

Penrose, Roland. *Joan Miró: Creación en el espacio,* Barcelona, Polígrafa. Spanish, English, French and German editions.

1967

Dupin, Jacques. *Miró,* Paris, Union Générale d'Éditions (Collection d'Art Unesco 10/18, 380); Mexico City-Buenos Aires, Hermes; New York, Mentor Unesco Art Book.
Roditi, Edouard. *Chagall, Ernst, Miró,* Paris, Sedimo.
Walton, Paul H. *Dalí, Miró*, New York, Tudor.

1968

Bucci, Mario. *Joan Miró,* Florence, Sadea-Sansoni; Barcelona, Nauta, 1970.

1969

Greenberg, Clement. *Joan Miró*, New York, Arno Press.

1970

Cirici-Pellicer, Alexandre. *Miró en su obra,* Barcelona, Labor; Catalan edition: *Miró llegit,* Barcelona, Edicions 62, 1971.
Penrose, Roland. *Miró,* London, Thames & Hudson; Barcelona, Daimon, 1976; Catalan and Spanish edition: London, Thames and Hudson, and Barcelona, Destino, 1985; French edition: Paris, Thames and Hudson, 1990.
Perucho, Joan. *Joan Miró i Catalunya,* Barcelona, Polígrafa.
Sweeney, James Johnson. *Joan Miró,* Barcelona, Polígrafa.
Tapié, Michel. *Joan Miró*, Milan, Fratelli Fabbri; Paris, Hachette-Fabbri; Paris, Celiv, 1989.

1971

Chilo, Michel. *Miró: L'artiste et l'œuvre,* Paris, Maeght Editeur (Archives Maeght, 2).
Corredor-Matheos, José. *Miró,* Madrid, Dirección General de Bellas Artes.
Melià, Josep. *Joan Miró,* Barcelona, Dopesa.
Rowell, Margit. *Miró,* New York, Harry N. Abrams.

1972
Dupin, Jacques. *Miró escultor*, Barcelona, Polígrafa.
Herrmanns, Ralph. *Natten och drommen,* Stockholm, Bonnier; *La nit i el somni,* Barcelona, Sala Gaspar.
Hommage à Joan Miró, Paris, *XXe Siècle,* special issue.
Joan Miró, Milan, Artelevi.
Leiris, Michel; Fernand Mourlot. *Joan Miró lithographe I (1930-1952).* Paris, Maeght; Barcelona, Polígrafa; Geneva, Weber Éditeur.
Taillandier, Yvon. *Miró à l'encre,* Paris, *XXe Siècle; Mirografías*, Barcelona, Gustavo Gili.
Tono, Yoshiaki. *Ernst, Miró,* Tokyo, Shueisha.
1973
Jouffroy, Alain; Joan Teixidor. *Miró sculptures,* Paris, Maeght Éditeur (2nd extended edition: Paris, Maeght, 1980); *Miró plastik*, Munich, F. Bruckmann KG; *Miró Sculpture,* New York, Leon Amiel.
Rubin, William S. *Miró in the Collections of the Museum of Modern Art,* New York, The Museum of Modern Art.
1974
Diehl, Gaston. *Miró,* Paris, Flammarion.
Dopagne, Jacques. *Miró,* Paris, Fernand Hazan.
Herrmanns, Ralph. *Affischer av Miró 1937-1973,* Stockholm, AH Grafik.
Joan Miró, Paris, Éditions des Musées Nationaux.
Miró, Bilbao, La Gran Enciclopedia Vasca (Maestros actuales de la pintura y escultura catalanas, 22).
Pierre, José José Corredor-Matheos. *Céramiques de Miró et Artigas,* Paris, Maeght; *Miró & Artigas: Keramik*, Berne, Benteli.
1975
Fundació Joan Miró. *Fundació Joan Miró. Centre d'Estudis d'Art Contemporani.* Inaugural exhibition. June 1975, Barcelona, Fundació Joan Miró.
Permanyer, Lluís. *Los años difíciles de Miró, Llorens Artigas, Fenosa, Dalí, Clavé, Tàpies,* Barcelona, Lumen.
Queneau, Raymond. *Joan Miró lithographe II (1953-1963),* Paris, Maeght Éditeur; Barcelona, Polígrafa; Geneva, Weber.
1976
Picon, Gaëtan. *Joan Miró: Carnets Catalans,* Geneva, Albert Skira (Les sentiers de la création); *Joan Miró: Catalan Notebooks,* New York, Rizzoli, 1977; *Joan Miró: Carnets catalans,* Barcelona, Polígrafa, 1980; *Joan Miró: Cuadernos catalanes,* Barcelona, Polígrafa, 1980.
Rowell, Margit. *Joan Miró: Peinture-poésie*, Paris, Éditions de la Différence.
Teixidor, Joan. *Joan Miró lithographe III (1964-1969),* Paris, Maeght; Barcelona, Polígrafa, 1978.
1977
Cirici, Alexandre. *Miró-Mirall,* Barcelona, Polígrafa; *Miró et son temps,* Paris, Société Française du Livre.
Raillard, Georges. *Joan Miró: Ceci est la couleur de mes rêves,* Paris, Seuil; *Conversaciones con Joan Miró,* Barcelona, Granica, 1978; *I colori dei miei sogni: Conversazione con Georges Raillard*, Milan, Emme Edizioni, 1979.
1978
Gimferrer, Pere. Miró, *colpir sense nafrar,* Barcelona, Polígrafa; *Miró y su mundo,* Barcelona, Polígrafa; *Miró, catalan universel,* Hier et Demain.

Joan Miró, Madrid, Rayuela (Cuadernos Guadalimar ; 19).
Sabater, Gaspar. *Joan Miró y Mallorca,* Palma de Mallorca, Cort.
1980
Corredor-Matheos, José. *Los carteles de Miró,* Barcelona, Polígrafa; *Miró's Posters,* Secaucus, NJ, Chartwell Books; *Les affiches originales,* Paris, Cercle d'Art.
1981
Calas, Nicolás; Elena Calas. *Joan Miró lithographe IV (1969-1972),* Paris, Maeght; Barcelona, Polígrafa; Geneva, Weber Éditeur.
Franqui, Carlos; Jacques Dupin; Sylvano Bussotti. *Miró, l'Uccello Luce,* Venice, La Biennale.
Iscariotti, Patrizia. *Miró*, Rome, Armando Curcio (I classici della pintura).
Prévert, Jacques. *Couleurs de Braque, Calder, Miró,* Paris, Maeght Éditeur.
Román, József. *Miró,* Budapest, Corvina Kiadó.
1982
Schmalenbach, Werner. *Zeichnungen aus den späten Jahren,* Berlin, Propyläen.
1983
Malet, Rosa Maria. *Joan Miró,* Barcelona, Polígrafa, Catalan, Spanish and English editions; French edition: Paris, Albin Michel; German and Italian editions: Barcelona, Polígrafa, 1985.
Miró, Madrid, Sarpe (Los genios de la pintura española, 11).
Miró lithographs: 40 works by Joan Miró, New York, Dover Publications.
1984
Català-Roca, Francesc. *Miró noranta anys,* Barcelona, Edicions 62-Fundació Joan Miró.
Dupin, Jacques. *Miró graveur I (1928-1960),* Paris, Daniel Lelong, French, English and German editions; Spanish edition: Barcelona, Polígrafa, 1987.
Serra, Pere A. *Miró i Mallorca,* Barcelona, Polígrafa; Paris, Cercle d'Art; *Miró and Mallorca,* New York, Rizzoli, 1986.
Weelen, Guy. *Miró,* Paris, Nouvelles Éditions Françaises, 1984; Cologne, Du Mont Buchverlag; Milan, Garzanti.
1986
Rowell, Margit. *Joan Miró: Selected Writings and Interviews,* Boston, G.K. Hall; *Joan Miró: Écrits et entretiens,* Paris, Daniel Lelong, 1995.
1987
Jouffroy, Alain. *Miró,* Paris, Fernand Hazan.
1988
Erben, Walter. *Joan Miró 1893-1983: Mensch und Werk*, Cologne, Benedikt Taschen.
Obra de Joan Miró: Dibuixos, pintura, escultura, ceràmica, tèxtils, Barcelona, Fundació Joan Miró (Abridged edition: *La Fundació Joan Miró i les seves col·leccions,* Barcelona, Fundació Joan Miró, 1990. Catalan, Spanish, French and English editions).
1989
Cramer, Patrick. *Joan Miró: Catalogue raisonné des livres illustrés,* Geneva, Patrick Cramer; *Joan Miró: The illustrated books. Catalogue raisonné*, Geneva, Patrick Cramer.
Dupin, Jacques. *Miró graveur II (1961-1973),* Paris, Daniel Lelong, French, English and German editions; Spanish edition: Barcelona, Polígrafa.
Raillard, Georges. *Miró,* Paris, Hazan (Les chefs d'œuvre); Spanish

edition: Madrid, Debate, 1993 (Grandes maestros de la Pintura moderna).
1990
Combalía, Victoria. *El descubrimiento de Miró: Miró y sus críticos, 1918-1929,* Barcelona, Destino.
Joan Miró, Paris, Éditions des Musées Nationaux, Grand Palais.
Sert, Josep Lluís. *Taller per a Joan Miró,* Palma de Mallorca, Col·legi Oficial d'Arquitectes.
1991
Bernier, Rosamond. *Matisse, Picasso, Miró as I knew them,* New York, Alfred A. Knopf.
Dupin, Jacques. *Miró graveur III (1973-1975),* Paris, Daniel Lelong, French, English and German editions; Spanish edition: Barcelona, Polígrafa.
Green, Christopher. *Picasso y Miró, 1930: El mago, el niño y el artista,* Valencia, IVAM-Generalitat Valenciana.
Green, Christopher; Hilton Kramer. *Joan Miró i la mort de la pintura: Dos excursos,* Barcelona, Barcanova.
1992
Cramer, Patrick. *Joan Miró lithographe V (1972-1975),* Paris, Maeght Éditeur. French, English and Spanish editions.
Fernández Miró, David. *David: Escritos de David Fernández Miró,* Barcelona, Fundació Joan Miró, Edicions 62; Palma de Mallorca, Fundació Pilar i Joan Miró.
Malet, Rosa Maria. *Joan Miró,* Barcelona, Edicions 62 (Col·lecció Pere Vergés de Biografies, 47).
Prete, Cecilia. *Miró,* Milan, Electa. Spanish edition: Madrid, Sociedad Editorial Electa España, 1995.
1993
Corbella, Domènec. *Entendre Miró: Anàlisi del llenguatge mironià a partir de la "Sèrie Barcelona" 1939-1944,* Barcelona, Publicacions de la Universitat de Barcelona.
Dupin, Jacques. *Joan Miró,* Barcelona, Polígrafa, Catalan, Spanish and English editions; French edition: Paris, Flammarion.
Gimferrer, Pere. *Les arrels de Miró,* Barcelona, Polígrafa; *Las raices de Miró,* Barcelona, Polígrafa; *The roots of Miró,* New York, Rizzoli; *Joan Miró: Auf den Spuren seiner Kunst,* Stuttgart, Daco-Verlag-Günter-Bläse.
Saura, Antonio. *Belvédère Miró,* Paris, L'Échoppe.
Scheidegger, Ernst. *Joan Miró a Catalunya: Huellas de un encuentro,* Paris, Maeght. Also French and English editions. German edition: Zurich, Ernst Scheidegger.
1994
Gassner, Hubertus. *Joan Miró: Der magische Gartner,* Cologne, Dumont.
Giralt-Miracle, Daniel. *El crit de la terra: Joan Miró i el Camp de Tarragona,* Barcelona, Columna (Tamarit, 4).
Santos Torroella, Rafael. *35 años de Joan Miró,* Barcelona, Parsifal Ediciones (Figuras, 30).
1995
Catoir, Barbara. *Miró on Mallorca,* Munich-New York, Prestel; *Miró auf Mallorca,* Munich-New York, Prestel.
Miró grabador en los fondos del Museo Nacional Centro de Arte Reina Sofía, Madrid, Museo Nacional Centro de Arte Reina Sofía.
1996
Punyet Miró, Joan. *Miró: L'Atelier,* Paris, Éditions Assouline; *Miró in his Studio,* London, Thames and Hudson.

Schildkraut, Joseph J.; Aurora Otero (eds.). *Depression and the Spiritual in Modern Art: Homage to Miró*, Chichester, etc., John Wiley & Sons.

1998

Combalía, Victoria. *Picasso-Miró: Miradas cruzadas,* Madrid, Electa.

Photographs

Raoul Barba: page 111
Neus D. Calvet: page 19
Colita: page 16
Daniel Font: page 14
F. Català Roca: pages 6, 16, 18, 101, 102, 113, 114-115, 117
Ferran Freixa: page 9
Joaquim Gomis: pages 8, 112
Joaquim Jansana and Montse Pastor: pages 9, 12
Man Ray: page 106
Pere Pratdesaba: pages 13, 20
Serra, Arxiu Històric de la Ciutat (Barcelona): page 108
Successió Miró: pages 107, 108

Board of Trustees of the Joan Miró Foundation